Option
Volatility
and Pricing
Strategies

Advanced Trading
Techniques for
Professionals

Sheldon Natenberg

Probus Publishing Company
Chicago Illinois

Library of Congress Cataloging-in-Publication Data

Natenberg, Sheldon.
    Option volatility and pricing strategies.

    Includes index.
    1. Options (Finance) I. Title.
HG6042.N38 1988   332.63'28   89-3994

ISBN: 1-55738-009-0

8   9   0

Dedication

To Paul, for convincing me to become an option trader;
To Hen and Jerry, for their financial support when I needed it;
And most of all to Leona, for her encouragement in good times and bad.

Contents

Preface   ix

1 The Language of Options   1
  Contract Specifications   2
  Exercise and Assignment   4
  Market Integrity   12
  Margin Requirements   14
  Settlement Procedures   15

2 Elementary Strategies   19

3 Introduction to Theoretical Pricing Models   41
  Expected Return   43
  Theoretical Value   44
  A Word on Models   46
  A Simple Approach   48
  The Black-Scholes Model   51
    Exercise Price   54
    Time to Expiration   54
    Price of the Underlying   55
    Interest Rates   56
    Volatility   57

4 Volatility   59
  Random Walks and Normal Distributions   60
  Mean and Standard Deviation   66
  Lognormal Distributions   70

                                                                     v

Volatility as a Standard Deviation   72
Volatility and Observed Price Changes   76
A Note on Eurodollar Volatility   78
Types of Volatilities   78
   Future Volatility   79
   Historical Volatility   79
   Forecast Volatility   81
   Implied Volatility   81
   Seasonal Volatility   86
Estimating Volatility   90
   Historical Volatility   90
   Marketplace Opinion of Future Volatility   92
   Volatility of Similar Commodities   92
Conclusion   93

5 Using an Option's Theoretical Value   **99**

6 Option Values andChanging Market Conditions   **115**
The Delta   116
   Rate of Change   116
   Hedge Ratio   119
   Theoretical or Equivalent Futures Position   119
The Gamma   121
The Theta   129
The Vega   132
The Rho   135

7 Introduction to Spreading   **145**
Why Traders Spread   151

8 Volatility Spreads   **155**
Backspread   156
Ratio Vertical Spread   159
Straddle   159
Strangle   161
Butterfly   164
Time Spreads   168
Diagonal Spreads   176
Classification of Volatility Spreads   176
Choosing an Appropriate Strategy   179
Adjustment   189
Graphing Spreads   191
Spread Order Entry   198

9 Risk Considerations   203
Choosing the Best Spread   203
Practical Considerations   214
How Much Margin for Error?   220
Net Short Contracts   220
What is a Good Spread?   222
Offsetting Spreads   222
How to Adjust   226
Style Considerations   229
Market Liquidity   230

10 Bull and Bear Spreads   235
Naked Positions   235
Ratioing a Spread Bullish or Bearish   236
Bull and Bear Butterflies and Time Spreads   238
Vertical Spreads   239
Buy and Sell Writes   251

11 Arbitrage Strategies   259
Synthetic Positions   259
Conversions and Reversals   263
Interest Considerations   266
Conversion/Reversal Risk   269
Interest Rate Risk   269
Execution Risk   269
Pin Risk   269
Futures Risk   271
Boxes   274
Jelly Rolls   277
Synthetic Volatility Spreads   280

12 Early Exercise of American Options   283
The Cox-Ross-Rubenstein Model   288
The Whaley Model   291
The Effect of Early Exercise on Vertical Spreads   293
A Comparison of European and American Option Values 295

13 Let the User Beware   299
Expiration Backspreads   317

Appendices

A: A Glossary of Option Terminology   323
B: The Mathematics of Option Pricing   335
C: Some Historical Volatilities   349
D: Characteristics of Volatility Spreads   361
E : What's the Best Strategy?   365
F : Synthetic and Arbitrage Relationships   369
G: A Guide to Option Software and Computer Services   375
H: Recommended Readings   385

Index   389

Preface

Within the last decade trading in options has increased at an explosive rate. Not only have traditional market participants, speculators, hedgers, and arbitrageurs all become actively involved in option markets, but the number of individual floor traders willing to risk their own capital in these markets has grown dramatically. Yet the trader entering an option market for the first time may find that his initial efforts are less than totally successful. Indeed, the learning period in options during which a trader gains full confidence in his ability to survive and thrive under all types of market conditions may require many months or even years of trading experience. Unfortunately, the great majority of traders do not survive this learning period. The unusual characteristics of options, the subtleties of the marketplace, and the unforeseen risks, all seem to conspire against the inexperienced trader and eventually lead to his demise.

Much of the pain experienced by a new trader could be avoided if the trader were better prepared for the realities of option trading. Unfortunately, existing option literature has tended to take either a highly theoretical approach best suited to an academic environment, or a simplistic approach presenting options as just another way of trading stocks or commodities. Neither approach is likely to meet the needs of the serious trader. The former approach is not only mathematically beyond the capabilities of most traders, but relies heavily on theoretical assumptions which are too often violated in the real world. The latter approach cannot possibly prepare a serious trader for the wide variety of strategies with which he must be familiar, nor with the very real risks to which he will be exposed.

This book was written with the hope of filling the void in the traditional option literature by combining theory and real-world practice. Moreover, it was written primarily with the serious trader in mind. This includes traders whose firms are actively involved in option markets, either by choice or by necessity, or individual traders who wish to make the most of the opportunities offered by options. This is not meant to discourage those who are casually or peripherally involved in options markets from reading this book. Additional insight into any subject is always worthwhile. But understanding options requires substantial effort. The serious trader, because his livelihood often depends on this understanding, will usually be more willing to invest the time and energy required to attain this goal.

In preparing the reader for the option marketplace, the author has tried to combine an intuitive approach to option theory with a discussion of the real-life problems with which he will be confronted. Of course, the reader who is comfortable with mathematics is in no way discouraged from delving more deeply into the theory of option pricing in many of the excellent academic presentations of the subject. But the important point is that such a rigorous approach is not necessary for success in option trading. Indeed, the great majority of successful option traders have never even looked at a mathematical presentation of option theory. Nor would many of them be capable of understanding the complex mathematics if they did.

Much of the presentation in this book will necessarily be colored by the author's personal experiences as a floor trader. Sophisticated hedging strategies, such as portfolio insurance, and complex intermarket spreading strategies are touched upon only briefly, if at all. Yet the principles of option evaluation which enable a floor trader to successfully participate in an option market are the same principles which will enable any participant to make the best use of options, regardless of the reasons for entering the market. Additionally, the author is able to place special emphasis on a lesson which floor traders quickly learn but which casual traders too often forget. Without a very healthy respect for the risks of option trading and a full understanding of risk management techniques, today's profits can quickly turn into tomorrow's losses.

Because of the more recent introduction of listed options on futures contracts and the increased interest in these markets, the author has tended to concentrate the examples in the text on these options. However, the principles which lead to success in futures options are equally valid in commodity, stock, and index option markets.

The core material in this book was developed in classes taught by the author to traders at the Chicago Mercantile Exchange and the Chicago Board of Trade. In expanding the material into book form the author has tried to draw on a wide variety of other sources. Foremost among these are the many floor traders who offered their comments and criticisms. In addition, special thanks go to Greg Monroe of the Chicago Board of Trade Education Department and Mark Rzepczynski of the Chicago Mercantile Exchange Research Department for their comments on the text, and to David Isbister of Monetary Investments International for preparation of some of the values used in the tables.

Finally, my thanks to the staff at Probus Publishing for their encouragement, patience, and assistance in dealing with a first time author.

Sheldon Natenberg
Chicago

1

The Language of Options

Every option market brings together traders and investors with different goals and trading styles. Some enter the market with an opinion on which way prices will move, and hope to use options to profit from this expectation. Some use options as insurance to protect existing commodity or security positions against adverse price movement. Some hope to take advantage of price discrepancies between similar or related products trading in the same or different markets. Some act as middlemen, buying and selling as an accomodation to other market participants, and hoping to profit from the difference between the bid and ask price.

Even though goals and trading styles differ, every trader's education must begin with an introduction to the terminology of option trading, and to the rules and regulations which govern trading activity. Without a facility in the language of options, a trader will find it impossible to communicate his desire to buy or sell to other traders. Without a clear understanding of the terms of an option contract and his rights and responsibilities under that contract, a trader cannot hope to make the best use of options, nor will he be prepared for the very real risks of trading.

Contract Specifications

Options come in two types. A *call option* is the right to buy or take a *long* position in a given stock, commodity, index, or futures contract at a fixed price on or before a specified date. A *put option* is the right to sell or take a *short* position in a given stock, commodity, index, or futures contract at a fixed price on or before a specified date.

Note the difference between a futures contract and an option. A futures contract *requires* delivery at a fixed price. The buyer and seller of a futures contract both have obligations which they must meet. The seller *must* make delivery and the buyer *must* take delivery of the commodity. The buyer of an option, however, has a choice. He can *choose* to take delivery (go long) or make delivery (go short). If the buyer chooses to take delivery or make delivery, the seller of the option is obligated to take the other side. In option trading all rights lie with the buyer, and all obligations with the seller.

The stock, commodity, index, or futures contract to be bought or sold under the terms of the option is the *underlying* contract or, more simply, the underlying. The *exercise price*, or *strike price*, is the price at which the underlying will be delivered should the owner of an option choose to exercise his right to buy or sell. The date after which the option may no longer be exercised is the *expiration date.*

If an option is purchased directly from a bank or other dealer, the quantity of the underlying to be delivered, the exercise price, and the expiration date can all be tailored to meet the buyer's individual requirements. If the option is purchased on an exchange, the quantity of the underlying to be delivered, as well as the exercise price and expiration date, are predetermined by the exchange.

As an example of an exchange traded option, the buyer of a crude oil October 19 call on the New York Mercantile Exchange has the right to take a long position in one October crude oil futures contract for 1000 barrels of crude oil (the underlying), at a price of $19 per barrel (the exercise price), on or before October expiration (the expiration date). The buyer of a Treasury Bond June 96 put on the Chicago Board of Trade has the right to take a short position in one June Treasury bond futures contract, with 8% coupon rate and $100,000 face value, at a price of $96,000, on or before June expiration.

The underlying futures month for an exchange traded futures option is usually identical to the expiration month of the option. The underlying contract for a crude oil October 19 call traded on the NYMEX is one October crude oil contract. The underlying contract for a Treasury Bond June 96 put on the CBOT is one June Treasury Bond contract (Figure1-1).

Recently, some exchanges have introduced *serial options*, whereby options with several different expiration dates have identical underlying contracts. When there is no futures contract with the same expiration month as the option, the underlying contract for that option is the nearest futures contract after the expiration of the option. For example, the underlying for a March Deutschemark option on the CME is one March Deutschemark futures contract. The underlying for a January or February Deutschemark option is *also* one March futures contract. With no January or February futures contracts available, March is the nearest futures month after expiration of the January and February options.

The exact expiration date of a futures option need not coincide with the delivery month specified by the underlying futures contract. In some cases, the expiration date of a futures option can predate the delivery month of the underlying futures contract by several weeks, so that the option expires in the month prior to the underlying futures month. A crude oil option on the NYMEX will typically expire the first week of the preceding month, so that an October option will actually expire the first week in September. A trader should always check with the exchange on which the option is traded to determine the exact expiration date.

CONTRACT SPECIFICATIONS

Crude Oil	October	19	Call
↑	↑	↑	↑
Underlying	Expiration Date	Exercise Price	Type
↓	↓	↓	↓
Treasury Bond	June	96	Put

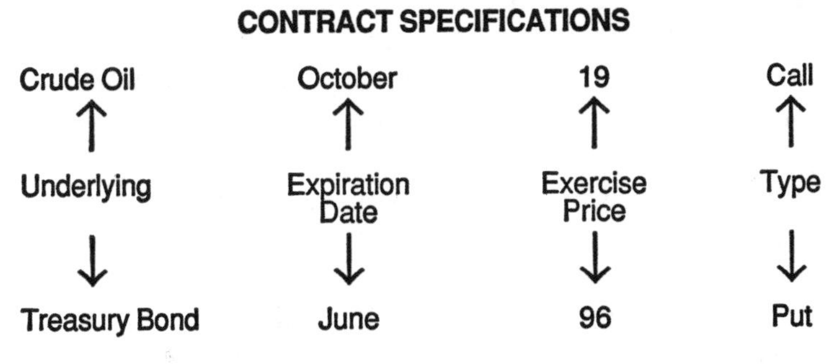

Figure 1-1

Exercise and Assignment

A trader who owns a call or put option has the right to *exercise* that option prior to expiration, thereby converting the option into a long underlying position, in the case of a call; or a short underlying position, in the case of a put (Figure 1-2). A trader who exercises a crude oil October 19 call has chosen to take a long position in one October crude oil futures contract at $19 per barrel. A trader who exercises a Deutschemark March 60 put has chosen to take a short position in one March Deutschemark futures contract at 60¢ per Deutschemark. Once an option has been exercised it ceases to exist, just as if it had been allowed to expire unexercised.

A trader who intends to exercise an option must submit an exercise notice to either the seller of the option, if purchased from a dealer, or to the guarantor of the option, if purchased on an exchange. When a valid exercise notice is submitted, the seller of the option has been *assigned*. Depending on the type of option, he will be required to take a long or short position in the underlying contract at the specified exercise price. (See Figures 1-3 through 1-6.)

In addition to its underlying contract, exercise price, expiration date, and type, an option is further identified by the conditions of exercise. An option is either *American*, whereby the holder can exercise his rights any time prior to expiration, or *European*, whereby the holder can exercise his rights only on expiration day.[1] The great majority of listed options throughout the world are American options, carrying with them the right of early exercise. Indeed, with the exception of certain index options, all futures options and stock options currently traded on U.S. exchanges are American.[2]

As in any competitive market, an option's price, or *premium*, is determined by supply and demand. Buyers and sellers make competing bids and offers until an equilibrium price is reached and a trade

---

[1]Since exchanges need time to process exercise and assignment notices, the holder of an exchange traded option must usually submit an exercise notice no later than the day prior to expiration.

[2]The S&P 500 index option traded on the Chicago Board Options Exchange and the Institutional Index option traded on the American Stock Exchange are both European exercise. Certain currency options traded on the Philadelphia Stock Exchange are also European.

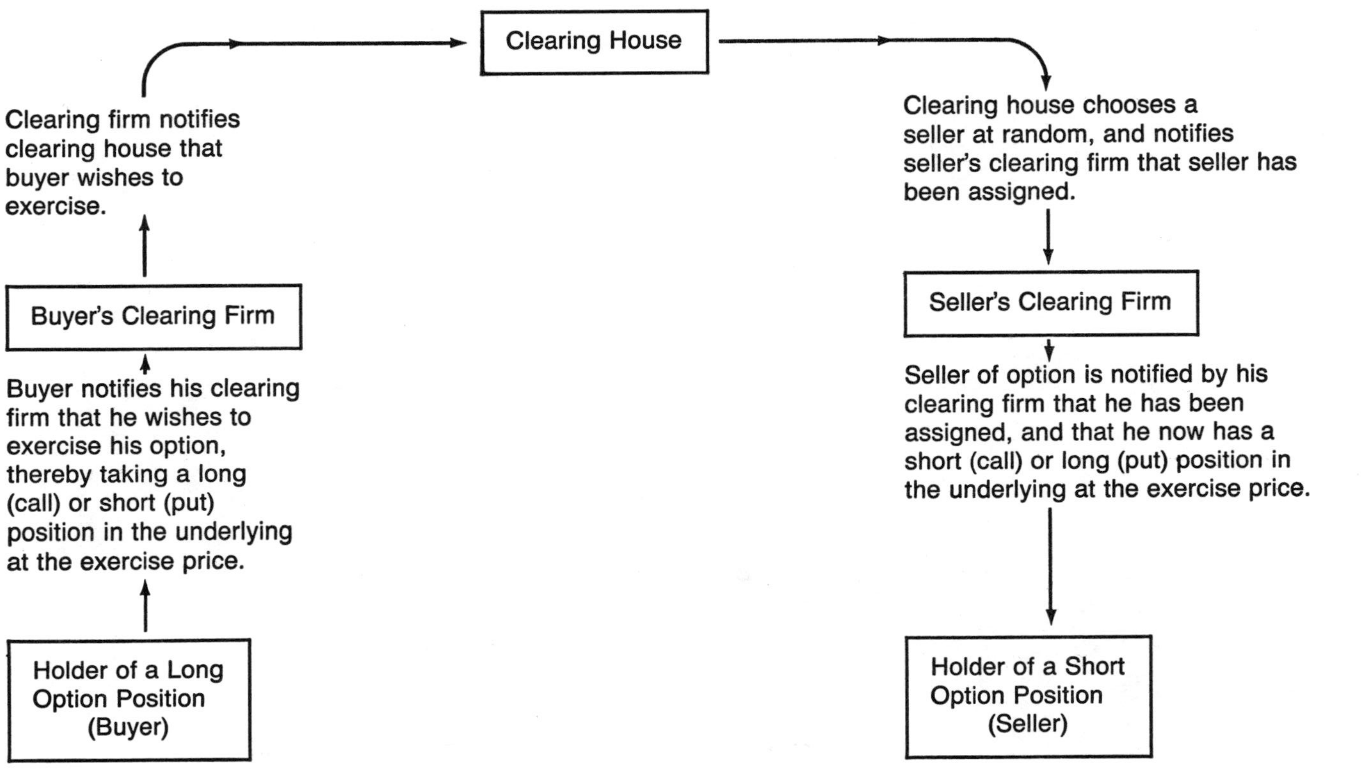
Clearing House
Clearing firm notifies clearing house that buyer wishes to exercise.
Buyer's Clearing Firm
Buyer notifies his clearing firm that he wishes to exercise his option, thereby taking a long (call) or short (put) position in the underlying at the exercise price.
Holder of a Long Option Position (Buyer)
Clearing house chooses a seller at random, and notifies seller's clearing firm that seller has been assigned.
Seller's Clearing Firm
Seller of option is notified by his clearing firm that he has been assigned, and that he now has a short (call) or long (put) position in the underlying at the exercise price.
Holder of a Short Option Position (Seller)

Figure 1-2

is made. The premium paid for an option can be separated into two components, the intrinsic and extrinsic value. An option's *intrinsic value* is the amount of capital which will accrue to a trader's account should he exercise the option and close out the position against the underlying contract at the current market price. For example, with gold at $450 per ounce, the intrinsic value of a $440 call is $10. By exercising his option, the owner of a $440 call can buy gold at $440 per ounce. If he then sells gold at the market price of $450 per ounce., $10 per ounce will enter his account. With Deutschemarks at 61.50¢, the intrinsic value of a 64 put is 2.50¢. By exercising his option, the owner of the 64 put can sell Deutschemarks at 64¢ per DM. If he then closes out the position by purchasing Deutschemarks at their current market price of 61.50¢, 2.50¢ per DM will enter his account.

A call will only have intrinsic value if its exercise price is less than the current price of the underlying contract. A put will only have intrinsic value if its exercise price is higher than the current price of the underlying contract. The amount of intrinsic value is the amount by which the call's exercise price is less than the current price, or the amount by which the put's exercise price is greater than the current price. No option can have an intrinsic value less than zero.

Very often an option's price in the marketplace will be greater than its intrinsic value. The additional amount of premium over the intrinsic value which traders are willing to pay is the *extrinsic value*, sometimes also referred to as the *time value* or *time premium*. Market participants are willing to pay this additional amount because of the protective characteristics afforded by options over an outright long or short position in the underlying contract.

An option's premium is always composed of precisely its intrinsic and extrinsic value. If a gold $440 call is trading for $15 with the current price of the underlying contract at $450 per ounce, the extrinsic value must be $5, since we know that the intrinsic value is $10. The two components taken together must add up to the option's total premium of $15. If the Deutschemark 64 put is trading for 3.50¢ with the underlying Deutschemark contract at 61.50¢, the option's extrinsic value must be 1¢, since we know that the intrinsic value is 2.50¢. The intrinsic and extrinsic values together must add up to the option's premium of 3.50¢.

An Order to Buy 10 Deutschemark September 62 Calls for 1.75 Each

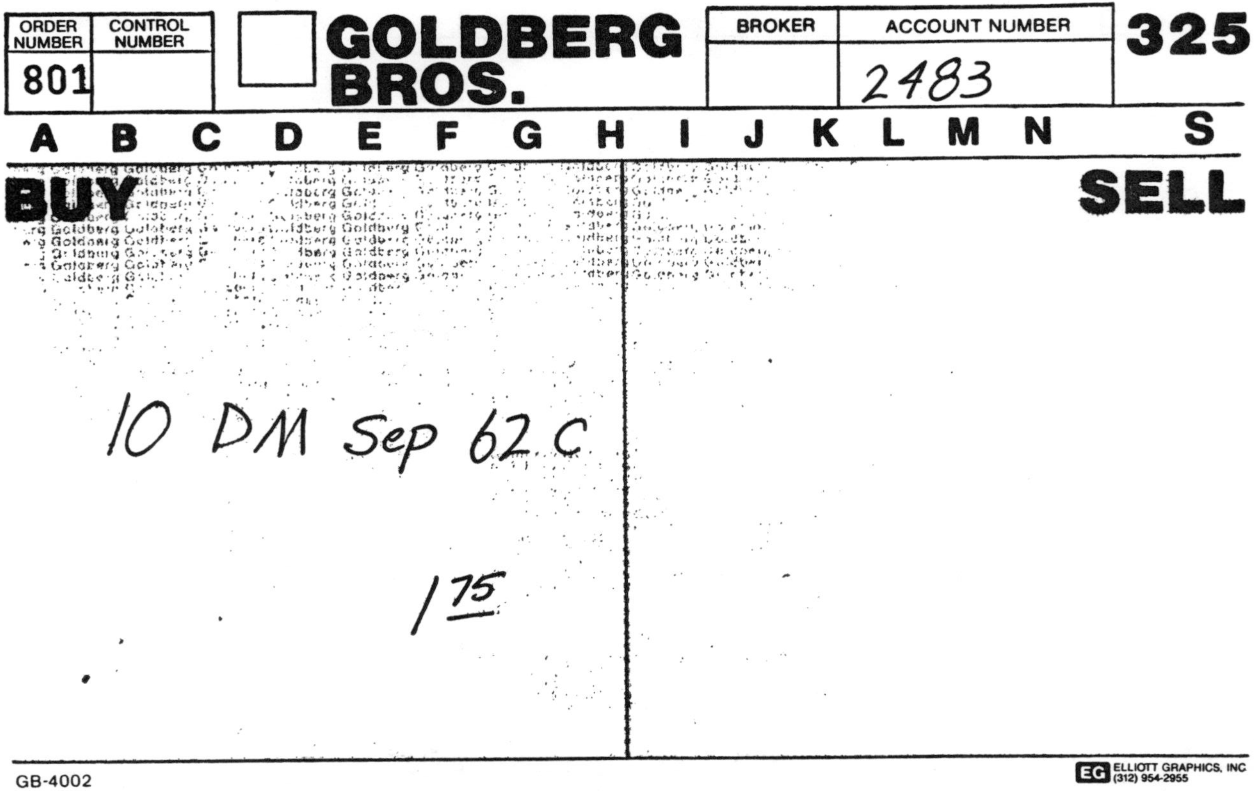

ORDER NUMBER	CONTROL NUMBER			GOLDBERG BROS.		BROKER	ACCOUNT NUMBER		325
801							2483		

A	B	C	D	E	F	G	H	I	J	K	L	M	N	S

BUY

SELL

10 DM Sep 62 C

1 75

GB-4002

EG ELLIOTT GRAPHICS, INC
(312) 954-2955

Figure 1-3

An Order to Sell 5 U.S. Treasury Bond March 96 Puts at 2 50/64 Each

GOLDBERG BROS.

ORDER NUMBER	CONTROL NUMBER		BROKER	ACCOUNT NUMBER	**325**
802				2483	

| A | B | C | D | E | F | G | H | I | J | K | L | M | N | S |

BUY

SELL

5 US Mar 96 P

$2\frac{50}{64}$

GB-4002

EG ELLIOTT GRAPHICS, INC
(312) 954-2955

Figure 1-4

An Exercise Notice for 10 Deutschemark September 62 Calls

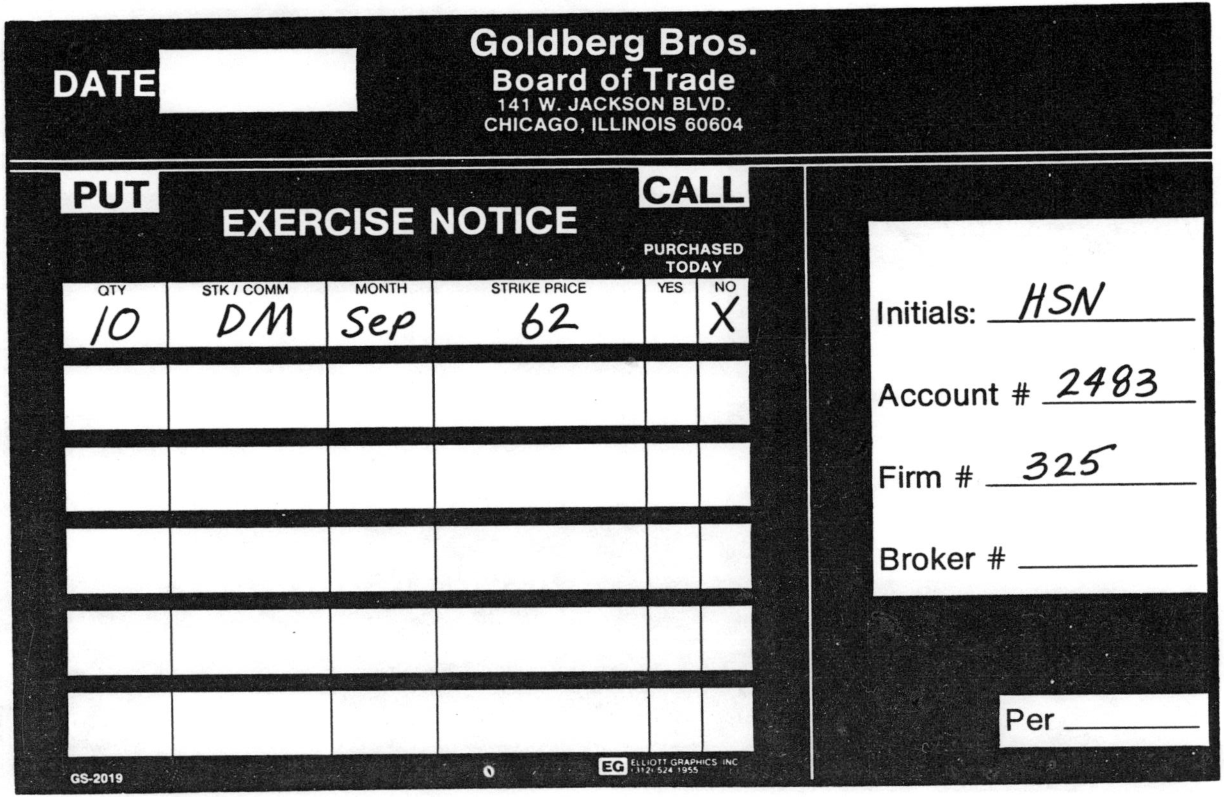

DATE

Goldberg Bros.
Board of Trade
141 W. JACKSON BLVD.
CHICAGO, ILLINOIS 60604

PUT   CALL

EXERCISE NOTICE

Initials: _HSN_

Account # _2483_

Firm # _325_

Broker # _____

Per _____

QTY	STK / COMM	MONTH	STRIKE PRICE	PURCHASED TODAY	
				YES	NO
10	DM	Sep	62		X

EG ELLIOTT GRAPHICS, INC.
(312) 524-1955

GS-2019

Figure 1-5

An Assignment Notice for 5 U.S. Treasury Bond March 96 Puts

DATE

Goldberg Bros.
Board of Trade
141 W. JACKSON BLVD.
CHICAGO, ILLINOIS 60604

Initials: _HSN_

Account # _2483_

Firm # _325_

ASSIGNMENT NOTICE

QTY	COMM	MONTH	STRIKE PRICE	PUT	CALL
5	US	Mar	96	X	

GB-4022

EG ELLIOTT GRAPHICS, INC.
(312) 954-2955

Figure 1-6

Even though an option's premium is always composed of its intrinsic and extrinsic value, it is possible for one or both of these components to be zero. If there is no intrinsic value, its price in the marketplace will consist solely of extrinsic or time value. If there is no extrinsic value, its price in the marketplace will consist solely of its intrinsic value. In the latter case, we say that the option is trading at *parity*.

While an option's intrinsic value can never be less than zero, it is possible for an option, if it is European exercise, to have a negative extrinsic value. (More about this when we look at early exercise in Chapter 12.) When this happens, the option can trade for less than parity. Usually, however, an option's premium will reflect some nonnegative amount of intrinsic and extrinsic value.

Any option which has a positive intrinsic value is said to be *in-the-money* by an amount equal to its intrinsic value. With gold at $450 per ounce, the $440 gold call is $10 in-the-money. With Deutschemarks at 61.50¢, the 64 Deutschemark call is 2.50¢ in-the-money. If an option has no intrinsic value, it is said to be *out-of-the-money*. The price of an out-of-the-money option consists solely of extrinsic value. In order to be in-the-money, a call (put) must have an exercise price lower (higher) than the current price of the underlying market. Note that if a call is in-the-money, a put with the same exercise price and underlying must be out-of-the-money. If a put is in-the-money, the call with the same exercise price must be out-of-the-money.

Finally, an option whose exercise price is identical to the current price of the underlying contract is said to be *at-the-money*. Technically, an option which is at-the-money is, by this definition, also out-of-the-money since it has no intrinsic value. We make the distinction between an at-the-money and out-of-the-money option because, as we shall see, an at-the-money option has the greatest amount of extrinsic value, and is usually traded very actively.

If we want to be very precise, the exercise price of an option must be identical to the current price of the underlying contract for the option to be at-the-money. However, for exchange-traded options the term is commonly applied to the call and put whose exercise price is closest to the current price of the underlying contract. With gold at $455 per ounce, and $20 between exercise prices (440, 460, 480, etc.), the $460 call and the $460 put would be considered the at-the-money options. These are the call and put with exercise price closest to the price of the underlying contract.

Market Integrity

An important consideration for every market participant is the integrity of the market. No trader will want to trade in a market where there is a chance that the opposing trader will default on a contract. If a trader purchases an option, he wants to be certain that the seller will fulfill the terms of the contract if the option is exercised.

In order to guarantee that the integrity of the market will be maintained, each options exchange has established several levels of responsibility for the fulfillment of the terms of an option. The first level of responsibility falls to the individual trader. If the seller of an option is assigned, he must be prepared to take the required long or short position in the underlying contract at the specified exercise price. In practical terms, this means a trader must have access to capital at least equal to the intrinsic value of the option.

If an individual trader is unable to fulfill the terms of the contract, the responsibility falls to the trader's clearing firm. A clearing firm is a member firm of the exchange which processes trades made by an individual, and which agrees to fulfill any financial obligation resulting from those trades. No individual may trade on an exchange without first becoming associated with a clearing firm.

If the clearing firm cannot fulfill the terms of the contract, the final responsibility rests with the clearing house. Each exchange has established, or has become a member of, a clearing house which guarantees the integrity of all trades. Once an option trade has been made, the connection between the buyer and the seller is severed, with the clearing house assuming the role of a buyer from every seller, and a seller to every buyer. If there were no central clearing house, the buyer of an option would be totally dependent on the good faith of the seller or the seller's clearing firm to fulfill the terms of the option. Because the clearing house guarantees every trade, all buyers of options can be certain that there will be an opposing party prepared to make or take delivery if an option is exercised. (See Figure 1-7.)

The Clearing Process

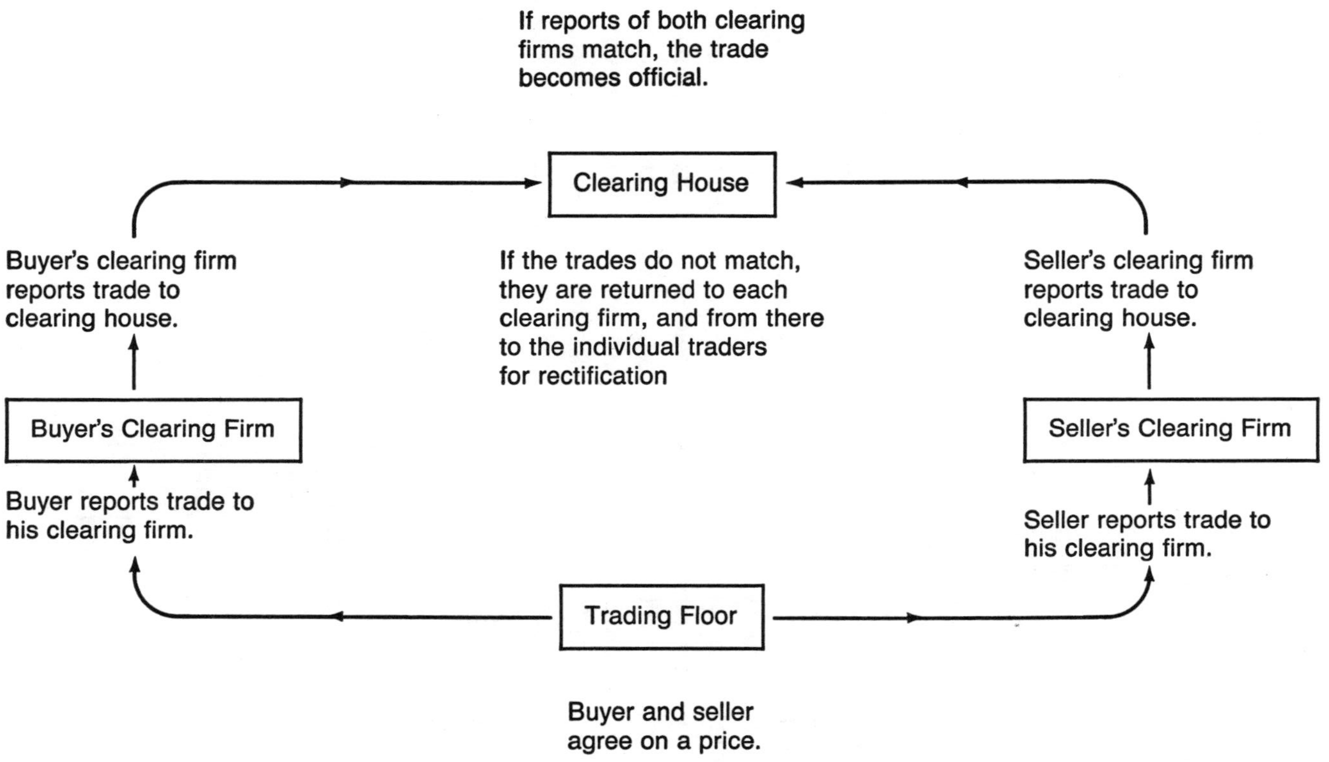

If reports of both clearing firms match, the trade becomes official.

Clearing House

If the trades do not match, they are returned to each clearing firm, and from there to the individual traders for rectification

Buyer's clearing firm reports trade to clearing house.

Seller's clearing firm reports trade to clearing house.

Seller's Clearing Firm

Seller reports trade to his clearing firm.

Buyer's Clearing Firm

Buyer reports trade to his clearing firm.

Trading Floor

Buyer and seller agree on a price.

Figure 1-7

This system of guarantees has thus far proved effective in ensuring the integrity of options exchanges. While individual traders and clearing firms occasionally fail, a clearing house has never failed in the United States.

Margin Requirements

Each exchange requires a trader to deposit with the clearing house some amount of *margin*, or good faith capital, each time he makes an opening trade on the exchange. Such deposits ensure that if the market moves adversely, the trader will still be able to fulfill any future financial obligations resulting from the trade.

In lieu of cash, margin requirements can often be met by depositing government treasury instruments or, less commonly, commercial securities. Clearing firms are required to collect these margin deposits from their traders and forward the funds to the clearing house. In theory, margin deposits with the clearing house still belong to the individual trader and, as such, any interest or dividends which accrue to the margin deposit also belong to the trader. Some clearing firms do not return this interest to the trader, claiming that it is part of the fee paid by the individual trader for the clearing services of the member firm. This can become a sensitive point between trader and clearing firm, and should be settled before an individual begins to trade.

Margin requirements for both futures and options are set by each exchange, using as guidelines the current value of the position as well as its potential risk. While a futures position generally has a fixed margin which does not fluctuate, the margin for an option position can change over time since the margin for an option often depends on the amount by which it is in- or out-of-the-money. Positions consisting of a combination of options, or options and futures, may have reduced margin requirments because the risk to one contract may be partially offset by the value of another contract. Additionally, traders who are exchange members often have reduced margin requirements. Every trader should become familiar with the margin requirements for the market in which he is trading. Doing so will ensure that he has sufficient capital to initiate positions and to hold those positions as long as he deems necessary.

Settlement Procedures

New option traders are often confused because settlement procedures may vary from one option exchange to another. Indeed, settlement procedures for an option and its underlying contract may even differ. Two methods are commonly used to settle exchange traded contracts—stock-type settlement and futures-type settlement.

Suppose a trader buys 100 shares of a $50 stock. The value of the stock is $5,000, and the buyer is required to pay the seller the full sale amount. If the value of the stock rises to $60 per share, the owner of the stock will show a profit of $10.00. Even so, he won't be able to actually spend the $10.00 profit until he formally liquidates the position by selling his 100 shares at $60 per share. This type of settlement procedure, where purchase requires full and immediate payment, and where profits and losses are not realized until the position is liquidated, is known as *stock-type settlement.*

In contrast to stock type settlement, *futures-type settlement* requires no initial cash payment. Additionally, all profits and losses are realized immediately even if the position is not liquidated. For example, if a trader buys a gold futures contract covering 100 ounce of gold for $450 per ounce, the value of the contract is $45,000. The buyer, however, is not required to pay the seller the full $45,000 value of the contract. In fact, the buyer does not have to pay any money at all. He is only required to deposit with the clearing house some amount of good-faith margin. Moreover, at the end of each trading day the trader will immediately realize any profits or losses resulting from movement in the price of the gold futures contract. If gold rises from $450 to $500 per ounce, $5,000 ($50 × 100 oz.) will be credited to his account, and he can make immediate use of these proceeds without liquidating the position. Of course, if the price of gold drops to $400 per ounce, he will realize an immediate loss of $5,000. If he does not have sufficient funds in his account to cover this loss, the clearing house will issue a *variation call.*

There is an important distinction between margin and variation calls. A margin call is issued by the clearing house to ensure that a trader can fulfill *future* financial obligations should the market move against him. Margin calls can be met with funds which, when deposited at the clearing house, still earn interest for the trader. A variation call is issued in order to fulfill *current* obligations in the form of *realized* losses. Variation calls must be met with a cash payment which is immediately deducted from the trader's account. If the trader has deposited securities as margin and receives a variation call, he must either deposit the additional variation amount in cash, or the clearing house will sell the securities in his account to cover the variation call. If the remaining securities and cash in the account is not sufficient to cover the current margin call, the trader may be forced to liquidate his position.

We make this very important distinction between stock- and futures-type settlement because some options are settled like stock while other options are settled like futures. It is important for a trader to know which he is trading. Currently all listed options in the United States, whether options on stock, futures, or indices, are settled like stock. Options must be paid for immediately and in full, and profits or losses will not be realized until the position is liquidated. In stock option markets, this is both logical and consistent, since both the underlying contract and options on that contract are settled using identical procedures. However, in U.S. futures options markets, the underlying contract is settled one way (futures-type selltlement), while the options are settled a different way (stock-type settlement). This can cause problems when a trader has bought or sold an option to hedge a futures position. Even if the profits from the option position exactly offset the losses from the futures position, the profits from the option position, because options are settled like stock, are only paper profits, while the losses from the futures position will require an immediate cash outlay to cover a variation call. If a trader is unaware of the different settlement procedures for options and the underlying futures contract, he can occasionally find himself with unexpected cash flow problems.

The settlement situation on many European exchanges has been simplified by making option and underlying settlement procedures identical. Stock options are settled like stock, and futures options are settled like futures. Under this method a trader is unlikely to get a surprise variation call from a position which he thinks is well-hedged.[3]

---

[3]There is currently a proposal before several U.S. futures exchanges to change to futures-type settlement for options on futures. As of this writing, no action has been taken on this proposal.

Before closing this chapter, it will be useful to define the terms *long* and *short* as they are used in option trading versus their use in futures trading. In a long futures position, a trader will profit if prices rise and lose if prices fall. In a short futures position, a trader will profit if prices fall and lose if prices rise. There is a tendency to carry this terminology over into the option market, by referring to any position which will profit from a rise in the price of the underlying commodity as a long position, and any position which will profit from a fall in price as a short position.

More generally, however, the terms long and short refer to the purchase or sale of a contract. If a trader is long a futures contract, he has purchased the futures contract. If he is short, he has sold it. This is the sense in which we apply these terms to option trading. A trader who is long an option has purchased the option, and a trader who is short an option has sold it. There is no confusion when we refer to a long call position, because the trader who is long a call also has a *long market position*. Calls will, in theory, rise in value if the underlying market rises. But a *long* put position is a *short* market position. A trader who has purchased (is long) a put wants the market to decline because a put will theoretically increase in value as the market declines. Throughout this text, whenever there is the possibility of confusion, an attempt will made to differentiate between a long and short market position versus a long and short option position.

2

Elementary
Strategies

The trader who enters an option market for the first time may find himself subjected to a form of "contract shock." Unlike a futures trader, whose choices are limited to five or six contracts, the option trader may have to deal with a bewildering assortment of contracts. With at least three different delivery months, with each month having 10 or more exercise prices, and with both calls and puts available at each exercise price, it is not unusual for an option trader to be faced with as many as 60 different option contracts.

Even if we eliminate the inactively traded options, a new trader may still have to deal with 20 or 25 different options. With so many choices available, he needs some logical method of deciding which options actually represent profit opportunities. Which should he buy? Which should he sell? Which should he avoid altogether? The choices are so numerous that many prospective option traders simply give up in frustration.

But for the trader who does persevere, a certain logic in the pricing of options begins to emerge. As he becomes familiar with this logic, he can begin to formulate potentially profitable strategies. Initially, he will concentrate on the purchase or sale of individual options. From there he will go on to simple spreading strategies, and eventually to more complex strategies involving many different contracts.

How might a beginning trader assess an option's value? One very simple pricing method might be to try to guess where the underlying futures contract wil be at expiration. If an option position is held to expiration, the option will be worth either zero if it is at- or out-of-the-money, or parity (intrinsic value) if it is in-the-money. The purchase of an option will be profitable if its trade price is less than its value at expiration, and the sale of the option will be profitable if its trade price is greater than its value at expiration.

For example, suppose that with two months to March expiration, and the March futures contract trading at 99.00, the following March options are available:

	85	90	95	100	105	110	115
Calls	14.05	9.35	5.50	2.70	1.15	.45	.20
Puts	.10	.45	1.55	3.70	7.10	11.35	16.10

If we believe that March futures will rise to at least 108.00 by expiration, we can buy a 100 call for 2.70. Our profit at expiration will be 8.00 (the option's intrinsic value) less 2.70 (the amount we paid for the option), or 5.30 points. In fact, given the above prices, we can profit by purchasing any call with an exercise price less than 110. The intrinsic value of each of these options at expiration will be greater than its current price in the marketplace.

What about the 110 and 115 calls? If we believe that 108.00 is a reasonable upside goal for March futures, but consider it unlikely that the price will ever rise above 110.00, then we will prefer to be sellers of the 110 and 115 calls. If we sell the 110 call for .45, and March futures never rise above 110.00, the 110 call will be worthless at expiration and we will get to keep the full premium of 45. We can also sell the 115 call for .20. Now we have an additional 5 point margin for error. If March futures never rise above 115.00, the 115 call will expire worthless and we will profit by the full premium amount of .20.

We can use the same reasoning to assess the potential profit from the purchase or sale of a put. As with a call, a put's intrinsic value at expiration must be greater than its trade price in order for the purchase of the put to be profitable. If the March futures contract rises to

108.00 by expiration, any put with an exercise price of 105 or less will be worthless. If we sell any of these puts, we will profit by the full amount of the premium. If we sell the 110 or 115 puts, they will not be totally worthless at expiration because, with March futures at 108.00, they will have intrinsic values of 2.00 and 7.00, respectively. However, this will still be less than their trade prices of 11.35 and 16.10. We will show a profit of 9.35 from the sale of the 110 put and 9.10 from the sale of the 115 put.

As we raise or lower our assumptions about the likely price of the underlying futures contract at expiration, we alter the likely profit or loss from any option position. If, instead of rising to 108.00, the March futures contract actually rises to 120.00, the purchase of the 100 call for 2.70 will result in a profit of 17.30 rather than 5.30. On the other hand, if the March futures contract falls to 90.00, the purchase of the 100 call will result in a loss of the full premium of 2.70. In the latter case, if we sell the 110 put for 11.35, instead of making 9.35 as we would with the March futures contract at 108.00, we will actually lose 8.65.

Using a value for an option of either zero or parity, we can draw a graph representing the profit or loss at expiration from any option trade which we might make today. Such graphs not only enable the beginning trader to assess the likely profitability of an option trade, but also help him understand some of the unusual characteristics of options. However, before looking at graphs of option positions, we begin by looking at the profit and loss graph of a futures position. At expiration, an option's value is totally dependent on the price of the underlying futures contract. If we really have an opinion on the likely price of the futures contract, we don't need to trade options at all. We can simply buy or sell futures contracts.

If we let the horizontal (X) axis represent the price of the futures contract, and the vertical (Y) axis represent the profit or loss from our position, Figure 2-1 shows the value at expiration of both a long and short position in a March futures contract taken at the current price of 99.00. Note that each graph is a smooth 45° line extending infinitely far in each direction. The potential profit or loss to each position is therefore unlimited. Note also that there is a continuous one-to-one relationship between change in the futures price and the value of the position. If we take a long position, for each point the futures

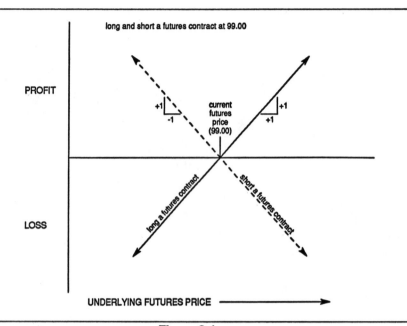

Figure 2-1

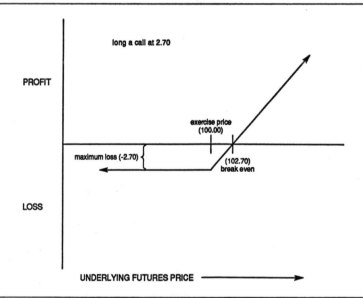

Figure 2-2

contract rises, we make one point; for each point the futures contract drops, we lose one point.[1] If we take a short position, we profit when the futures price drops, and lose when the futures price rises. But, there is still a one-to-one relationship between price movement in the futures contract and the profit or loss to our position.

Using the same evaluation method, Figure 2-2 shows the profit or loss at expiration from the purchase of a 100 call at 2.70. Now, however, the graph is no longer a straight line. With March futures anywhere below 100, the 100 call will be worthless, and we will lose the full 2.70 which we paid for the call. Above 100.00, where the call goes into-the-money, it begins to increase in value at the same rate as a long futures position; in this case, the position gains one point in value for each point that the underlying futures contract rises. If the futures contract rises to 102.70, the 100 call will be worth 2.70 (its intrinsic value), and we will break exactly even. Above 102.70 the purchase of the 100 call will be profitable, and its profit potential, like that of a long futures position, will be unlimited.

The profit and loss graph of a long call position will always have the same general shape as the graph in Figure 2-2. The position will always have limited downside risk and unlimited upside profit potential. The exact location of the graph will be determined by the exercise price (the point at which the graph bends) and the price of the option (the maximum risk). Graphs of long positions in the 95, 100, and 105 calls are shown in Figure 2-3.

Figure 2-4 shows the profit and loss from short positions in the 95, 100, and 105 calls. These are simply inversions of the long call graphs. The positions now have profit limited to the amount of premium for which we sold the option, as well as unlimited risk similar to a short position in the March futures contract.

Figure 2-5 shows long positions in the 95, 100, and 105 put. The risk/reward characteristics of these positions are similar to long call positions, but now the limited risk is on the upside, and the unlimited reward is on the downside. The position will break even if the March

---

[1] Of course a commodity price cannot fall below zero, so the downside profit or loss potential to a position is actually limited. However, if the price of a commodity does drop to zero, it will probably seem like an unlimited profit or loss to most traders.

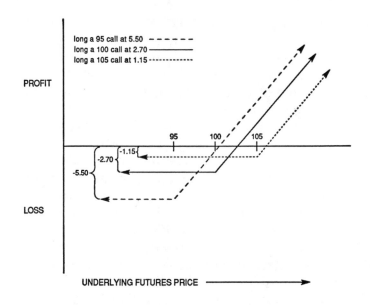

Figure 2-3

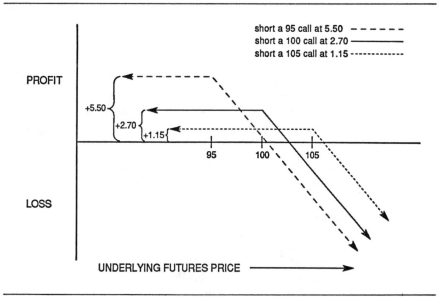

Figure 2-4

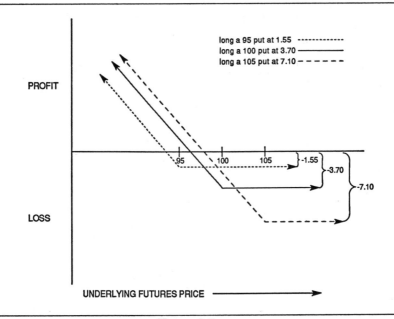

Figure 2-5

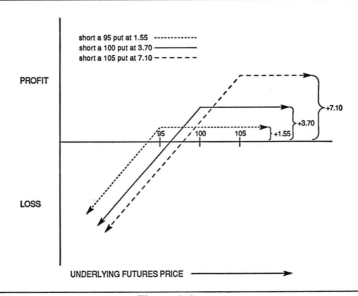

Figure 2-6

futures contract falls below the exercise price by exactly the amount of the option's trade price. Below that break even price, the long put position will act like a short futures position, gaining one point in value for each additional point the futures contract declines.

The short put positions in Figure 2-6 are inversions of the graphs in Figure 2-5. Each position has upside profit potential limited to the amount of the trade price, and unlimited downside risk equivalent to a long position in the March futures contract.

Figures 2-4 through 2-6 point up one of the important chracteristics of options: buyers of options have limited risk and unlimited reward; sellers of options have limited reward and unlimited risk. More specifically, net buyers (sellers) of calls have unlimited upside reward (risk), and net buyers (sellers) of puts have unlimited downside reward (risk).

At this point all new traders tend to have the same reaction: Why would anyone ever want to do anything other than buy options? After all, a buyer of options has limited risk and unlimited profit potential, while a seller has limited profit potential and unlimited risk. Who in their right mind would choose the latter over the former?

The prospect of unlimited risk certainly seems a good reason to avoid a trade. In fact, if a trader gives some thought to the matter, he will realize that almost any trade in a commodity market, or futures market, or stock market, entails unlimited risk. A violent adverse move, which does not give a trader time to cover his position, is always possible (as witness October 19, 1987). Yet traders take long and short positions in stocks and commodities all the time. The only explanation must be that they believe the chances of sustaining an unlimited loss must be very small, and that the profit potential is worth the risk.

Option traders learn that the limited or unlimited risk/reward characteristics of a trade are not the only considerations. Equally important is the likelihood of a profit or loss. As an example, suppose a trader is considering a trade with only two outcomes: in one case he will double his money; in the other case he will lose everything he owns. It may seem that a rational trader will avoid such a trade because of the potentially unlimited risk. But suppose the probability of the trader losing everything is one chance in a billion. Suppose, in fact, that the exact circumstances which can cause the loss have never happened before. Now how does the trade look? The reward is still limited and the risk unlimited. Yet most traders would probably make the trade in spite of the potentially disastrous results.

Every trader must consider not only the limited versus unlimited risk/reward characteristics of a trade, but also the likelihood of each of those outcomes. Is the reward, even a limited one, sufficient to offset the risk, even an unlimited one? Sometimes it is; sometimes it isn't.

When considering an option trade, we need not restrict ourselves to the purchase or sale of individual options. We can also combine option positions to form new positions with their own unique characteristics. Figure 2-7 shows the profit and loss at expiration from the combined purchase of a 100 call and a 100 put for 2.70 and 3.70, respectively. Here we have paid a total of 6.40, which will be our maximum loss if both options expire worthless. This will happen only if March futures are right at 100.00 at expiration. Above 100.00, the put will be worthless, but the call will begin to act like a long futures position, gaining one point in value for each point the March futures contract rises. Below 100.00 the 100 call will be worthless, but the 100 put will begin to act like a short futures position, gaining one point in value for each point the March futures contract falls. In order to break even, the position must be worth 6.40 at expiration. This will occur if either the 100 call goes 6.40 into-the-money (March futures at 106.40) or the 100 put goes 6.40 into-the-money (March futures at 93.60). Below 93.60 or above 106.40 the profit potential is unlimited, since the position is net long both puts and calls.

The position in Figure 2-7 might be sensible if we feel that a large move is likely in March futures, but we are uncertain as to the direction of the move. Of course, we might also take the opposite view, that March futures are unlikely to either fall below 93.60 or rise above 106.40. Under those conditions we will prefer to sell the 100 call and put (Figure 2-8). Now our profit is limited to the total premium of 6.40, while our risk is unlimited in either direction. But if we feel strongly that the March futures contract will stay in the 93.60-106.40 range, the risk might be worth taking.

We might also take a view similar to that in Figure 2-8, that the March futures contract is unlikely to make a big move in either direction. But because there is always a chance we can be wrong, we might

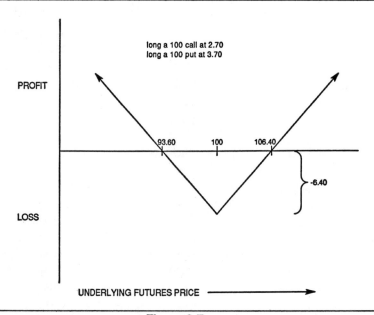

long a 100 call at 2.70
long a 100 put at 3.70

PROFIT

93.60   100   106.40

-6.40

LOSS

UNDERLYING FUTURES PRICE ⟶

Figure 2-7

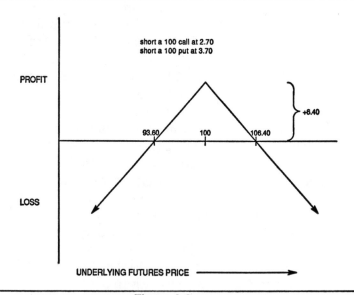

short a 100 call at 2.70
short a 100 put at 3.70

PROFIT

+6.40

93.60   100   106.40

LOSS

UNDERLYING FUTURES PRICE ⟶

Figure 2-8

want to increase our margin for error by increasing our range of profitability beyond the 93.60-106.40 area. One way to accomplish this is by selling a 95 put at 1.55 and a 105 call for 1.15. This position (Figure 2-9) will realize its maximum profit of 2.70 anywere within the 95-105 range where both options will expire worthless. We won't begin to lose money until the March futures contract falls below 92.30, where the 95 put will be 2.70 in-the-money, or rises above 107.70, where the 105 call will be 2.70 in-the-money. There is, as always, a tradeoff for this increased range of profitablility. Our maximum profit now is only 2.70, whereas in Figure 2-8 it was 6.40. In order to reduce our risk, we must also reduce our profit. Option traders are constantly required to make these types of tradeoffs between risk and reward. Sometimes, if the potential reward is big enough, it may be worth taking a big risk. At other times, if the potential reward is small, the accompanying risk should also be small.

The positions in Figures 2-7, 2-8, and 2-9 have either unlimited risk or unlimited reward because they are either net long or net short options. If we purchase and sell equal numbers of options of the same type (either calls or puts), we can also create positions which have both limited risk and limited reward. For example, we might buy a 90 call for 9.35 and sell a 100 call for 2.70. If March futures finish below 90, both options will be worthless and we will lose our total investment of 6.65. If March futures finish above 100, the 90 call will be worth exactly 10 points more than the 100 call, and we will realize the maximum profit of 3.35 (10.00 - 6.65). Between 90 and 100, the position will be worth some amount between zero and 10.00 points. In order to do no worse than break even, we must recoup our original investment of 6.65. We will be able to do this if March futures are at 96.65 or higher. The 90 call, which we own, will then be at least 6.65 points in-the-money (Figure 2-10). Like the outright purchase of a call, this position wants the market to rise so that we will realize our maximum profit of 3.35. Here, however, we are willing to give up the unlimited upside potential associated with the outright purchase of the 90 call in return for the partial downside protection afforded by the sale of the 100 call. The position is bullish, but with both limited risk and limited reward.

We can also create a bearish position with both limited risk and limited reward by purchasing a put with a higher exercise price and

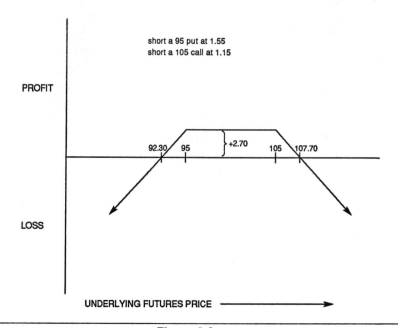

short a 95 put at 1.55
short a 105 call at 1.15

PROFIT

92.30   95   +2.70   105   107.70

LOSS

UNDERLYING FUTURES PRICE ⟶

Figure 2-9

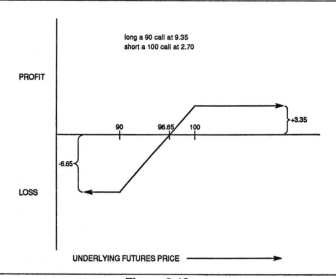

long a 90 call at 9.35
short a 100 call at 2.70

PROFIT

90   96.65   100   +3.35

-6.65

LOSS

UNDERLYING FUTURES PRICE ⟶

Figure 2-10

selling a put with a lower exercise price. We might, for example, buy a 105 put for 7.10 and sell a 100 put for 3.70, for a total debit of 3.40. If March futures are below 100 at expiration, the position will be worth 5.00, and we will realize our maximum profit of 1.60. If March futures are above 105, both options will be worthless, and we will lose our entire investment of 3.40. The position will do no worse than break even if March futures are at 101.60 or below, for then the 105 put will be 3.40 in-the-money (Figure 2-11). Like the outright purchase of a put, this position is bearish. However, we have chosen to give up the unlimited downside potential associated with the outright purchase of the 105 put in return for the partial upside protection afforded by the sale of the 100 put.

From the foregoing examples, we can formulate some simple rules for drawing these expiration profit and loss graphs:

1. If the graph bends, it will do so at an exercise price. Therefore, we can calculate the profit or loss at each exercise price involved and connect these points a straight lines.
2. If the position is long and short equal numbers of calls (puts), the downside (upside) risk and reward will be limited to the total debit or credit required to establish the position.
3. Above the highest exercise price all calls will go into-the-money, so the entire position will act like a futures position which is either long or short futures equal to the number of net long or short calls. Below the lowest exercise price all puts will go into-the-money, so the entire position will act like a futures position which is either long or short futures equal to the number of net long or short puts.

To see how we can use these rules to construct an expiration graph, consider the following position:

> long a March 95 call at 5.50
> short 3 March 105 calls at 1.15

The first step is to determine the profit or loss at each exercise price involved. If March futures finish at 95 (the lower exercise price), both the 95 call and the 105 calls will be worthless. Since the entire

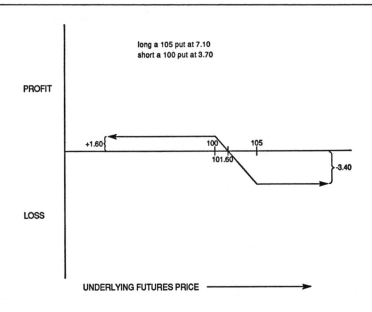

PROFIT

long a 105 put at 7.10
short a 100 put at 3.70

+1.60

100   105
101.60

-3.40

LOSS

UNDERLYING FUTURES PRICE ⟶

Figure 2-11

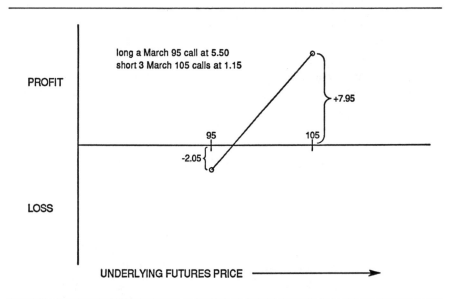

PROFIT

long a March 95 call at 5.50
short 3 March 105 calls at 1.15

+7.95

95   105

-2.05

LOSS

UNDERLYING FUTURES PRICE ⟶

Figure 2-12A

position was established for a debit of 2.05 (-5.50 + 3 × 1.15), the position will show a loss at 95 of 2.05. If March futures finish at 105 (the higher exercise price), the 95 call will be worth 10.00 points and the 105 calls will still be worth zero. The position will be worth the 10.00 point value less the initial 2.05 debit, or 7.95. We can plot and connect these two points on a graph (Figure 2-12a).

Second, we see that there are no puts involved in this position, so the maximum downside loss we can incur is the 2.05 debit required to establish the position. This loss will occur anywhere below the lowest exercise price—in this case 95 (Figure 2-12b).

Above 105, both the 95 and 105 calls will go into-the-money, so that all options will begin to act like long futures contracts. Since we are long one 95 call and short three 105 calls, we are net short 2 futures contracts. Therefore, for each point increase in the the futures price bove 105, our position will lose two points. The graph will continue down and to the right infinitely far at a slope of 1 to -2 (Figure 2-12c).

Applying this method to a more complex example, what would be the expiration graph of the following position?

> short a March 90 call at 9.35
> long 2 March 100 calls at 2.70
> short 4 March 95 puts at 1.55
> long 2 March 100 puts at 3.70

First, what happens at the three exercise prices involved? At 90 we have:

90 call	+9.35
100 calls	-2 × 2.70
95 puts	-4 × 3.45
100 puts	+2 × 6.30
Total	+2.75

At 95 we have:

90 calls	+4.35
100 calls	-2 × 2.70
95 puts	+4 × 1.55
100 puts	+2 × 1.30
Total	+7.25

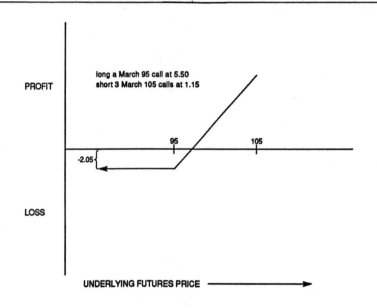

Figure 2-12B

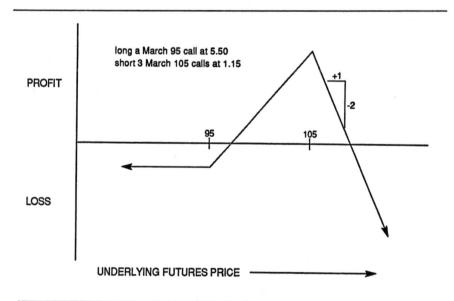

Figure 2-12C

At 100 we have:

90 calls	-.65
100 calls	-2 × 2.70
95 puts	+4 × 1.55
100 puts	-2 × 3.70
Total	-7.25

We can plot and connect the profit and loss points at each of these exercise prices (Figure 2-13a).

Next, below 90 all calls will be worthless and all puts will act like short futures contracts. Since we are net short 2 puts, the graph will act like a position which is long 2 futures. For each point that March futures fall below 90, we will lose 2 points. The graph will continue down and to the left infinitely with a slope of -1 to -2 (Figure 2-13b).

Finally, above 100 all puts will be worthless and all calls will act like long futures contracts. Since we are net long 1 call, our position will act like a position which is long 1 futures contract. For each point that March futures rise above 100, we will make 1 point. The graph will continue up and to the right infinitely, with a slope of 1 to 1 (Figure 2-13c).

Using this method, we can draw the expiration profit or loss of any position, no matter how complex. The position may consist of underlying futures contracts, plus calls and puts on that futures contract at different exercise prices. But as long as the options expire at the same time, the value of the position will be determined by the price of the underlying futures contract at expiration.

Using options and futures, it is also possible to create positions which mimic other option or futures positions. For example, what are the characteristics of the following position?

> long a March 100 call at 2.70
> short a March 100 put at 3.70

With March futures above 100 at expiration, the put will be worthless and the call will act like a long futures contract. With March futures below 100, the call will be worthless and the put will act like a short futures contract. However, since the position is *short*

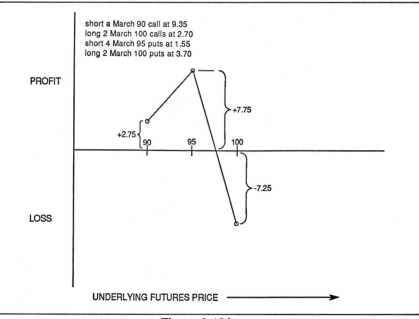

short a March 90 call at 9.35
long 2 March 100 calls at 2.70
short 4 March 95 puts at 1.55
long 2 March 100 puts at 3.70

PROFIT

+7.75

+2.75

90   95   100

-7.25

LOSS

UNDERLYING FUTURES PRICE ⟶

Figure 2-13A

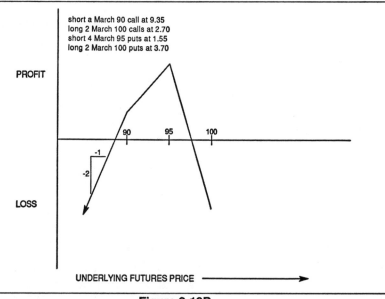

short a March 90 call at 9.35
long 2 March 100 calls at 2.70
short 4 March 95 puts at 1.55
long 2 March 100 puts at 3.70

PROFIT

90   95   100

-1

-2

LOSS

UNDERLYING FUTURES PRICE ⟶

Figure 2-13B

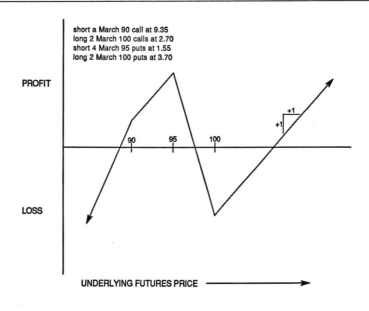

short a March 90 call at 9.35
long 2 March 100 calls at 2.70
short 4 March 95 puts at 1.55
long 2 March 100 puts at 3.70

PROFIT

90   95   100

LOSS

UNDERLYING FUTURES PRICE ⟶

Figure 2-13C

the 100 put, it will act like a long futures contract. In other words, this position will mimic a long futures position regardless of where March futures are at expiration (Figure 2-14). The only real difference between the option position and a long futures position is that the option position will also create a credit of 1 full point.

Or consider the following position:

> long a March 90 put at 45
> short a March 100 call at 2.70
> long a March futures contract at 99.00

The value of this position at expiration is given in Figure 2-15. Note the similarity between this position and the one in Figure 2-10. The only difference appears to be that we replaced a long 90 call with the combination of a long 90 put and a long March futures contract. Therefore, a long 90 put and a long March futures contract together must mimic a long 90 call. As proof, the reader should draw the expiration profit and loss graph of the following two positions:

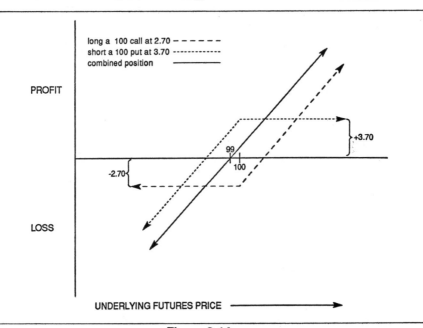

long a 100 call at 2.70 – – – – – –
short a 100 put at 3.70 --------------
combined position ————

Figure 2-14

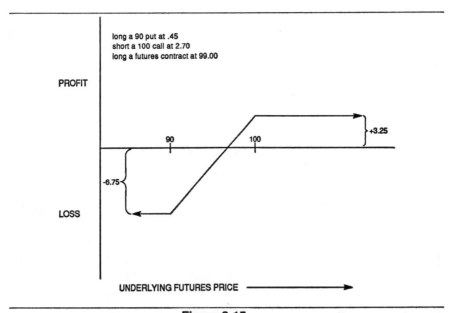

long a 90 put at .45
short a 100 call at 2.70
long a futures contract at 99.00

Figure 2-15

1. long a 90 call at 9.35

2. long a 90 put at .45 and long a March futures contract at 99.00

He will find that, although the credit or debit created by the two trades are different, the general shapes of the graphs are very similar.

The reader who is new to options may find it useful to sit down with the business section of a newspaper, and create and graph a variety of option and futures positions on a given commodity.[2] (See Figure 2-16.) This will enable him to become comfortable with many of the concepts introduced in the first two chapters, and will make the subsequent material that much easier to understand.

While elementary strategies are important in introducing the new trader to options, in real life no active trader tries to initiate a strategy based on where he thinks the underlying futures contract will be at expiration. Even if he were to initiate such a position, he would be foolish to simply walk away from the market and come back at expiration to find out whether he had made or lost money. As market conditions change, a position which seemed sensible yesterday may not seem quite so sensible today. Based on new conditions the trader may want to—indeed, may have to—alter his strategy. This is true not only for option traders. A futures trader who takes a long postion in the belief that a commodity will rise in price would be foolish not to reassess his position if the commodity were to unexpectedly drop several points. An option trader who sells 105 calls in the belief that the underlying futures contract will never rise above 105, would likewise be foolish not to reassess the situation if the futures contract were to make a rapid upward move from 99.00 to 104.00. He may still believe that the futures contract cannot rise above 105.00, but he is unlikely to have the same degree of conviction. *Every trader reserves the right to make a more intelligent decision today than he made yesterday.*

The serious trader must be able to identify potentially profitable strategies given current market conditions. But he must also be able adjust to changing market conditions, and to take protective measures when the market moves adversely. In the next chapter will begin our investigation of basic option pricing theory, and show how this theory can be used to help a trader achieve these goals.

---

[2]*Investors Daily, The New York Times,* and *The Wall Street Journal* all carry extensive listings of commodity futures and futures options.

Futures

WEDNESDAY, JUNE 1, 1988

—Season— High	Low	High	Low	Close	Chg.	Open Interest
CRUDE OIL (NYM)						
42,000 gallons; $ per barrel						
20.17	14.85 Jul	17.70	17.56	17.58	+.07	61,109
20.10	14.80 Aug	17.85	17.69	17.72	+.01	59,880
19.72	14.95 Sep	17.95	17.73	17.77	−.04	20,586
19.70	14.90 Oct	17.99	17.76	17.79	−.07	12.222
18.42	14.90 Nov	17.93	17.89	17.80	−.09	7,063
18.35	14.99 Dec	18.00	17.89	17.80	−.11	6,720
18.20	15.18 Jan	17.98	17.93	17.77	−.11	1,949
18.10	15.15 Feb	17.95	17.65	17.74	−.11	1,776

Est. sales 44,859. Tue.'s sales 35,744.
Tue.'s open int 174,306, up 1, 198.

GOLD (COMEX) 100 troy oz.; $ per troy oz.

523.00	399.00 Jun	459.00	455.60	457.60	+2.60	9,408
458.50	458.40 Jul	....	....	459.90	+2.60	160
527.00	425.00 Aug	463.30	460.30	462.40	+2.60	52,683
533.50	429.00 Oct	468.40	465.80	467.30	+2.50	12,677
546.00	430.80 Dec	473.50	470.50	472.30	+2.40	23,958
549.50	446.00 Feb	479.50	476.00	477.50	+2.20	9,610
550.00	451.00 Apr	....	....	482.80	+2.00	7,128
570.00	455.50 Jun	485.80	485.80	488.30	+1.80	10,216
575.00	482.20 Aug	....	....	494.10	+1.60	5,894
575.50	466.30 Oct	....	....	500.30	+1.40	7,249
513.00	406.00 Dec	....	....	506.60	+1.20	5,380
516.00	502.00 Feb	....	....	512.90	+1.00	1,898
....	.... Apr			519.30	+.80	....

Est. sales 36,000. Tue.'s sales 31,639.
Tue.'s open int 146,461, off 2,872.

U.S. TREASURY BONDS (CBT) 8%-$100,000 prin.; pts. and 32d's of 100%

99-23	66-25 Jun	87-18	86-5	87-17	+1-23	123,719
99-12	74-20 Sep	86-20	85-10	86-19	+1-22	188,973
99-2	74-1 Dec	85-25	84-15	85-23	+1-22	27,352
95-10	73-20 Mar	84-29	83-23	84-29	+1-22	10,570
94-4	73-11 Jun	84-8	83-8	84-4	+1-21	5,983
93-16	72-26 Sep	83-15	83-12	83-13	+1-20	396
92-22	72-18 Dec	82-24	82	82-24	+1-19	793

Est. sales 410,000. Tue.'s sales 253,513.
Tue.'s open int 358,097, off 2,616.

Options

WEDNESDAY, JUNE 1, 1988

CRUDE OIL (NYM) 42,000 gallons; $ per barrel

Strike	Calls-Last			Puts-Last		
Price	Jul	Aug	Sep	Jul	Aug	Sep
12	r	r	r	0.01	r	r
13	r	r	r	0.01	0.01	0.04
14	r	r	r	0.01	0.02	0.07
15	2.59	2.76	2.87	0.01	0.04	0.11
16	1.59	1.83	2.00	0.01	0.11	0.24
17	0.60	1.05	1.26	0.02	0.33	0.51
18	0.03	0.47	0.69	0.45	0.75	0.93
19	0.01	0.17	0.35	1.43	1.45	1.59
20	0.01	0.05	0.16	r	r	2.40
21	0.01	r	0.07	r	r	r

Estimated volum 16,539
Prev. day calls vol. 7,699. Open int. 80,718
Prev. day puts vol. 4,183. Open int. 100,332

GOLD (COMEX) 100 troy oz.; $ per troy oz.

Strike	Calls-Last			Puts-Last		
Price	Aug	Oct	Dec	Aug	Oct	Dec
380	82.40	87.30	$	0.10	0.30	s
390	72.40	77.30	82.30	0.20	0.50	1.20
400	62.40	67.30	72.30	0.30	0.80	1.70
420	42.60	47.60	54.00	0.60	1.70	3.40
440	24.10	30.30	37.50	1.70	3.90	6.30
460	8.30	15.50	22.80	5.90	8.40	10.90
480	2.70	7.30	13.10	20.30	19.80	20.40
500	1.00	3.30	7.20	38.60	35.00	34.00
520	0.50	1.50	3.90	57.60	53.20	50.00
540	0.10	0.80	2.10	77.60	72.70	67.70
560	0.10	0.50	1.30	97.60	92.70	87.70
580	0.10	0.20	$	117.60	112.70	s
600	0.10	0.10	$	137.60	132.70	s

Estimated volume 8,500
Prev. day calls vol. 5,908. Open int. 45,724.
Prev. day puts vol. 1,895. Open int. 27,294.

U.S. TREASURY BONDS (CBT) 8%-$100,000 prin.; pts. and 64th's of 100%

Strike	Calls-Last			Puts-Last		
Price	Sep	Dec	Mar	Sep	Dec	Mar
70	r	r	r	0-02	0-05	s
72	$	$	$	0-03	0-10	s
74	12-38	$	$	0-03	0-15	s
76	r	$	$	0-05	0-20	0-52
78	8-40	8-02	$	0-08	0-35	s
80	6-51	6-25	$	0-16	0-57	1-40
82	5-00	4-56	$	0-31	1-20	s
84	3-26	3-40	3-40	0-56	2-00	2-61
86	2-06	2-37	2-50	1-35	2-54	s
88	1-11	1-46	$	2-36	3-62	s
90	0-40	1-12	$	3-62	5-24	s
92	0-19	0-50	1-02	5-46	6-60	s
94	0-10	0-32	$	7-34	$	s
96	0-06	0-22	0-38	9-30	$	s
98	0-04	0-16	0-28	11-29	$	s
100	0-02	0-10	$	13-27	$	s
102	0-01	0-06	$	$	$	s
104	0-01	0-04	$	$	$	s

Estimated volume 80,000
Prev. day calls vol. 21,923. Open int. 191,105.
Prev. day puts vol. 19,799 Open int. 201,421.

Figure 2-16

3

Introduction to Theoretical Pricing Models

In the previous chapter we looked at some simple option strategies a trader might pursue given an opinion on a commodity's likely price movement. Whatever the basis for the opinion, it will probably be expressed in terms such as "good chance," "highly unlikely," "possible," "improbable," and so forth. The problem with this approach is that opinions cannot be easily expressed in numerical terms. What really represents a good chance? What does highly unlikely mean? If we want to approach options markets logically we must find some way to quantify our opinions about price movements.

In addition to making a decision about the direction in which a market might move, the option trader has another problem: the speed of the market. A futures trader who believes it likely that a commodity will rise in price within a specified period can be reasonably certain of making a profit. He simply buys the commodity, waits for it to reach his target price, then sells the commodity for a profit.

The situation is not so simple for the option trader. Suppose a trader believes that a commodity will rise from $100, its present price, to $120 within the next four months. Suppose also that a $110 call expiring in three months is available at a price of $4. If the commodity goes to $120 by expiration, the purchase of the $110 call will result in a profit of at least $6 ($10 intrinsic value less the $4 cost of the option). But is this profit a certainty? What will happen if the price of the commodity remains below $110 for the next three months and only reaches $120 after the option expires? Then the call will be worthless at expiration, and the trader will lose his $4 investment.

Perhaps the trader would do better to purchase a $110 call which expires in six months rather than three months. Now he can be certain that when the commodity reaches $120, the call will be worth at least $10 in intrinsic value. However what if the price of a six month call is $12? In that case he might still show a loss. There is no guarantee that the option will ever be worth more than its $10 intrinsic value when the commodity price reaches $120.

The futures trader is interested almost exclusively in the direction of the market. The option trader is also interested in market direction, but he must give at least equal consideration to how fast the market will move. If both the futures trader and the option trader take a long market position in their respective instruments and the market does in fact move higher, the futures trader is assured of a profit while the option trader may show a loss. This is the primary reason speculators who purchase options are likely to end up losers. Not only must a speculator be right about market direction, he must also be right about market speed. Only if he is right on both counts can he expect to make a profit. Indeed the speed of the market is of such importance in option trading that, as we shall see, some option strategies depend only on the speed of the market and not at all on direction.

The option trader who wants to approach option markets logically is faced with the task of analyzing several different factors:

1. The commodity's present price.

2. The exercise price.

3. The time to expiration.

4. The direction in which he expects the market to move.

5. The speed at which he expects it to move.

Ideally, he would like to be able to express each of these factors numerically, push these numbers into a formula, and thereby derive a value for the option. The trader would then know whether the purchase or sale of the option was likely to be profitable. *This is essentially the goal of theoretical evaluation: to analyze an option based on current market conditions as well as expectations about future conditions.*

Expected Return

Suppose you are allowed to roll a 6-sided die and each time you roll you will receive a dollar amount equal to the number which comes up. If you roll a one, you get $1; if you roll a two, you get $2; and so on up to six, in which case you get $6. If you were to roll the die an infinite number of times, on the average, how much would you expect to receive per roll?

We can calculate the answer using some simple arithmetic. There are six different numbers which can come up, each with equal probability. If we add up the six numbers $1 + 2 + 3 + 4 + 5 + 6 = 21$ and divide this by the number of possibilities the result is $21/6 = 3\ 1/2$. That is, on the average you can expect to get back $3 1/2 per roll. This is the average or *expected* return. If someone were to charge you for this opportunity, what might be a fair price? If you were to purchase the chance to roll the die for less than $3 1/2, you would expect to be a winner in the long run; if you were to pay more than $3 1/2, you would expect to be a loser in the long run. If you paid exactly $3 1/2, you would expect to break even. Note the qualifying phrase "in the long run." The expected return of $3 1/2 is a realistic goal only if you are allowed to roll the die many times. If you are allowed to roll only once, you cannot count on getting back $3 1/2. Indeed, on any one roll it is impossible to get back exactly $3 1/2 since no face of the die has exactly 3 1/2 spots. Nevertheless if you pay less than $3 1/2 for even one roll of the die, the odds are on your side because you have paid less than the expected return.

In a similar vein, consider a roulette bet. A roulette wheel has 38 slots, numbered 1 through 36, 0, and 00. Suppose a casino allows a player to choose a number. If the player's number comes up, he receives $35; if any other number comes up, he receives nothing. What is the expected return from this proposition? There are 38 slots on the roulette wheel, each with equal probability, but only one slot will result in a return of $35 to the player. If we multiply the $35 return by the one chance in 38 of winning we get $35 \times 1/38 = \$.9211$, or about 92 cents. A player who pays 92 cents for the privilege of picking a number at the roulette table can expect to break just about even in the long run.

Of course no casino will let a player buy such a bet for 92 cents. Under those conditions the casino would make no profit. In the real world a player who wants to purchase such a bet will have to pay more than the expected return, typically $1. The 8 cent difference between the $1 price of the bet and the 92 cent expected return represents the profit potential or *edge*, to the casino. In the long run, for every dollar bet at the roulette table the casino can expect to keep 8 cents.

Given the above conditions any player interested in making a profit would rather switch places with the casino so that he could be the house. Then he would have the edge on his side by selling bets which are worth 92 cents for $1. Alternatively, he would like to find a casino where he could place this 92 cent bet for less than its expected return, perhaps 85 cents. Then the player would have a 7 cent edge over the casino.

Theoretical Value

The theoretical value of a proposition is the price one would be willing to pay in order to just break even in the long run. Thus far there have been no considerations other than the expected return, so the theoretical value of each proposition has been identical to its expected return. The theoretical value of the dice bet was $3 1/2$; the theoretical value of the roulette bet was 92 cents.

Suppose that in our roulette example the casino decides to change the rules slightly. The player can now buy a roulette bet for its expected return of 92 cents and, as before, if he loses the casino will immediately take his 92 cents. Under the new rules however, if he wins the casino will send him his $35 winnings in two months. Do you still think both the player and the casino will break even? Where did the the player get the 92 cents with which he purchased the bet? In the immediate sense he may have taken it out of his pocket. But a closer examination may reveal that he withdrew the money from his savings account. Since his winnings won't be paid to him for two months, he will have to take into consideration the two months interest he would have earned had he left the 92 cents in the bank. This is an additional cost of buying the roulette bet. If interest rates are 6% annually, the interest loss over two months is $1\% \times 92$ cents, or about 1 cent. If the player purchases the bet for its expected return of 92 cents, he will still be a 1 cent loser in the long run because of the cost of carrying the 92 cent debit for two months. The casino, on the other hand, will be a winner because it can take the 92 cents, put it in a savings account, and at the end of two months collect a 1 cent profit from the interest.

Under these new rules the theoretical value of the bet is now the expected return of 92 cents less the 1 cent carrying cost, or about 91 cents. If a player pays 91 cents today and receives his winnings in two months, neither he nor the casino can expect to make any profit in the long run.

An investment is really a bet that an asset will go up or down in price over some period of time. Other factors beside the probability of a particular price outcome may also effect the value of the bet. In the above example, we had to take into consideration carrying costs. An investment in a stock will also depend on the expected dividend payout to stockholders. Since commodities do not pay dividends, our primary concerns in evaluating commodity options will be expected return and carrying costs.

Exchange representatives will perhaps object to the casino analogy. They prefer that investing not be thought of as gambling, but rather in more socially acceptable terms. There is certainly no desire here to assess the moral implications of options trading. The fact remains that the same laws of probability which enable a casino to set the odds for different games of chance also enable a trader to analyze an option's value. In this respect market makers and local traders act as the house. Through their bids and offers they set the prices of the various bets in the marketplace. The off-the-floor trader, in his role as the player, looks at each commodity option market as an individual casino in which he hopes the bets have somehow been mispriced.

The concept of theoretical value based on probability is quite common in many aspects of business. If the reader is uncomfortable with the gambling analogy, he can think of an option as an insurance policy which requires payment of a premium. Through the use of statistical tables and probability theory, actuaries at any large insurance company attempt to calculate the likelihood that the company will have to pay off on an insurance policy. They can then take into consideration what the insurance company will earn on any money which it is able to invest, and arrive at a theoretical value for the policy. The policy can then be offered to prospective customers at an additional cost, which represents the theoretical edge to the insurance company.

In the same way, the goal of option evaluation is to determine through the use of theoretical pricing models, the theoretical value of an option. The trader can then make an intelligent decision as to whether an option is either overpriced or underpriced in the marketplace.

A Word on Models

Before continuing, a few observations on models in general will perhaps be worthwhile.

A model is a scaled down or more easily managed representation of real life. The model may be a physical one, such as a model airplane or building; or a mathematical one, such as a formula. In each case, the model is constructed to enable us to better understand the world in which we live. *However, it is unwise, and sometimes dangerous, to assume that the model and the real world which it represents are identical in every way.* They may be similar, but it is unlikely that the model will duplicate exactly every feature of the real world.

All models, if they are to be effective, require certain prior assumptions about the physical world. Mathematical models require the input of numbers which quantify these assumptions. If we feed incorrect data into the model, we can expect incorrect answers. As every model user knows: garbage in—garbage out. These general observations about models are equally true for option pricing models. An option model is only a representation of how options may be evaluated under certain conditions. At any single moment there is no guarantee that theoretical prices and actual prices in the marketplace will bear any logical resemblance.

There is a great deal of disagreement among traders as to the usefulness of option pricing models. Some traders feel that models are no more than hocus-pocus and have no relationship to what goes on in the real world. After all, models don't trade options, people do. Other traders feel that once they have a sheet of theoretical values, all their problems are solved. They take the view that the model never lies.

The reality lies somewhere between these two extremes.

A new option trader is like someone entering a dark room for the first time. Without any guidance, he will grope in the dark and may eventually find what he is looking for. The trader who is armed with a basic understanding of theoretical pricing models enters the same room with a small candle. He can make out the general layout of the room and is unlikely to fall over a piece of furniture and hurt himself. However the dimness of the candle prevents him from making out every detail in the room, and some of what he does see may be distorted. Nevertheless, a trader is more likely to find what he is looking for with a small candle than with no illumination at all.

The problems with theoretical pricing models arise most often after a trader has acquired some sophistication. As he gains confidence, he begins to increase the size of his positions. When this happens, his inability to make out every detail in the room, as well as the distortions caused by the flickering candle flame, take on increased importance. Now a misinterpretation of what he thinks he sees can lead to financial disaster, since any error in judgement will be greatly magnified.

The sensible approach is to use the model, but with an awareness of what it can and cannot do. Option traders will find that theoretical pricing models are invaluable tools to understanding the pricing of options. Even the most experienced and successful traders who are familiar with the subtleties of the markeplace, still make use of theoretical pricing models from time to time. However, an option trader, if he is to make the best use of a theoretical pricing model, must also be aware of its weaknesses and limitations. Otherwise he may be no better off than the trader groping in the dark.

A Simple Approach

Suppose we try to adapt the concepts of expected return and theoretical value to options. If we could calculate the expected return for an option, then take into account carrying costs, we could come up with a theoretical value. Let's take a simple example. Assume that a certain commodity is now trading at $100 and that on some date in the future, which we will call expiration, it will take on one of five different prices: $80; $90; $100; $110 or $120.

Assume moreover, that each of the five possible prices is equally likely, i.e. 20%. The prices and probabilities might be represented by the line in Figure 3-1.

$80	$90	$100	$110	$120
20%	20%	20%	20%	20%

Figure 3-1

If we take a long position in the commodity at today's price of $100, what will be the expected return from this position at expiration? *Answer:* 20% of the time the commodity price will be $80 for a loss of $20; 20% of the time the price will be $90 for a loss of $10; 20% of the time the price will be $100 for no profit or loss; 20% of the time the price will be $110 for a profit of $10; and 20% of the time the price will be $120 for a profit of $20. The arithmetic can be written as:

-($20 ×20%) – ($10 × 20%) +0 + ($10 × 20%) + ($20 × 20%) = 0

Since the losses exactly offset the profits, the expected return from a long position in the commodity is zero. The same reasoning will show that the expected return from a short position is also zero. If we take either position we can expect to just break even in the long run.

Now suppose we take a long position in a $100 call expiring on the given date. If the price of the futures contract is $80, $90, or $100 at expiration the call will be worthless. If the futures price is $110 or $120, the call will return $10 and $20, respectively. This can be written:

$$(20\% \times 0) + (20\% \times 0) + (20\% \times 0) + (20\% \times \$10) + (20\% \times \$20) = \$6$$

Because the call can never be worth less than zero the expected return is now a positive number, $6.

If we want to use this approach in a theoretical pricing model, we might propose a series of possible prices and probabilities for the commodity at expiration. Then, given an exercise price, we can multiply the return at each price outcome by its associated probability, add up all of these numbers, and thereby obtain an expected return for the option.

How might we have to alter our approach to make it more realistic? For one thing, while there are no carrying costs associated with a futures contract, in U.S. markets options on futures are settled in cash like stock. If, for example, interest rates are 6% annually (1/2% per month), and expiration is two months away, we will have to discount the $6 expected return by the 6 cent carrying cost. The theoretical value of the option will then be $5.94.

What other changes might we have to make? We assumed that all five price outcomes are equally likely. Is this a realistic assumption? Suppose we were told that only two prices were possible at expiration, $110 and $250. With the commodity trading at $100 today, which price outcome is more likely? Our intuition tells us that price outcomes which are far away from today's price are less likely than price outcomes which are close to today's price. $250, being further from today's price, is therefore less likely than $110. To account for this, perhaps price outcomes in our scenario should be concentrated around the present price of the commodity. A more realistic distribution of probabilities might be those in figure 3-2:

$80	$90	$100	$110	$120
10%	25%	30%	25%	10%

Figure 3-2

Now the expected return from a $100 call is:

$$(10\% \times 0) + (25\% \times 0) + (30\% \times 0) + (25\% \times \$10) + (10\% \times \$20) = \$4.50.$$

If carrying costs are 1% as before, the theoretical value of the $100 call will be approximately $4.45.

Note that because our probabilities are arranged symetrically around the present price of the commodity, the expected return from a long or short position in the commodity is still zero.

Next, it might occur to us that there is a bottom line below which the price of a commodity cannot fall, namely zero. On the other hand the price is unlimited on the upside. Perhaps the price probabilities shouldn't be distributed symetrically around the present price but should exhibit an upward bias. This also conforms to our experience with inflation, that prices tend to move upward over time. The price of a commodity next year is likely to be greater than the price this year, even if all fundamental factors remain the same. If we skew our probabilities to the upside we might get a line such as in Figure 3-3.

$80	$90	$100	$110	$120
10%	20%	25%	25%	20%

Figure 3-3

Using these new probabilities the expected return from a $100 call will be:

$$(10\% \times 0) + (20\% \times 0) + (25\% \times 0) + (25\% \times \$10) + (20\% \times \$20) = \$6.50$$

Discounting the expected return by the 1% carrying cost, we get a theoretical value of approximately $6.43.

Notice that using the last probability line the expected return from a long position in the actual commodity is no longer zero:

$$-(10\% \times \$20) - (20\% \times \$10) + (25\% \times 0) + (25\% \times \$10) + (20\% \times \$20) = \$2.50$$

This means, based on the data above, we can now expect a return of $2.50 simply by taking a long position in the commodity.

Even with allowances for carrying costs, for the fact that price outcomes are concentrated around the present price of the commodity, and for a likely upward bias in prices, one major problem still remains. In our simplified approach there are only five possible price outcomes, while in the real world there are an infinite number of possibilities. In order to make our model really accurate we will have to construct a line with every possible price outcome, together with a probability associated with each price.

This may seem an impossible task, but it is in fact the basis for all theoretical pricing models: to determine the possible prices and then to determine the probability associated with each price. If we can do that, we can calculate the expected return at expiration, discount the expected return by the carrying costs, and thereby obtain a theoretical value for the option.

The Black-Scholes Model

In 1973 Fischer Black and Myron Scholes introduced the first really practical theoretical pricing model for options. Prior to this, evaluation methods required the solution of complex mathematical equations. Since such methods were slow and costly, a trader who tried to use them quickly found that profit opportunitities disappeared faster than the evaluation methods could identify them. However, the Black-Scholes Model, with its relatively simple arithmetic and limited number of easily observable inputs, proved ideal for use in the real world. Although other models have since been developed to overcome some of the deficiencies of the original model, the Black-Scholes Model still remains the most widely used method by which options are evaluated.

The Black-Scholes Model was originally developed to evaluate European call options (no early exercise is permitted) on non-dividend paying stocks. In 1976 Fischer Black made slight modifications to adapt the model for the evaluation of options on futures contracts. The changes centered on the cash settlement feature of stocks versus the futures-type settlement of futures contracts. The modified version for options on futures is officially known as the Black Model, but most traders simply refer to both versions, whether for options on stocks or futures, as the Black-Scholes Model. We shall adhere to this terminology.

The great majority of options traded today are American options (early exercise is permitted). For this reason, it may seem that the Black-Scholes Model is poorly suited for use in the real world. However, the Black-Scholes Model has proven so easy to use that many traders do not believe the slightly more accurate values derived from an American option pricing model are worth the effort. As we shall see, the additional early exercise value associated with futures options is so small that there is virtually no difference between values derived from the Black-Scholes Model and values derived from an American exercise model.[1]

Due to its widespread use and its importance in the development of other pricing models, we will for the moment restrict ourselves to a discussion of the Black-Scholes Model. Only in Chapter 12, when we look at the early exercise of American options, and Chapter 13, when we question some of the basic assumptions in the Black-Scholes Model, will look at alternative methods of pricing options.

The development of the Black- Scholes Model is based on much the same reasoning we introduced earlier in this chapter:

1. Determine all the possible prices and associated probabilities for an underlying instrument at expiration.
2. Calculate the expected return on an option.
3. Discount the option's expected return by the carrying costs.

Black and Scholes originally worked only with call values, but put values can be derived in much the same way. Alternatively, we shall see in Chapter 11 that there is a unique relationship between an underlying futures contract, and a call and a put with the same exercise price and expiration date. This relationship makes it possible to derive a put value simply by knowing the associated call value.

In order to calculate a theoretical value using the Black-Scholes Model, we need to know five characteristics of an option and its underlying contract:

---

[1]Unless otherwise specified, the option values used in this book were generated using the Black-Scholes Model.

1. The option's exercise price
2. The time to expiration
3. The price of the underlying contract
4. Interest rates
5. The volatility of the underlying contract

If we know each of these five inputs, we can feed them into the theoretical pricing model, and thereby generate a theoretical value (Figure 3-4).

Exercise Price
Time to Expiration
Underlying Futures Price   → Theoretical Pricing Model   → Theoretical Value
Interest Rates
Volatility

Figure 3-4

Black and Scholes also incorporated into their model the concept of the *riskless hedge*. For every option position there is a theoretically equivalent position in the underlying contract such that, as the price of the underlying contract moves up or down, the option position will gain or lose value at exactly the same rate as the underlying position. To take advantage of a theoretically mispriced option, it is necessary to establish a hedge by offsetting an option position by this theoretically equivalent underlying position. The correct proportion of underlying contracts to option contracts needed to establish this riskless hedge is known as the *hedge ratio*.

Why is it necessary to establish a riskless hedge? Recall that in our simplified approach to option pricing an option's theoretical value depended on the probability at expiration of various price outcomes in the underlying contract. In the real world, as market conditions change the probability of each price outcome also changes. If a commodity is currently trading at $100 and we assign a 25% probability to $120, we might drop the probability to 10% for $120 if the price of the commodity falls to $80. By initially establishing a riskless hedge, and then by adjusting the riskless hedge as market conditions change, we are taking into consideration these changing probabilities. The only time when the hedge ratio need not be adjusted is at the moment of expiration. At that moment, the hedge ratio will be either zero (the option is out-of-the-money and requires no hedge against the underlying contract), or one (the option is in-the-money and requires a hedge of one underlying contract per option contract).

In this sense, an option can be thought of as a substitute for a similar position in the underlying contract. A call is a substitute for a long futures position; a put is a substitute for a short futures position. Whether it is better to take a position in the option or the underlying futures contract depends on the price of the option in the marketplace. If calls can be purchased for less than theoretical value, it will, in the long run, be more profitable to take a theoretically equivalent long market position by purchasing calls than by purchasing the underlying futures contract. In the same way, if puts can be purchased for less than theoretical value, it will, in the long run, be more profitable to take a theoretically equivalent short position by purchasing puts than by selling the underlying futures contract.

Since the theoretical value obtained from a pricing model is no better than the inputs into the model, a few comments on each of these inputs will be worthwhile.

Exercise Price
There ought never be any doubt about the exercise price of an option. It is fixed by each exchange on which the option is traded and may not vary over the life of the option. If one purchases a Deutschemark June 55 call on the Chicago Mercantile Exchange it will not turn into a June 56 call tomorrow. There may be a problem during the trading and confirmation process whereby the exercise price is mistakenly communicated as 56. But that is a communication problem and not the result of a fluctuating or variable exercise price.

Time to Expiration
Like the exercise price, the option's expiration date may not vary over the life of the contract. Our June 55 call will not suddenly turn into a May 55 call tomorrow. Of course each day that passes brings us closer to expiration so in that sense the time to expiration is constantly

decreasing. However the expiration date, like the exercise price, is set by the exchange and will not change.

Time to expiration is entered into the Black-Scholes Model as a percentage of the year. 91 days to expiration would be entered as approximately 25% of a year and 182 days would be entered as approximately 50% of a year. It may seem initially that we have a problem as to the correct number of days to feed into the model. For volatility purposes in assessing the "speed" of the market we are only interested in trading days. Only on those days can the price of the underlying contract actually change. This might lead us to drop weekends and holidays from our calculations. On the othe hand, for interest rate purposes we must include every day. After all, if we borrow money from a bank we get charged interest on weekends and holidays, no matter that these are not business days.

It turns out that this is not really a problem. It is possible to calculate the "speed" of the market using only business days, and then make allowances for the fact that no trading takes place on weekends and holidays. There is always the possibility that the number of business days to expiration may change because of some freak event. Exchanges have been known to close because of power failures, snow storms, or hurricanes. If there are 100 trading days to expiration and an exchange closes for a day, the time to expiration has been reduced by only 1%. But if there are only two days remaining to expiration and an exchange closes, the number of trading days has been reduced by 50%. This can greatly effect an option trader's positions, and indeed such situations have occurred.

This does not mean that one need constantly worry about the natural disasters that may affect the number of trading days to expiration. These events occur so infrequently as to play only a minute role in option evaluation. Moreover, there is no way to quantify them so that they can be input into a theoretical pricing model.

Price of the Underlying

We have seen that the correct use of an option's theoretical value requires us to hedge the option position with an opposing trade in the underlying contract. Therefore the underlying price we feed into our theoretical pricing model ought to be the price at which we think we can make the opposing trade. If we intend to purchase calls, we will have to hedge by selling futures contracts. In that case, we ought to use the bid price of the futures as that is the only price at which we can be certain of selling futures contracts. On the other hand, if we intend to sell calls, an opposing trade requires us to purchase futures contracts. In this case, we ought to use the ask price for theoretical evaluation as that is the only price at which we can be certain of buying futures contracts.

In practice the bid and offer are constantly changing, and most traders will simply use the last trade price as the basis for theoretical evaluation. But the last trade price may not always reflect the present market. Even the settlement price quoted in a newspaper may not accurately reflect the market at the close of business. The last trade price may show 99.04. By contrast, the bid and offer at the time may have been 99.04 bid, 99.08 offered. A trader who hoped to buy at 99.04 would have almost no chance of being filled. For this reason experienced traders will rarely trade options without knowing the exact bid and offer in the underlying market. This may require a steady flow of information from the marketplace.

Interest rates

Since the purchase or sale of options will result in a debit or credit to a trader's account, the carrying costs on a debit position or the interest earned on a credit position must also play a role in option evaluation. This is a function of interest rates over the life of the option. Most traders cannot borrow and lend at the same rate, so the correct interest rate will, in theory, depend on whether the option trade will create a debit or credit balance. In the former case the trader is interested in the borrowing rate, while in the latter case he is interested in the lending rate.

Fortunately the interest rate component plays a very small role in the theoretical evaluation of options on futures, certainly much smaller than the interest rate component in the evaluation of stock options. To understand why, recall that an option can be thought of as a substitute for taking an equivalent market position in the underlying contract. The value of the option will therefore depend, among other factors, on the cost of carrying a position in the underlying contract to expiration. Since the purchase of stock requires an immediate cash outlay (stock type settlement), an increase in interest rates will make call options on stock more desirable. By purchasing a call instead of stock a trader can avoid the interest charges associated with carrying a long stock position. The situation is just the reverse for puts. An increase in interest rates will make puts less attractive. All traders desiring to take a short position in the stock will prefer to sell the stock and collect greater interest on the funds received from the stock sale.

Futures contracts, on the other hand, require no cash outlay (futures type settlement). Any increase or decrease in interest rates will affect only the cost of carrying the option, not the cost of carrying an equivalent position in the underlying futures contract. Since the cost of an option is very small in relation to the value of the futures contract for which it is a substitute, the interest rate component in evaluating options on futures contracts will also be small. What little effect there is will be reflected in lower option values for both calls and puts when interest rates are high (traders are less willing to lay out cash to own options), and higher option prices when interest rates are low (traders are more willing to lay out cash to own options).[2]

What interest rate should a trader use in evaluating options on futures? Since interest rates play only a minor role, a trader will not go far wrong if he simply uses some interest rate in general agreement with the marketplace. A sensible guideline might be to use the rate for treasury bills maturing closest to the option expiration date. For a 60-day option, use the rate for 60-day treasury bills; for a 90 day option, use the rate for 90-day treasury bills.

Volatility

Of all the inputs required in option evaluation, volatility is the most difficult for traders to understand. At the same time, as any experienced trader will attest, volatility often plays the most important role. Changes in our assumptions about volatility can have a dramatic effect on our evaluation of an option, and the manner in which the marketplace assesses volatility can have an equally dramatic effect on an option's price. For these reasons, we will devote the next chapter to a detailed discussion of volatility.

---

[2]There is at this writing a proposal before the CFTC to change the settlement of options on futures in the U.S. from stock type to futures type settlement. If this proposal is implemented, the interest rate component in theoretical pricing models will effectively be zero. This settlement procedure is already in effect in the London futures markets.

4

Volatility

W hat is volatility, and why is it so important to an option trader? The option trader, like the futures trader, is interested in the direction of the market. Unlike the futures trader, the option trader is also extremely sensitive to the speed of the market. If the market for a commodity fails to move at a sufficient speed, options on that commodity will have less value because of the reduced likelihood of the market going through an option's exercise price. In a sense, volatility is a measure of the speed of the market. Markets which move slowly are low volatility markets; markets which move quickly are high volatility markets.

One might guess intuitively that some commodities are more volatile than other commodities. Between 1980 and 1982 the price of gold moved from $300 per ounce to $800 per ounce, more than doubling its price. Yet few traders would predict that Treasury bonds might go from 90 to 180 in a similar period of time. The Treasury bond market tends to move more slowly than the gold market and is therefore less volatile.

We would like to feed into a theoretical pricing model our intuitive feelings about how fast a market tends to move. If we could tell the model to assume a highly volatile market, or a relatively quiet market, then any evaluation of options on that market would be more accurate than if we simply ignored the volatility. Since option pricing models are based on mathematics, we need some way to quantify the volatility component so that we can feed it into the model in numerical form.

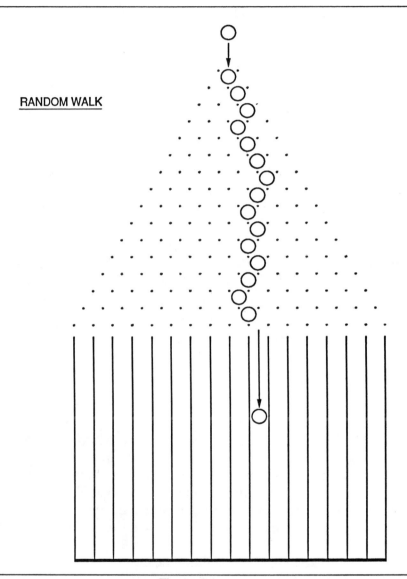

Figure 4-1

Random Walks and Normal Distributions

Visualize for a moment a pinball maze, such as in Figure 4-1. When a ball is dropped into the maze at the top it moves downward, pulled by gravity until it encounters a nail, where it may go either left or right. Each time the ball falls down a level it encounters another nail, moves either left or right, and falls down to a new level. Finally it reaches the bottom of the maze where it falls into one of the troughs. The path the ball takes through the maze is known as a *random walk*.

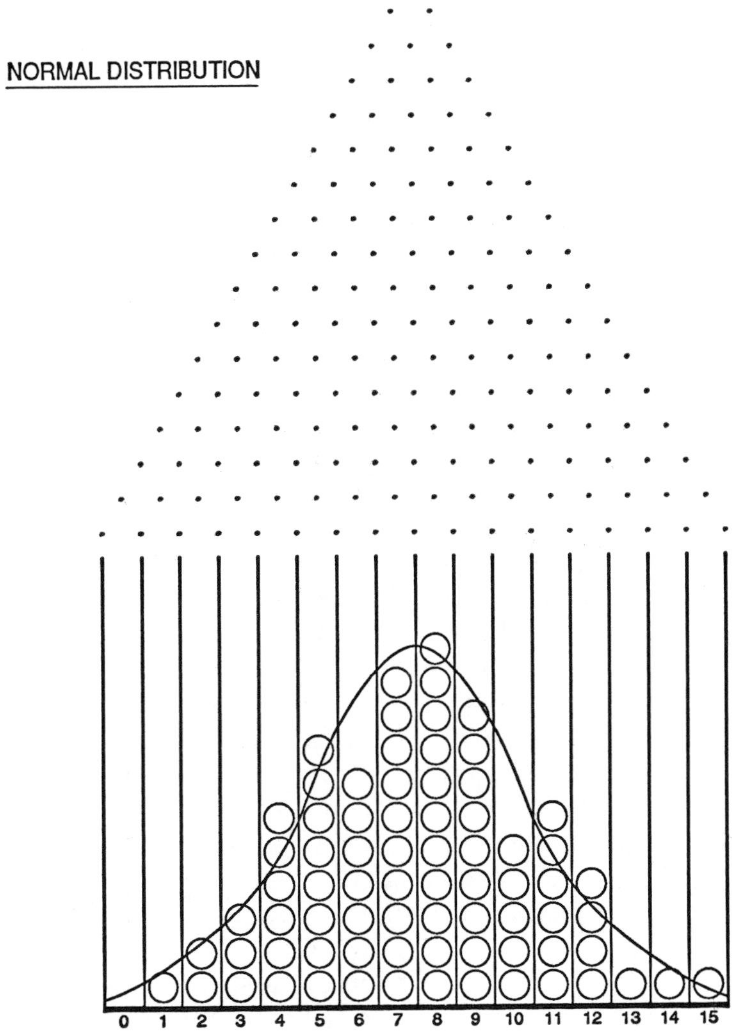
NORMAL DISTRIBUTION
0 1 2 3 4 5 6 7 8 9 10 11 12 13 14 15

Figure 4-2

Once the ball enters the maze nothing can be done to artificially alter its course, nor can one predict ahead of time the path the ball will take through the maze.

If enough balls are dropped into the maze they will begin to form a curve at the bottom, such as in Figure 4-2. Note that the curve is symmetrical with its peak at approximately the center of the maze. This type of curve is known as a *normal distribution,* or bell-shaped curve. Such a curve is always symmetrical (if we flipped it from side to side its shape would be the same), it has its peak in the center, and its tails flare outward at identical rates.

The curve in Figure 4-2 might also represent the results of flipping a coin 15 times, and we can number the troughs to represent the number of heads which occurred after each 15 flips. A ball which ended up in trough zero would indicate no heads and 15 tails; a ball in trough 15 would indicate 15 heads and no tails. Of course we would be surprised to flip a coin 15 times and get either 15 heads or 15 tails. Assuming the coin is perfectly balanced, some result in the middle of these two extremes, perhaps 8 heads and 7 tails, or 9 heads and 6 tails, is more likely.

Normal distribution curves are used to describe the likely outcome of random events. Any student whose teacher graded an examination on a bell-shaped curve knew that most of the scores would be grouped near the average and would receive C's. Fewer scores above and below the average would receive B's and D's. Only a small number of students, whose scores were far removed from the average, would receive A's or F's.

Suppose we change our maze slightly by closing off a row of nails so that a ball must drop down two levels before it can go left or right (Figure 4-3). If we drop enough balls into this maze they will also begin to form a curve. Since the sideways movement of the ball is restricted, this curve will have a higher peak and narrower tails than the curve in Figure 4-2. Even though the shape of the curve is altered, it still represents a normal distribution, although a distribution of a slightly different shape.

Finally, suppose we block off some of the spaces between nails so that each time a ball drops down a level it must move two nails to the left or right before it can fall down to a new level (Figure 4-4). Again, if we drop enough balls into the maze they will begin to form a normal distribution. However, this curve will have a much lower peak

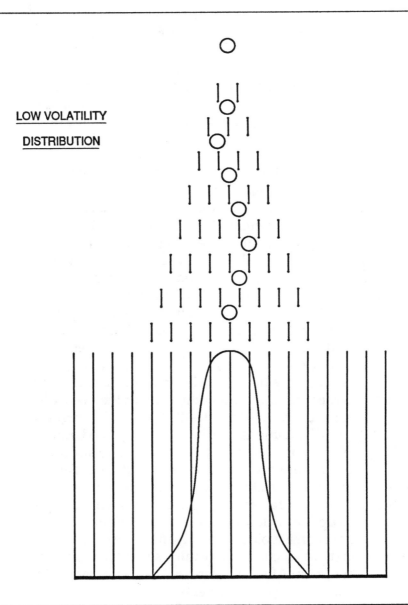

LOW VOLATILITY

DISTRIBUTION

Figure 4-3

and its tails will spread out much more quickly than either the curve
in Figure 4-2 or 4-3.

Suppose now we think of the ball's sideways movement as the price movement of a commodity, and its downward movement as the passage of time. If we assume that each day the commodity can go up or down $1, the price distribution after 15 days might be represented by the curve in Figure 4-2. If we assume the price can go up or down $1 every two days, the price distribution might be represented by the curve in Figure 4-3. Finally, if we assume the price can go up or down $2 each day, the distribution might be represented by the curve in Figure 4-4.

With the commodity presently at $100 and 15 days to expiration how might we evaluate a $105 call? One way is to look at the possible price distribution of the commodity after 15 days. We can do this by comparing the three different distribution curves. If the distribution is as in Figure 4-3, then the underlying commodity has almost no chance of reaching $105. Therefore no trader will be willing to pay much for the option. If the distribution is as in Figure 4-2 there is some chance the commodity will reach $105 and result in the call finishing in-the-money. Now traders will be willing to pay something more for the option. Finally, if the distribution is as in Figure 4-4 there is a very real likelihood that the option will finish in-the-money. In that event the value of the call will increase dramatically. (See Figure 4-5.)

If we assume only that the price movement of the commodity resembles a random walk, and nothing about the likely direction of the market, the curves in Figures 4-2, 4-3, and 4-4 might represent possible price distributions in a low volatility, moderate volatility, and high volatility market respectively. In a low volatility market, the price movements are severely restricted, and consequently all options will command relatively low premiums. In a highly volatile market the chances for extreme price movements are greatly increased, and options will command high premiums.

Since the different volatility curves in Figure 4-5 are symmetrical, it may seem that an increase in volatility should have no effect on the value of an option. After all, increased volatility may increase the likelihood of large upside movement, but this should be offset by the greater likelihood of large downside movement. Here, however, there is an important difference between a futures position and an option position. Unlike a futures contract, an option's potential loss is limited. No matter how far down the market goes, a call option

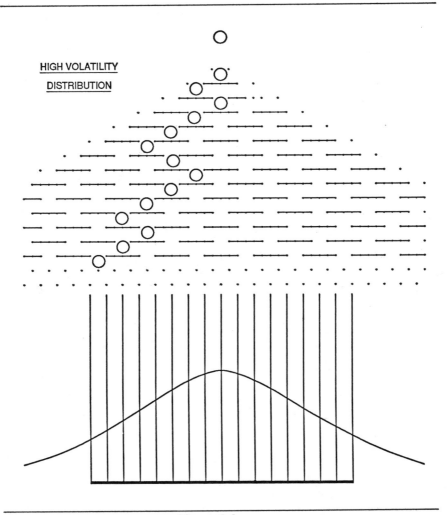

Figure 4-4

can only go to zero. However, like a futures contract, its value is still unlimited on the upside. An increase or decrease in volatility will have no effect on the chances of winning or losing any one bet, but it will change the total expected return. The odds against a roulette player winning any one bet are 38 to 1. Yet if he has purchased the bet for less than its theoretical value, he can still expect to be a winner in the long run.

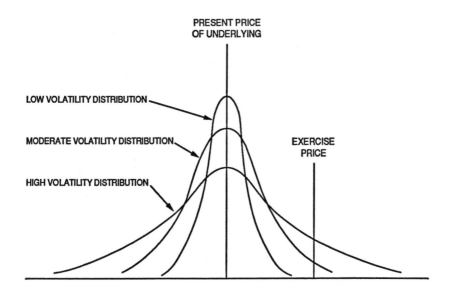

PRICE DISTIBUTION AT EXPIRATION

Figure 4-5

This leads to an important distinction between futures and option evaluation. The expected return from a futures position depends primarily on where the peak of the distribution curve is located. The expected return from an option position depends not only on where the peak of the distribution curve is located, but also how fast the curve spreads out.

Mean and Standard Deviation

Suppose we want to use this concept of price movement based on normal distribution curves in a theoretical pricing model. To do this we need a way to describe the curve in numerical terms so that we can feed the numbers into our model.

A normal distribution curve can be described by two numbers, its *mean* and *standard deviation*. The mean is the average outcome, and locates the peak of the curve. The standard deviation describes how fast the curve spreads out. Curves with a high standard deviation spread out very quickly as in Figure 4-4; curves with a low standard deviation spread out very slowly as in Figure 4-3.

While the mean, or average, is commonly used in technical analysis, the standard deviation may be a new concept to many traders. One need not know how either of these numbers are calculated in order to successfully trade options. (For those who are interested, some sample calculations are given in Appendix B.) It will, however, be very useful to an option trader to understand exactly what these numbers mean in terms of likely price movements.

Let's go back and use the trough numbers 0 through 15 in Figure 4-2. We said that these numbers might represent the number of heads resulting from 15 flips of a coin. Alternatively, they might also represent the number of times a ball went to the right at each nail as it dropped down through the maze. The first trough is assigned zero since any ball that ends up there will have gone left at every nail. The last trough is assigned 15 since a ball will have gone right at every nail in order to end up there.

If we are told that the mean and standard deviation for the curve in Figure 4-2 are 7.50 and 3.00, respectively, what does this tell us about the distribution? (The actual mean and standard deviation of 7.53 and 2.95 are calculated in Appendix B. Here, for simplicity, we will simply round them to 7.50 and 3.00.) The mean tells us the average outcome. In this case a mean of 7.50 says that, on the average, a ball will drop exactly between troughs 7 and 8. (This is not an actual possibility. However, we noted in Chapter 3 that the average outcome does not have to be a possible outcome for any one event.)

The standard deviation not only tells us how fast the distribution curve spreads out, it also tells us something about the probability of a ball ending up in a specific trough or group of troughs. Specifically, the standard deviation tells us the probability of a ball ending up in a trough a specified distance from the mean. For example, we may want to know the likelihood of a ball falling down through the maze and ending up in a trough lower than 5 or higher than 10. We can do this by first asking how many standard deviations the ball must move away from the mean to reach our goal. Once we know this, we can calculate the probability associated with that number of standard deviations.

The exact probability associated with a specific number of standard deviations can be calculated on a computer or found in mathematical tables.

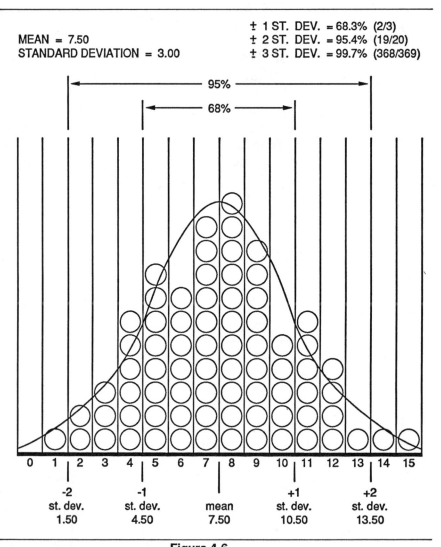

MEAN = 7.50
STANDARD DEVIATION = 3.00

± 1 ST. DEV. = 68.3% (2/3)
± 2 ST. DEV. = 95.4% (19/20)
± 3 ST. DEV. = 99.7% (368/369)

95%

68%

| 0 | 1 | 2 | 3 | 4 | 5 | 6 | 7 | 8 | 9 | 10 | 11 | 12 | 13 | 14 | 15 |

-2
st. dev.
1.50

-1
st. dev.
4.50

mean
7.50

+1
st. dev.
10.50

+2
st. dev.
13.50

Figure 4-6

However, the following approximations will act as a good guideline for option traders:

±1 standard deviation takes in approximately 68.3% (about 2/3) of all occurrences

±2 standard deviations takes in approximately 95.4% (about 19/20) of all occurrences

±3 standard deviations takes in approximately 99.7% (about 368/369) of all occurrences.

Now let's try to answer our question about the probability of getting a ball in a trough lower than 5 or higher than 10. We can designate the divider between troughs 7 and 8 as the mean of 7 1/2. The divider between troughs 4 and 5 can be designated 4 1/2. 4 1/2 is 3 troughs away from the mean of 7 1/2. How many standard deviations is 3 troughs? Since the standard deviation is 3.00, three troughs is exactly 1 standard deviation away from the mean. For a ball to drop into a trough lower than 5 it has to move at least one standard deviation to the left. This is shown in Figure 4-6.

The same calculations will show that the divider between troughs 10 and 11, which we can designate 10 1/2, is also 1 standard deviation from the mean. For a ball to drop into a trough higher than 10 it must move at least one standard deviation to the right.

For a ball to fall into troughs 0 through 4 or 11 through 15 it must move more than 1 standard deviation from the mean. If 1 standard deviation takes in 68.3%, then outside 1 standard deviation must include everything else, or 31.7%. Therefore, any ball dropped into the maze has a 31.7% chance of ending up in a trough lower than 5 or higher than 10. This is about 1 chance in 3.

Suppose someone were to offer you 30 to 1 odds that you couldn't drop a ball into the maze and get it specifically in troughs 14 or 15. Is this a fair bet? Note in Figure 4-6 that to reach troughs 14 and 15, a ball must move to the right more than 2 standard deviations. What is the likelihood of a ball moving beyond 2 standard deviations? Going back to our approximations, 2 standard deviations takes in 95.4%, or about 19 out of every 20 occurences. Therefore we ought to get a ball beyond 2 standard deviations about 1 time in 20. Note that beyond 2 standard deviations also takes in troughs 0 and 1. Here the bet includes only trough 14 and 15. The correct odds are half of 20 to 1, or 40 to 1. The offered odds are therefore insufficient and will represent a losing proposition in the long run for anyone who accepts them.

In Chapter 3 we said that our goal in option evaluation is to assign a probability to an infinite number of possible price outcomes. If the possible prices of a commodity are distributed along a normal distribution curve, using the probabilities associated with normal distributions enables us to do just that. In our simple pinball distribution we were limited to 16 possible outcomes. A normal distribution curve enables us to make the jump from a finite number of outcomes to an infinite number. Using the formulas which describe normal distributions (these can be found in books on probability theory) a probability can be calculated for an infinite number of outcomes. This is exactly what we are looking for.

Lognormal Distributions

Is it reasonable to assume that commodity prices are normally distributed? Note that because a normal distribution curve is symmetrical, it allows for outcomes from minus to plus infinity. This means that the curve allows for negative commodity prices. Is this realistic? Additionally, the curve says that the chances of an asset going down in price are exactly the same as the chances of it going up. Yet our experience with inflation seems to indicate otherwise. Over long periods of time we expect upward pressure on all prices. What we need is a curve which does not allow for negative prices and which assumes that there is also an upward tendency in prices. Does such a curve exist?

Suppose that instead of thinking of a commodity's price movement in total dollar terms, we think of it in percentage terms. That is, we will allow a commodity's price to move up or down, but rather than an equal dollar amount, we will allow it to move up or down an equal percentage of its current price. If a $100 commodity is allowed to move up or down 5%, at its current price it may move up or down $5. However, if the same commodity falls to $50 and we allow the same 5% price movement, it may only move up or down $2.50. In the other direction, if the commodity price jumps to $200, a 5% price change will result in a $10 move.

If we assume a percentage price movement rather than a total dollar price movement, as the commodity's price drops its ability to change price, as measured in total dollars, is severely restricted. In fact, as the price approaches zero it will not be able to change at all. On the upside, as the price increases, its dollar price movements will become greater, even though the percent change remains the same. A curve which assumes a distribution such as this is a *lognormal* distribution. (See Figure 4-7.) It assumes that price changes are calculated in percent, and that these percent changes are distributed normally. If we assume that a commodity's price is changing continuously, then the possible dollar prices of the commodity will be distributed lognormally.[1]

We can now summarize the assumptions about prices made in the Black-Scholes and most other theoretical pricing models:

1. Price changes are random and cannot be artificially manipulated, nor can one predict beforehand which way they will move.

2. The percent changes in commodity's price are distributed normally.

3. The dollar changes in a commodity's price are distributed lognormally.

The first of these assumptions may meet with resistance from some traders. Technical analysts in particular believe that by looking at past price activity one can predict future price movement. One can chart support and resistance points, double tops and bottoms, head and shoulders, and many similar formations which predict future price trends. We will leave debate on this question to others. The important point here is that the Black-Scholes Model, as well as other theoretical pricing models, make the assumption that price changes are random and cannot be predicted.

The lognormal distribution of prices assumed in the Black-Scholes Model helps explain why options with higher exercise prices seem to carry more value than options with lower exercise prices. For example, suppose a certain commodity is at exactly 100. If there are

---

[1]This is analogous to compounding interest continuously rather than at discrete intervals.

LOGNORMAL DISTRIBUTION

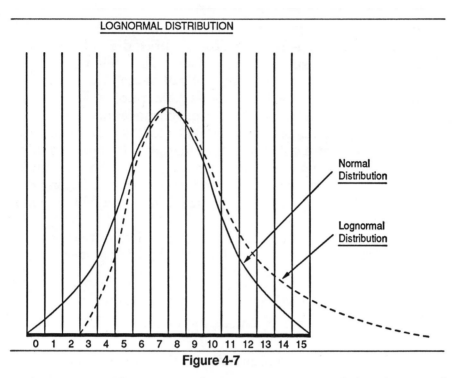

Figure 4-7

no interest considerations and we assume a normal distribution of possible commodity prices, then the 105 call and the 95 put, being equally far out of the money, should have identical theoretical values. In fact, under the assumptions of the Black-Scholes Model the 105 call will always have a greater theoretical value. The lognormal distribution allows for greater upside price movement than downside price movement in the underlying commodity. Consequently the 105 call will have a greater possibility of price appreciation than the 95 put. Of course, if one were to assume a normal distribution of prices, then both options would indeed have the same value.

Volatility as a Standard Deviation

Now that we have a method for describing price distributions, how do we feed this information into a theoretical pricing model? First we must enter a mean. When we enter the present price of a commodity into a theoretical pricing model we are actually entering the mean of a price distribution. Since theoretical pricing models assume that the expected return from a position in the underlying is zero, the peak of the curve will be the present price of the underlying plus carrying costs. Carrying costs for futures are zero, so the peak of our curve will be exactly the current price of the futures contract.[2]

Next we must enter a standard deviation or, as we will now refer to it, a volatility. *The volatility number associated with a commodity is a one standard deviation price change, in per cent, at the end of one year.* If the commodity is currently trading at $100 and has a volatility of 20%, one year from now we expect the same commodity to be trading between $80 and $120 ($100 ± 20%) approximately 68% of the time, between $60 and $140 [$100 ± (2 × 20%)] approximately 95% of the time, and between $40 and $160 [$100 ± (3 × 20%)] approximately 99.7% of the time.

If we come back in one year and find the above commodity trading at $35, does this mean that the volatility of 20% was wrong? A price change of more than 3 standard deviations may be unlikely, but one shouldn't confuse unlikely with impossible. Flipping even a perfectly balanced coin 15 times may result in 15 heads. Unlikely, but not impossible, although the odds against it are more than 32,000 to 1. With our commodity perhaps this was the 1 time in 369 that we were due for a move beyond 3 standard deviations. This does not exclude the possiblity that we may have had the wrong volatility. But we wouldn't know this without looking at price changes of the commodity over many years so that we have a representative price distribution.

Almost no listed options have life spans as long as a year, so a one-year standard deviation may not be of practical value to an option trader. Even a month or a week may be too long a period for some traders to work with. (Indeed, 30 seconds can seem like an eternity to a trader with a large position.) What does a one year's standard deviation tell us about price changes over some shorter period of time, say a week or a day? In the Black-Scholes Model time and volatility are related by a square root factor. To change a yearly volatility to a volatility over some shorter period of time, we must divide the yearly volatility by the square root of the number of trading periods in a year.

---

[2]For stocks, the peak of the curve would have to take into account carrying costs on the stock as well as any expected dividend payouts.

Suppose we are interested in a daily volatility. How many daily trading periods are there in a year? Since prices can only change on business days we can throw out all the weekends and holidays. If we do this, we are left with approximately 256 trading days in a year.[3] The square root of 256 is 16. Therefore, to change any yearly volatility figure to a daily volatility we must divide by 16.

Going back to our $100 commodity with a volatility of 20%, what is a 1 standard deviation price change over a day's time? 20%/16 = 1 1/4%. Therefore a 1 standard deviation price change is 1 1/4% × $100, or $1.25. We expect to see a price change of $1.25 or less 2 days out of every 3, and $2.50 or less 19 days out of 20. Only 1 day in 20 do we expect to see a price change of more than $2.50.

We can go through similar calculations for weekly standard deviations. To do this, we note that there are 52 weekly trading periods in a year. Dividing our annual volatility by the square root of 52, or approximately 7.2, we get 20%/7.2 = 2.78%. For our $100 commodity we expect to see a weekly price change of $2.78 or less 2 weeks out of every 3, and a change of $5.56 or less 19 weeks out of every 20. Only 1 week in 20 do we expect to see a price change of more than 2 standard deviations, or more than $5.56.

This volatility/time relationship allows us to calculate a 1 standard deviation price change for any length of time. For example, if there are 35 days remaining to expiration, what is a 1 standard deviation price change between now and expiration for a $65 commodity with an annual volatility of 14%?

365/35	= 10.43 (the number of trading periods in a year)
Square Root of 10.43	= 3.23
14%/3.23	= 4.33% (1 standard deviation price change in per cent over a 35 day period)
4.33% × $65	= $2.81 (1 standard price change in dollars over a 35 day period)

---

[3]The actual number of trading days in a year is somewhere between 250 and 252. However, we use 256 because its square root is a whole number, and therefore easier to work with.

We might also want to work backwards. Given a volatility and a hoped-for price change, how likely are we to see this change? Suppose we are looking for a $20 price change between now and expiration in a $150 commodity. If the commodity has an annual volatility of 12% and there are 80 days to expiration, what is the probability of actually getting this $20 price change?

365/80	= 4.56 (number of trading periods in the year)
Square Root of 4.56	= 2.14
12%/2.14	= 5.61% (1 standard deviation price change in per cent)
5.61% × $150	= $8.42 (1 standard deviation dollar price change over 80 days)

If 1 standard deviation is $8.42 then $20/$8.42 = 2.38 standard deviations. Here we must go to a math table to find the probability associated with 2.38 standard deviations. This number is 98.27%. We therefore have a 1.73% chance, or only about 1 chance in 58, of seeing $20 price change. If we are specifically looking for a $20 increase in price, the chances are exactly half of 2.38 standard deviations, or about 1 time in 116.

We have used the phrase "price change" in conjunction with volatility. Exactly what do we mean by this? Do we mean the high/low during some period? Do we mean open to close price variations? While there have been attempts to measure volatility in other ways,[4] the standard method has been to calculate volatility from settlement to settlement price changes. When we say that a 1 standard deviation price change over a day's time is .75, we mean a price

---

[4]There have been some attempts to calculate volatility from intraday price movements. See for example: Parkinson, Michael, "The Extreme Value Method of Estimating the Variance of the Rate of Return," *Journal of Business*, 1980, vol. 53, no. 1, pp. 61-64; Garman, Mark B. and Klass, Michael J., "On the Estimation of Security Price Volatilities from Historical Data," *Journal of Business*, 1980, vol. 53, no. 1, pp. 67-78; and Beckers, Stan, "Variance of Security Price Returns Based on High, Low, and Closing Prices," *Journal of Business*, 1983, vol. 56, no. 1, pp. 97-112.

change of .75 from one day's price settlement to the next day's price settlement. The intra-day price movement may be a good deal greater than .75. However on expiration day (or the last trading day prior to expiration) the settlement price will determine the final value of all options on the underlying contract. If we own a 110 call with the futures contract at 115 at the close on the last trading day of the option, then 115 is the theoretical price at which we can sell the futures contract to ensure a 5-point credit when we exercise our call. In addition, settlement-to-settlement eliminates the problem of determining exactly where the underlying price is at any specific moment during the trading day. For these reasons, settlement-to-settlement makes a convenient unit of time over which to measure price changes.

Volatility and Observed Price Changes

If a trader has an opinion about the volatility of a commodity, and knows the approximate probability associated with each standard deviation, he will be able to form a picture of the price movements he expects to see in that commodity. He can then decide whether his opinion is supported by what he actually sees in the marketplace.

For example, suppose a certain commodity is trading at $50.00 and a trader is using a 20% volatility for theoretical evaluation. A 1 standard deviation daily price change is 20%/16 = 1.25% or, in dollar terms, about $.63. Suppose that during a five-day period a trader notes the following settlement to settlement price changes:

$$+.32, -.15, -.61, -.25, +.45$$

Are these five price changes consistent with a 20% volatility? He expects to see a price change of more than .63 (1 standard deviation) about 1 day in 3, or over a five-day period between 1 and 2 times. During this five-day period he did not see a price change of this magnitude even once. The greatest movement was .61, and that is still less than 1 standard deviation. What conclusions can the trader draw from this?[5] One thing is certain: these five price changes are not con-

---

[5]5 days is admittedly a small sample from which to draw a conclusion about volatility. The reasoning, however, is still valid.

sistent with a 20% volatility. The trader might explain this discrepancy in one of two ways. On the one hand, perhaps this was an unusually quiet week for business reasons (perhaps it was a holiday week); and next week when trading returns to normal, the market will go right back to price movements which are more consistent with a 20% volatility. If the trader comes to this conclusion then perhaps he ought to continue to use 20% for his calculations. On the other hand, if he can see no logical reason for the market being less volatile than he expects, then he may simply be using the wrong volatility. If he comes to this conclusion, perhaps he ought to look for a new volatility number which is more consistent with the observed price changes. If he continues to use 20% in the face of price changes which are significantly less than those predicted by a 20% volatility, he will begin to lose money on his trades. Or, depending on the strategies he is pursuing, he may show a profit, though not as great a profit as he would show, had he chosen a more accurate volatility.

Exactly what volatility is associated with the five price changes in the last example? Without doing some rather involved calculations it is difficult to say. (The answer is actually 13.8%.) However, if he knows beforehand approximately what price changes he expects, a trader can easily see that the changes are not consistent with a 20% volatility over the five day period.

Let's look at another example. Suppose a trader noted the following five daily price changes for a $100 commodity:

$$-1.15, +.35, +1.64, -.50, +.98$$

Are these price changes consistent with a 12% volatility? At 12% a 1 standard deviation price change is $12\%/16 \times 100 = .75$. In five days we expect to see a price change of more than .75 between one and two times. Yet here we had a price change of more than .75 three days out of five, and once the price change was more than 1.50 (two standard deviations) which we would not expect to see more than one day in twenty. Again, if the trader does not have some reason to believe that these five price changes occurred during an extraordinary week (perhaps a one-time government report was issued), then he ought to consider changing his volatility figure so that it is more consistent with the observed price changes.

A Note on Eurodollar Volatility

If Eurodollars are at 93.00 and we assume a volatility of 16%, we can apply the same method previously described to calculate a daily 1 standard deviation price change: $16\%/16 \times 93.00 = .93$. As any trader will attest, a daily price change of .93 in Eurodollars is wildly improbable. How can we account for this illogical answer? The reason here is that Eurodollars (and also Treasury Bills) are indexed from 100.00. This simply means that the interest rate associated with a Eurodollar contract is 100.00 less the value of the contract. It also means that, barring the unlikely advent of negative interest rates, such contracts can never have values greater than 100.00. In this respect 100 acts as a limiting value for Eurodollars in the same way that zero acts as a limiting value for other commodity contracts. We can integrate this change into our model by assuming that the price of the Eurodollar contract is actually the difference between the present contract value and 100.00. If the contract is at 93.00, for theoretical evaluation purposes we must use a price of 100 - 93.00, or 7.00, in our pricing model. If we define the price of the contract as 7.00, a 1 standard deviation price change is $16\%/16 \times 7.00 = .07$. This is a more realistic answer than .93.

If we index Eurodollar prices from 100.00 then, to be consistent, we must also index exercise prices from 100.00. Therefore a 93.50 exercise price in our pricing model is actually a 6.50 (100 - 93.50) exercise price. To intelligently use a theoretical pricing model to evaluate Eurodollar options we must always index both the contract price and exercise price from 100.

Types of Volatilities

When traders gather to discuss volatility, even experienced traders may find that they are not always talking about the same thing. If one trader asks another about the volatility of a certain commodity and receives the answer "20%," this may mean one thing to the trader who asked the question and quite a different thing to the trader who gave the answer. We can avoid this confusion by defining the various types of volatilities traders work with.

Future Volatility

We begin with future volatility. This is what every trader wants to know, the volatility that best describes the future distribution of prices in an underlying commodity. If a trader knows the future volatility he can evaluate all options on that commodity with increased confidence. He will then be in a position to compare the values of the options with their prices in the marketplace and, as we shall see, turn the difference into a cash profit. Of course, traders rarely talk about the future volatility since it is impossible to know what the future holds.

Historical Volatility

Even though he cannot know the future, a trader must still try to make an intelligent guess about what the future holds. To do this in option evaluation, as in other disciplines, he must first look at the past. What has historically been the volatility of a certain commodity? If over the past 10 years the volatility of Treasury Bonds has never been higher than 25%, a 30% guess for future volatility hardly makes sense. This does not mean that 30% is impossible (in option trading the impossible always seems to happen sooner or later) but based on past performance, and in the absence of any extraordinary circumstances, a guess of 25% or less is more realistic than a guess of 30%.

When a trader examines historical volatility he has a number of ways calculate this number. First he must decide how far back in time to go. Does he want to look at the volatility over the last 10 days, or over the last 6 months, or over the last 5 years? Just how far back is it necessary to go to get an accurate historical picture? An option trader is likely to begin by looking at the volatility over a long period of time (at least a year) since this will enable him to identify any short-term aberrations from the norm. On the other hand, a trader must also worry about short term changes in volatility, so he will also want detailed information on the most recent volatility. If the volatility of a commodity has averaged 25% over the last year but only 15% over the last 30 days, a trader might logically alter his volatility estimate to take into account the most recent information. Even though over long periods of time the commodity has a volatility of 25%, in light of the recent volatility, a guess of less than 25%—say 20%—may be more logical for short-term options. On the other hand, if the trader is dealing in longer term options a guess closer to the long term historical volatility of 25% may be best.

Once a trader has decided on the period over which he wants to look at historical volatility, he must also decide at what intervals he will take his price measurements. If he is interested in the volatility over the last 10 weeks, the volatility figure he arrives at if he measures price changes at the close of every day may differ from the volatility he arrives at if he measures price changes at the end of every week. Prices can fluctuate wildly from day to day yet end up unchanged for the week. If this is true, the volatility figure resulting from daily price changes will be much higher than the volatility figure resulting from weekly price changes.

One might conclude from this that there are an infinite number of ways to calculate historical volatility over the same period, and that each method will yield a different historical volatility figure.

However, the evidence strongly suggests that as long as price changes are measured at regular intervals the annualized volatilities resulting from these different intervals will be very similar. A good example is the graph of historical corn volatility in Figure 4-8. The broken line is the historical volatility calculated from daily price changes over a 50-day period. The dotted line is the historical volatility for the same 50-day period, but here the volatility was calculated from weekly price changes. The graphs occasionally diverge, but for the most part they show the same general volatility levels and trends. In other words, if a commodity is volatile from day to day, it is likely to be equally volatile from week to week.

As a general rule, services which supply historical volatilities base their calculations on daily settlement-to-settlement price changes. If this is not the case, the information will usually be accompanied by an explanation as to the intervals which were used. For example, if a service gave the historical volatility during the month of August as 20%, then it can be assumed that the calculations were made using the daily settlement-to-settlment price changes for all the business days during that month.

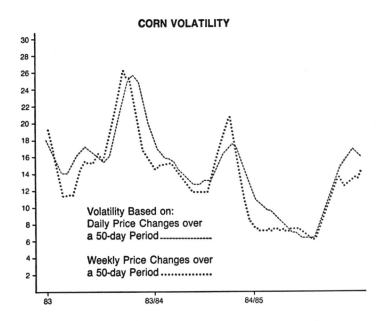

Figure 4-8

Forecast Volatility

Even though forecasting the future is an inexact science at best, there are services which will attempt to do so. Using analytical tools and mathematical formulae, such services will attempt to forecast the volatility of a commodity. The forecast periods usually cover the lifetime of options on that commodity, but may also cover specific daily, weekly, or monthly periods. Depending on his confidence in the forecaster, a trader's guess about the future volatility of a commodity might also take this forecast into consideration. An example of forecast volatility is given in Figure 4-9.

Implied Volatility

Future, historical, and forecast volatility are all numbers which are associated with an underlying contract, and say something about how prices of that contract are distributed over time. A different type

Midland Bank FX Volatility Forecasts

	Spot Price 17/8/86	Volatilities 3- month	6- month
British pound	1.5130	13.5-14.5	13.2-14.2
D-Mark	2.2150	14.4-15.4	14.2-15.2
Swiss franc	1.8270	14.5-15.5	14.0-15.0
Canadian $	1.3870	6.0-7.0	6.0-7.0
Japanese yen	166.40	14.7-15.7	13.9-14.9
French franc	7.0650	14.8-15.8	14.8-15.8
Dutch guilder	2.4960	14.5-15.5	14.5-15.5

Volatilities are normalized standard deviations against US$.

Courtesy of *Futures and Options World* (London).

Figure 4-9

of volatility, the implied or implicit volatility, is associated solely with an option.

Suppose a certain futures contract is trading at 98.00 with interest rates at 6%, and our best guess for the contract's future volatility is 15%. If a 105 call is available with three months to expiration we can use these inputs in a theoretical pricing model to evaluate this option. In this case, the Black-Scholes Model will yield a theoretical value of .72. Having done this, we might then compare the theoretical value of the 105 call with the option's price in the marketplace. Instead of trading at .72, which is our theoretical value, we find that the option is actually trading at 1.13.

If we make the assumption that the marketplace is using the same theoretical pricing model as we are, how might we account for this difference?

The time to expiration and exercise price are fixed in the option contract, so these factors cannot account for the discrepancy. If we assume that the price of the underlying contract has remained unchanged at 98.00, this also cannot be the cause. Perhaps our problem is the interest rate component. But, as we have noted, interest rates do not greatly affect the value of a futures option. This leaves only one input which can account for the difference, and that is volatility. In some sense the marketplace must be evaluating the 105 call using a volatility other than 15%.

To find out what that volatility might be, we can ask the following question: What volatility must we feed into our theoretical pricing model, along with the other given inputs (time to expiraton, exercise price, underlying futures price, and interest rates) in order to come up with a theoretical value for the 105 call which is equal to the price of the call in the marketplace (1.13)? If we work with a computer programmed with the Black-Scholes Model we will find that the answer is 17.9%. This number is the *implied volatility* of the 105 call at a price of 1.13. It is the volatility we must feed into our theoretical pricing model to arrive at a theoretical value identical to the option's price in the marketplace. (See Figure 4-10.)

When we solve for the implied volatility of an option we are assuming that the theoretical value (the option's price) is known, and that the volatility is unknown. At any instant an option has an implied volatility based on its price in the marketplace, the time to expiration, the exercise price, the price of the underlying contract, interest rates, and the theoretical pricing model being used. Given these factors we can, in theory, invert our theoretical pricing model to solve for the one unknown, volatility.

Using the Model to Solve for a Theoretical Value

Knowns	*Unknowns*
Exercise Price (105)	Theoretical Value
Time to Expiration (3 months)	(?? = .72)
Futures Price (98.00)	
Interest Rates (6%)	
Volatility (15%)	

Using the Model to Solve for an Implied Volatility

Knowns	*Unknowns*
Exercise Price (105)	Implied Volatility
Time to Expiration (3 months)	(?? = 17.9%)
Futures Price (98.00)	
Interest Rates (6%)	
Option Price (1.13)	

The implied volatility is the volatility needed in a theoretical pricing model to yield a theoretical value identical to the price of the option in the marketplace.

Figure 4-10

Services which supply implied volatilities may give the implied volatility for each option on a given underlying contract, or they may only give one single implied volatility figure for all the options on the same underlying future contract. In the latter case, the figure will usually represent an average of the implied volatilities of all the options on the same underlying future contract. This figure will be weighted using some criteria, such as volume of options traded, open interest, or as is most common, assigning the greatest weight to the at-the-money options.

The implied volatility in the marketplace is constantly changing because option prices as well as the inputs into the theoretical pricing model are constantly changing. It is as if the marketplace were constantly taking a poll among all the participants to come up with a consensus volatility for the underlying contract. This is not a true poll since all traders do not huddle together and eventually vote on a correct volatility. However, as bids and offers are made, the trade price of an option will represent an equilibrium between supply and demand. This equilibrium price can be translated into an implied volatility.

Even though the term premium actually refers to an option's price, traders tend to refer to the implied volatility of options as the *premium* or *premium level*. If the current implied volatility is historically high, or high relative to the recent volatility of the underlying futures contract, a trader might say that premium levels are high; if implied volatility is unusually low, he might say that premium levels are low.

If a trader could look into a crystal ball and see the future volatility of an underlying contract he would be able to evaluate accurately all options on that contract. He might then look at the dollar difference between the option's theoretical value and its market price, selling any options which were overpriced and buying any options which were underpriced. If given the choice between selling one of two overpriced options he might simply sell the option most overpriced in total dollars.

Another way to evaluate the price of an option in the marketplace might be to compare its implied volatility to either a volatility forecast or to the implied volatility of other options on the same underlying. Going back to our example of the 105 call, we might say that with a theoretical value of .72 and a price of 1.13 the 105 call is .41 overpriced. But in volatility terms it is 2.9% overpriced since its theoretical value is based on a 15% volatility (the trader's volatility estimate) while its price is based on a volatility of 17.9% (implied volatility). Due to the unusual characteristics of options, it is often more useful for the serious trader to consider an option's price in terms of its implied volatility rather than in terms of its dollar price.

For example, suppose a Treasury Bond 98 call is trading for 3-32 ($3,500) with a corresponding implied volatility of 12.5%. Suppose also that a 102 call on the same underlying futures contract is trading for 1-16 ($1,250) with an implied volatility of 13.5%. In total dollar terms the 102 call is $2,250 cheaper than the 98 call. An experienced trader, however, will conclude that in theoretical terms the 98 call is less expensive than the 102 call because the implied volatility of the 98 call is a full percentage point less than the implied volatility of the 102 call. This does not mean that the 98 call is a good buy while the 102 call is a poor buy. Both calls may be either underpriced or over-priced depending on the future volatility. But in relative terms, the 98 call is a better value (or a less poor value) because its implied volatility is lower.

While option traders may at various times refer to any of the four types of volatilities, two of these stand out in importance. The future volatility of a commodity, if we were somehow able to know it, would enable us to determine the *value* of all options on that com-modity. The implied volatility tells us the *price* of each option in the marketplace. These two numbers are what every trader is concerned with, value versus price. If we know both the value and price of a product, then we know whether we want to be a buyer or a seller of that product. Of course, since future volatility cannot be known we use historical and forecast volatility to help us make the most intel-ligent decision we can about the future. But in the final analysis, it is still the future volatility in which we are interested.

To help clarify the differences among the four types of volatility, we might consider an analogy to weather forecasting. Suppose a trader living in Chicago gets up on a July morning and must decide what clothes to wear that day. Will he consider putting on a parka? This is not a logical choice since he knows that *historically* it is not suf-ficiently cold in Chicago in July to warrant wearing such a heavy coat.

Next, he might turn on the radio to listen to the weather *forecast*. The weatherman is predicting clear skies with temperatures in the 90's. Based on this information our trader has reached a decision: he will wear a short sleeve shirt with no sweater or jacket, and he certainly won't need an umbrella. However, just to be sure, he will probably walk over to the window and look outside to see what the people in the street are wearing. What might be his reaction if everyone is wearing a coat and carrying an umbrella? The people outside are *implying* different weather than is forecasted. What clothes should the trader then wear? He must make some decision, but whom should he believe, the weather forecaster or the people in the street? There can be no correct answer simply because the trader will not know the *future* weather until the end of the day.

Perhaps the people in the street really do know something about the local weather that the forecaster does not know. Then the trader would be foolish not to take their implied forecast into consideration. On the other hand, perhaps the people in the street all listened to a radio weatherman who has a history of playing practical jokes.

The decision on what clothes to wear, just like every trading decision, depends on a great many factors. Not only must the decision take into consideration the benefits of being right, but also the consequences of being wrong. If the trader fails to take an umbrella and it rains, that may be of little consequence if a bus picks him up right outside his door and drops him off right outside his place of work. On the other hand, if he has to walk three blocks in the rain, he might catch the flu and be away from work for a week. The choices are never easy, and one can only hope to make the best decision from the available information.

Seasonal Volatility

There is one other type of volatility with which a trader may have to deal. Certain agricultural commodities, such as soybeans, corn, and wheat, are very sensitive to volatility factors arising from severe seasonal weather conditions. Such severe weather occurs especially during the summer months when drought can destroy major portions of a crop and cause crop prices to swing wildly. For this reason, grains show a significant increase in volatility during the months of July and August. Conversely, they show a significant decrease during the early spring months, before American planting has begun but after the South American crop has been harvested. Given these factors, a trader must automatically assign a higher volatility to any option contract which extends through the summer months. If, in January, a trader has assigned a volatility of 15% to a May soybean contract, he will certainly choose a higher figure (perhaps 20%) for a November contract. He knows that the November contract includes the summer months, while the May contract does not. The effect of seasonal volatility on soybeans is shown in Figure 4-11.

Why have we gone into such detail in our discussion of volatility? An option trader can, if he chooses, base his strategies solely on market direction. But if he has a thorough understanding of volatility, he has an additional variable with which to work. He can in effect approach the market from two directions instead of one. Many traders find it far easier to work exclusively with volatility, rather than try to guess market direction. Moreover, volatility strategies can be extremely profitable and, when chosen intelligently, can even reduce a trader's risk exposure. These two variables, market direction and volatility, enable the option trader to pursue many strategies not available to the pure futures or cash trader.

Changing our assumptions about future volatility can have a dramatic effect on the value of options. Look at Figure 4-12, prices, theoretical values, and implied volatilities for options on Deutschemark futures on 16 March 1987. Note the dramatic change in theoretical values as the volatility is increased in increments of 3 percentage points. The 55 call and put, which are at-the-money, change by approximately .30 ($375) for each 3 percentage point change in volatility. Out-of-the-money options, such as the 51 and 52 puts and the 58 call, do not show as great a dollar change, but in percentage terms their sensitivity is even greater. As volatility increases from 9% to 12%, these options double in value, and almost double again as it is increased from 12% to 15%.

And a 3 percentage point change in volatility is not at all uncommon. Indeed, the volatility of some commodities can show swings of 10 and 15 percentage points in a relatively short time.

Given its importance, it is not surprising that the serious option trader spends much of his time thinking about volatility. Using historical, forecast, implied, and, in the case of agricultural products, seasonal volatility, he must try to make an intelligent decision about

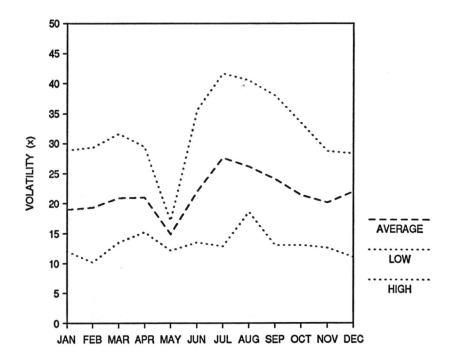

Nearby Soybean Volatility (1979-1983)

Courtesy of Chicago Board of Trade.

Figure 4-11

future volatility. From this, he will look for option strategies which will result in a profit if he is right, but which will not result in a disastrous loss if he is wrong. Because of the difficulty in predicting volatility, the trader must always look for strategies which will leave the greatest margin for error. No trader will survive very long pursuing strategies based on a volatility estimate of 15% if such a strategy results in a loss when volatility actually turns out to be 16%. Given the shifts that occur in volatility, a one percentage point margin for error is no margin at all.

16 March 1987
June Deutschemarks at 54.89;   Time to expiration = 81 days;   Interest rate = 6.25%

Exercise Price	Settlement Price	Implied Volatility	Theoretical value if...		
			Volatility = 9%	Volatility = 12%	Volatility = 15%
Calls					
51	3.93	10.9	3.87	3.97	4.12
52	3.06	11.0	2.96	3.12	3.33
53	2.28	11.1	2.12	2.36	2.61
54	1.58	10.8	1.41	1.70	1.99
55	1.05	10.8	.86	1.17	1.47
56	.67	11.0	.48	.76	1.05
57	.41	11.3	.24	.47	.73
58	.25	11.6	.11	.27	.49
Puts					
51	.12	11.7	.04	.13	.28
52	.22	11.2	.11	.27	.48
53	.41	11.0	.26	.49	.75
54	.70	10.7	.54	.82	1.11
55	1.16	10.8	.97	1.17	1.58
56	1.76	11.0	1.57	1.86	2.15
57	2.49	11.2	2.32	2.55	2.81
58	3.31	11.5	3.17	3.34	3.56

Figure 4-12

Estimating Volatility

Historical Volatility

Since volatility is so important in option pricing, perhaps we ought to try to develop a rational method for making our volatility estimates. What might be a logical approach? First, we would certainly want to look at the historical volatility of the underlying market. By looking at the historical volatility over a long period of time, we can establish some likely limits for a volatility estimate. This is important because most commodities seem to have a characteristic volatility. That is, if one looks at the historical volatility of a commodity over long periods of time there is usually an average volatility to which the volatility tends to revert if it strays very far away. A commodity with a long-term historical volatility of 20% may go to 30% or 10%, but it is unlikely to remain there for an extended period. In all likelihood, it will eventually return to its 20% average. There are of course exceptions to this generalization. Occasionally a commodity will show a long-term shift in its volatility characteristics. In that case, the volatility will not return to its historical average, but will instead establish a new average.

If the current volatility of an underlying contract is significantly different than the historical average, we still have the problem of deciding how quickly the volatility will return to its historical average. Will it be one month from now, or three months, or six months? The answer can greatly influence a trader's strategies. Perhaps we can make a more intelligent volatility estimate if we know which way the commodity's volatility is trending. Is it moving further away from its historical average, or is it moving back toward the average? We can answer this question by looking at volatility figures which cover a shorter, and more recent, period of time. If our historical volatility average is based on volatility over the last year, perhaps we should also look at volatility over the last month, or the last week. These figures will help us analyze the volatility trend.

Suppose a commodity has the following historical volatilities:[6]

---

[6]Historical volatilities normally cover a specified number of trading days. Therefore, the 10 day volatility covers 2 calendar weeks, the 50 day volatility covers 10 calendar weeks, and the 250 day volaitlty covers the last year.

last 10 days...22%
last 50 days...25%
last 250 days...16%

The recent volatility of this commodity (last 10 and last 50 days) has been higher than its historical average (last 250 days). But note that the last 10 days have been less volatile than the last 50 days, so the volatility does seem to be trending back towards the historical average.

One simple method of coming up with a consensus estimate of all these numbers might simply be to average them out:

$$(22 + 25 + 16) / 3 = 21$$

If we do this, then 21 will be our best guess about future volatility. However, we can perhaps do better by considering the future period for which we are attempting to estimate volatility. Are we trying to estimate volatility in order to evaluate 1-month options, or 4-month options, or 7-month options? If we are trading long-term options, there is a greater likelihood that the volatility of the underlying contract over that period will be close to its historical average. On the other hand, if we are trading short-term options the most recent volatility will be very important since that is likely to best reflect the current volatility climate. We can take these factors into consideration by weighting the historical volatilities according to our trading horizon. If we are trading very long-term options, we can give the greatest weight, say 50%, to the long-term volatility; and lesser weight, say 25% each, to our more recent volatilities:

$$(50\% \times 16) + (25\% \times 25) + (25\% \times 22) = 19.75$$

19.75% now represents an intelligent guess for long-term options.

If we are attempting to evaluate shorter term options, we will give the greatest weight to the more recent volatilities. An intelligent weighting scheme might be to give the greatest weight to the historical volatility which covers a period equal to the life of the option. Therefore, in our example, if we are trading 50 (trading) day options, we can give the greatest weight to the 50 day historical volatility. Then we might have:

$$(25\% \times 16) + (50\% \times 25) + (25\% \times 22) = 22.0$$

Marketplace Opinion of Future Volatility

Another consideration in our estimate might be the opinion of the marketplace about future volatility. We can include this opinion in our estimate by giving some weight to the current implied volatility. This assumes, not unreasonably, that option prices reflect traders' expectations about future price movement, and that these expectations will play some role in the future volatility. How much weight should we give to the implied volatility? Here there are a wide range of opinions; with some traders giving very little weight to implied volatility, and others giving almost all the weight to implied volatility. A reasonable figure might be somewhere between 25% and 50%, using a smaller weight when the historical figures yield a clear estimate and a larger weight when the historical figures are inconclusive.

Recall the example where we estimated a volatility of 22% for a 50 day option based on historical volatilities. Suppose the implied volatility of the option in which we are interested is 26%, and that we intend to give a 30% weighting to the implied volatility:

$$70\% \times 22 + 30\% \times 26 = 23.2.$$

23.2% is now the volatility estimate we will use to evaluate our trading strategies.

Volatility of Similar Commodities

There is one additional factor we may wish to consider in making our volatility estimate, and that is the volatility characteristics of other similar commodities. While similar commodities may have different historical volatilities, their volatilities will all tend to trend in the same direction together. If Deutschemarks become highly volatile, then it is likely that Swiss Francs and Japanese Yen will also become volatile. If corn becomes volatile, in all likelihood so will soybeans and wheat. The same is true for the debt instruments (treasury bonds, treasury notes, and Eurodollars), as well as for the metals (gold and silver). Given this fact, a volatility estimate might give some weight to the volatilities of other similar commodities. If such commodities are unusually volatile or unusually quiet in relation to the commodity which is being analyzed, then one might wish to increase or decrease the volatility estimate accordingly. The amount of the increase or decrease will depend on the degree of volatility correlation with the other similar commodities. If the historical volatility of Deutschemarks has consistently been two percentage points less than the historical volatility of Swiss Francs, then a volatility estimate of 10% for Deutschemarks and an estimate of 15% for Swiss Francs might be adjusted to take into consideration the historical volatility spread. In that case, perhaps a better estimate is 11% for Deutschemarks and 14% for Swiss Francs.

Conclusion

As one can see, making an intelligent volatility estimate can turn into a complex exercise because of the many different factors involved. Which historical data should one use? How should it be weighted? How much weight should be given to implied volatility? What is the volatility relationship with other similar commodities? It can be discouraging indeed to put a great deal of time and effort into making a volatility estimate, and then have it turn out to be totally wrong. This doesn't mean that the effort is not worthwhile. In the long run a sensible volatility estimate will enable a trader to choose strategies with the best risk/reward characteristics. But one must accept the fact that estimating volatility is at best difficult, and on occasion terribly frustrating.

A practical solution to many of the problems of estimating volatility might be to construct graphs of volatility. Most traders find it easier to identify patterns by looking at a graph rather than by looking at a collection of numbers. Not only can a graph help us identify the short- and long-term volatility characteristics of a commodity, it can also help us identify trends and make projections that would otherwise be difficult using only raw numerical data. An added plus is that many commodity traders use some form of technical analysis to forecast price trends, and it may be possible to use many of the same tools to forecast volatility. The analogy here is not perfect since price movement and volatility are two different, though related, concepts. Still, there is the suspicion that common formations such as support and resistance, head and shoulders, double tops and bottoms, and trend lines might also be useful in volatility analysis.

While price changes in a commodity are easily plotted, volatility figures can be calculated in a variety of ways, depending on the period over which the volatility is calculated and the intervals used to measure the price changes. Even with these obstacles, the serious trader might do well to construct graphs of historical volatility and try to draw some inferences about the properties of volatility. Several graphs of historical gold volatility during 1987 are given in Figure 4-13. These graphs are based on 10-day, 50-day, and 150-day volatilities. In order to smooth out some of the extreme fluctuations, particularly in the 10 day volatility, the data points represent a 5-day moving average.

Finally, because some option strategies depend not only on estimating a future volatility, but also on making a judgement about how implied volatility is likely to fluctuate, a graph of implied volatilities over time might also be useful. Figure 4-14 shows graphs of the implied volatilities of the three nearest expiration months in gold options throughout 1987. As with the historical volatilities, these graphs have been smoothed out using 5 day moving averages. Based on Figures 4-13 and 4-14, the reader might consider the following questions:

1. How widely can gold volatility, both historical and implied, fluctuate?

2. What is a reasonable margin for error in estimating volatility?

3. Can trends be identified which would help the trader make accurate volatility projections?

4. How closely do historical and implied volatilies correlate?

5. Which historical volatility seems to correlate best with implied volatility?

6. Does implied volatility change more or less quickly than historical volatility?

7. Does implied volatility lead or lag behind historical volatility?

One point is very important: the option trader must always keep an open mind about volatility. As we shall see, volatility can often be traded as if it were itself a commodity. It is, in a sense, possible to buy or sell volatility, so that one will profit from an increase or decrease in volatility. While most professional traders tend to sell volatility, no intelligent trader is *always* short or *always* long volatility. Sometimes volatility is clearly rising and a trader will attempt to buy it, and sometimes volatility is falling and a trader will attempt to sell it.

Even if one is able to accurately estimate the volatility of a commodity over a specific period, one still has to decide if the price at which volatility can be bought or sold is favorable. For example, if the volatility estimate for a commodity over a certain period is 25% and the implied volatility of options covering that period is 20%, then it does indeed make sense to buy volatility. If, however, implied volatility is also at 25% there will be no profit opportunity since the value of the options based on the estimated volatility (25%) is identical to the price of the options as reflected in the implied volatility (also 25%).

Historical Volatilities—COMEX Gold (near contract)—1987

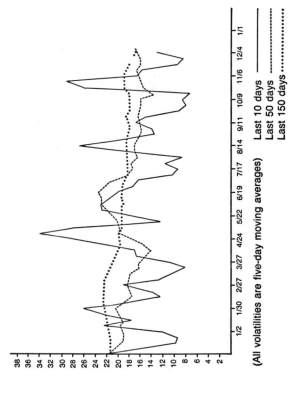

(All volatilities are five-day moving averages)

Last 10 days
Last 50 days
Last 150 days

Figure 4-13

Implied Volatilities—COMEX Gold (three near-term contract)—1987

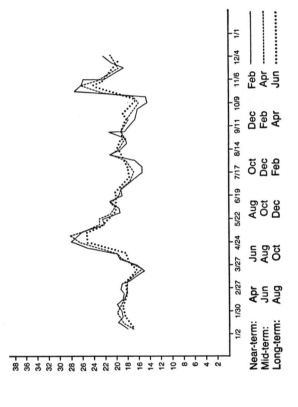

Near-term:	Apr	Jun	Aug	Oct	Dec	Feb
Mid-term:	Jun	Aug	Oct	Dec	Feb	Apr
Long-term:	Aug	Oct	Dec	Feb	Apr	Jun

Figure 4-14

5

Using an Option's
Theoretical Value

From a theoretician's point of view, the Black-Scholes Model represents a novel solution to a complex problem. Moreover, the model requires a limited number of inputs and relatively simple mathematical calculations. These factors have made the Black-Scholes Model the most popular of all option pricing methods.

While a trader might appreciate the artistic merits of the model, it is still the actual performance of the model in the marketplace that interests him. Is it really possible to profit from price descrepancies between model-generated values and market prices of options?

Questions concerning the accuracy of model generated values arise most often from questions about the accuracy of the volatility component. Let us therefore make the following assumptions:

1. Price distribution of an underyling contract is accurately represented by a lognormal distribution.
2. We actually know the future volatility of an optionable contract.

If we make these assumptions, and the Black-Scholes Model does indeed work, we ought to be able to turn any difference between an option's price and its theoretical value into a cash profit. How can we do this?

Suppose the following conditions exists:

> Commodity Price   = 101.35
> Interest   = 8.00%
> Time to Expiration = 70 days

We can choose any exercise price we like, so the only input needed for accurate evaluation of options on this commodity is volatility. Since we have made the assumption that we actually know the future volatility, let's imagine that we have a crystal ball into which we can look to determine the future volatility. When we do this, we see a volatility figure of 18.3%. Now we have all the necessary inputs for theoretical evaluation, and it only remains to choose a specific option.

Let us focus on the 100 call. Using our model, and our known inputs, now including volatility, we find that the 100 call has a theoretical value of 3.88. When we check its price in the marketplace we find that it is being offered at 3.25. How can we profit from this discrepancy?

We saw in Chapter 3 that the purchase or sale of theoretically mispriced options requires us to establish a riskless hedge by taking an opposing position in the underlying contract. When this is done, for small changes in the price of the underlying contract, the increase or decrease in the value of the option position will exactly offset the increase or decrease in the value of the opposing position in the underlying contract. Such a hedge is unbiased or *neutral*, as to the direction of movement in the underlying contract.

The number which enables us to establish a riskless hedge under current market conditions is a by-product of the theoretical pricing model and is known as the *hedge ratio*, or more commonly, the *delta*. We will discuss the delta in greater detail later but certain characteristics of the delta will be important in our present example:

1. The delta of a call option is always between 0 and 1.00.

2. The delta of an option changes as market conditions change.

3. A futures contract always has a delta of 1.00.

Option traders commonly drop the decimal point when discussing deltas, a convention which we shall also follow. Therefore the delta of a call option will be between 0 and 100, and a futures contract will always have a delta of 100.[1]

Going back to our example, in order to make use of the theoretical value of 3.88 we also need to know the delta, in this case 57 (.57). This means that for each option we purchase we must sell .57 of a futures contract to establish an unbiased or neutral hedge. Since the purchase or sale of fractional futures contracts is not permitted, we will buy 100 of the 100 calls and sell 57 futures contracts.

Contract	Contract Delta	Delta Position
Buy 100 100 calls	57	+5700
Sell 57 futures	100	–5700

Note that the delta position on each side of the hedge is the contract position (positive for buy, negative for sell) multiplied by the contract delta. The total delta position is then the sum of these two numbers. In our example, when we add +5700 and -5700 the total delta position is zero, and we say that the hedge is *delta neutral*. If the total delta position had been positive then the hedge would have indicated an upward bias; a negative delta position would have indicated a downward bias.

Having established a neutral hedge we must now deal with the fact that a theoretical value is based on probability. The roulette player who is able to purchase a roulette bet for less than its theoretical value can only expect to show a profit if he is allowed to play many, many times. On any one turn of the wheel the most likely outcome is that he will lose since there are 37 ways for him to lose but only one way for him to win. The same is true for our hedge. Probability figures are only valid in the long run. In the short run any one outcome may result in a loss.

---

[1]This convention originally arose in stock options, where an underlying stock contract consisted of 100 shares of stock. It became common to equate one delta with each share of stock.

Is there any way we can reduce the possibility of luck going against us in this one instance? We can do this only if we are given the chance to make many bets with the same favorable odds. The more bets we make, the better our chances of making a profit identical to the theoretical edge of the hedge. One way to accomplish this is by approaching the hedge as a continuing series of small bets. This can be done by reassessing our delta position at regular intervals, and then making adjustments in our delta position as market conditions change.

Suppose that one week later the futures price in our example moves from 101.35 to 102.26. At this point we can feed new inputs into our theoretical pricing model:

$$
\begin{array}{ll}
\text{Commodity Price} & = 102.35 \\
\text{Interest} & = 8.00\% \\
\text{Time to Expiration} & = 63 \text{ days} \\
\text{Volatility} & = 18.3\%
\end{array}
$$

Note that we have made no change in the interest rate or volatility. The theoretical pricing model assumes that these two inputs remain constant over the life of the option. Based on these new inputs we can calculate a new delta for the 100 call, in this case 62. Now our delta position is:

Contract	Contract Delta	Delta Position
Long 100 100 calls	62	+6200
Short 57 futures	100	-5700

Our total delta position is now +500. This is the end of one bet, with another bet about to begin.

Whenever we begin a new bet we must always return to an unbiased, or delta neutral, position. In our present example it will therefore be necessary to reduce our position by 500 deltas. There are a number of different ways to do this, but in order to keep our present calculations as simple as possible we will make the necessary trades in the futures market; a futures contract always has a delta of 100.

Here we wish to go short 500 deltas, so we will have to sell 5 futures contracts. Now our delta position is:

Contract	Contract Delta	Delta Position
Long100 100 calls	62	+6200
Short 62 futures	100	–6200

We are again delta neutral and ready to begin a new bet which, as before, depends only on the volatility of the underlying futures contract and not its direction.

The extra five futures contracts which we sold were an *adjustment* to our position. Adjustments are trades which are not necessarily made for the purpose of adding to our theoretical edge, although in some cases they may also have that effect. Rather, they are made primarily for the purpose of maintaining a delta neutral position. In this case the sale of five extra futures contracts has no effect at all on our theoretical edge since futures contracts have no theoretical value. The trade was made solely for the purpose of adjusting our hedge to remain delta neutral.

This brief example illustrates the principles underlying the use of any option's theoretical value:

1. Purchase (sell) undervalued (overvalued) options.

2. Establish a delta neutral hedge against the underlying futures contract.

3. Adjust the hedge at regular intervals to remain delta neutral.

Regarding point 3, theoretical pricing models actually assume that the hedge is being continually adjusted at every instant in time. Such continuous adjustments are impossible in the real world since a trader can only trade at discrete time intervals. By making adjustments at regular intervals we are conforming as best we can to the constraints of the theoretical pricing model.

Using our principles, how would the adjustments look if we were to carry the hedge to expiration? The results are given Figure 5-1. In this example adjustments were made at weekly intervals. After each interval the delta of the 100 call was calculated based on the time remaining to expiration, the current futures price, and a fixed interest rate of 8.00% and volatility of 18.3%. The total delta position was then calculated and the required number of futures contracts either bought or sold to return to a delta neutral position. After week 1 we were 500 deltas long and had to sell 5 futures; after week 2 we were 1600 deltas short and had to buy 16 futures; and so on through each of the ten weeks to expiration.

What do we plan to do with our position at the end of ten weeks when the options expire? At that time we will close out the position by:

1. Letting any out-of-the-money options expire worthless.

2. Selling any in-the-money options at parity or, equivalently, exercising them and offsetting them against the underlying futures contract.

3. Liquidating any extra long or short futures at the market price.

Week	Futures Price	Delta of 100 Call	Total Delta Position	Adjustment in Futures	Total Adjustment Futures
0	101.35	57	0		
1	102.26	62	+500	sell 5	short 5
2	99.07	46	−1600	buy 16	long 11
3	100.39	53	+700	sell 7	long 4
4	100.74	55	+200	sell 2	long 2
5	103.59	74	+1900	sell 19	short 17
6	99.26	45	−2900	buy 29	long 12
7	98.28	35	−1000	buy 10	long 22
8	99.98	50	+1500	sell 15	long 7
9	103.78	93	+4300	sell 43	short 36
10	102.54			buy 36	

Figure 5-1

Let's go through this procedure step by step. At the end of ten weeks (expiration) the futures price is 102.54. We can liquidate our 100 calls by either selling them at parity (2.54), or by selling futures at 102.54 and exercising our calls. Either method will result in 2.54 points credit to our account. However, since we originally paid 3.25 points for each option we are effectively losing .71 per option, or a total of $100 \times -.71 = -71.00$.

As part of our original hedge we also sold 57 futures at 101.35. At expiration we had to pay 102.54 to buy them back, for a loss of $57 \times -1.19 = -67.83$. Therefore our total profit and loss on the original hedge was $-71.00 - 67.83 = -138.83$. This certainly does not appear to have been successful. Based on our theoretical evaluation we expected to make money, and here we have a sizeable loss.

However, the original hedge was not our only transaction. We were also buying and selling futures contracts throughout the ten-week life of the hedge. Note that each time the futures price rose our delta position became positive and we were forced to sell futures; and each time the futures price fell our delta position became negative and we were forced to buy futures. Because our adjustments depended on the delta position, we were forced to do what every trader wants to do: buy low, sell high.

What was the result of all our buying and selling of futures contracts in order to maintain a delta neutral position? In fact, it resulted in a profit of 208.06 points. (The reader may wish to confirm this by adding up the results of all the adjustments in Figure 5-1.) This profit more than offset the loss resulting from the original hedge.

Were there any considerations other than the hedge and adjustments affecting our final profit or loss? Originally we bought calls and sold futures. The purchase of options requires a cash outlay (stock-type settlement) and we must therefore take into consideration the interest loss, or carrying cost, of the option position. We initially bought 100 calls at 3.25 each for a total outlay of 325.00. Based on our assumption of an 8.00% interest rate, the carrying costs on 325.00 for 10 weeks is $.08 \times 10/52 \times 325.00 = 5.00$.

We can now summarize the complete profit and loss from our position:

Hedge	Adjustments	Carrying Costs
$100 \times -\ .71\ = -71.00$		
$57 \times -1.19 = \underline{-67.83}$		
-138.83	$+208.06$	-5.00

The total profit is $-138.83 + 208.06 - 5.00 = +64.23$.

How much did the theoretical pricing model predict we would make? We bought 100 calls worth 3.88 for 3.25. Our original theoretical edge was .63 per call, for a total of $100 \times +.63 = +63.00$. In other words, the theoretical model came very close to predicting our actual profit from the position.

Just as in this example, the profit and loss from every hedge will be made up of three components:

1. The hedge profit and loss.

2. The adjustment profit and loss.

3. The interest profit and loss.

It is impossible to determine beforehand what proportion each component will contribute to the total P & L of the hedge. In our example the only profitable component was adjustments; but one can just as easily construct examples where the profit comes from the original hedge, or where some of the profit comes from the hedge and some from the adjustments. The important point to remember is that, if a trader's inputs into the theoretical pricing model are correct, in some combination he can expect to show a profit (or loss) approximately equal to that predicted by the theoretical pricing model.

Where did the volatility figure of 18.3% come from? Since we made the assumption that we knew the future volatility of the commodity, we had to know the price changes beforehand. Simply put, the author took the ten price changes in Figure 5-1 and, using a volatility calculation based on the logarithmic returns of these price changes, calculated an annualized volatility. The complete calculations in this example are given in Appendix B.

Why didn't our example yield a profit of exactly 63.00 points, the amount predicted by the model? As we emphasized in Chapter 3, a theoretical pricing model is only an approximation of what happens in the real world under certain conditions. We tried to eliminate some of the error in the model by calculating the future volatility beforehand. But other problems, arising from the nature of volatility, may also lead to errors (more about this in Chapter 13). Additionally, some rounding error inevitably creeps into this type of calculation. In our example we rounded the volatility calculation to one decimal point, and the delta figures to the nearest whole number. We might have generated a more accurate theoretical value had we carried out all our calculations to several decimal places.

Given these inherent limitations in the model, how much faith can one put in model-generated theoretical values? If one expects 100% accuracy from the model in every possible instance, then any theoretical pricing model is bound to be a severe disappointment (not to mention extremely dangerous). However, if a trader understands the limitations of the model, the dependence of the model on accurate inputs, and the isolated instances when the model is likely to generate highly inaccurate values, the model can be an invaluable tool in identifying potential profit opportunities and predicting the likely magnitude of the profit.

We assumed in our example that a trader realized 100% of the profit or loss from any trade, and that no external factors would affect his profit or loss. This is because theoretical pricing models assume that all markets are *frictionless*, that there are no external considerations which might affect the profit and loss. The primary assumptions in a frictionless market are:

1. All traders can borrow and lend money at the same rate, and that rate is constant throughout the life of the option.
2. Transaction costs are zero.
3. There are no tax considerations.

All traders will immediately realize that markets are not frictionless since each of the above assumptions is violated to a greater or lesser degree in the real world. Individual market makers cannot generally borrow or lend money at the same rate as a large brokerage house. If the trader has a debit balance it will cost him more to carry that debit; if he has a credit balance he will not earn as much on that credit. There is a spread, and perhaps a fairly large one, between a trader's borrowing and lending rate. Fortunately, the interest rate component in theoretical evaluation of futures options is relatively small. Even though it may vary from trader to trader, it will be only very slight in relation to the profit and loss from the other components.

Transaction costs, on the other hand, can be a very real consideration. If such costs are too high, the hedge in Figure 5-1 might not be a viable strategy for a retail customer; all of the profits could be eaten up by brokerage fees. The choice of strategies will depend not only on the customer's initial transaction costs, but also on the subsequent cost of making adjustments. This last cost is a function of the trader's willingness to adjust since more adjustments will increase the transaction costs. Of course a customer who establishes a theoretically profitable hedge, but refrains from adjusting, still has positive theoretical edge. But his disinclination to adjust means that there is greater risk of not realizing a profit on this one hedge. Adjustments do not in themselves alter the expected return; they simply reduce the probability of short-term bad luck.

Do transaction costs also significantly affect the profit and loss of a professional trader, one who is an exchange member? Every trader, even an exchange member, is required to pay fees to the exchange's clearing house, to the exchange itself, and to the clearing member which processes his trades. Such fees might typically total a dollar per contract. Even though an active trader's transaction costs may be a large dollar amount, the costs will still be small in relation to the profit he expects to realize from his trading activities. Unlike the retail customer, the professional trader will rarely consider transaction costs when trading.

Tax consequences may also be a factor for the active trader. When positions are initiated, when they expire, how the positions overlap, and the relationship between different instruments (options, futures, stock, physical commodities, and so on) may all have different tax consequences. Since each trader has unique tax considerations and this book is intended as a general guide to strategies, we will simply assume that every trader wishes to maximize his theoretical profit and that he will worry about taxes afterwards.

Returning now to our example in Figure 5-1, note that after the hedge was intitiated the trader's profit was not affected by what subsequently transpired in the option market. Once the hedge was established the trader's only concern was the volatility, or price fluctuations, in the underlying futures contract. These price fluctuations determined how much and how often he would have to adjust and, in the final analysis, it was the adjustments which determined the profitability of the hedge. The hedge was really a race between the loss in time value of the 100 calls and the profits resulting from the adjustments. In very simple terms, the theoretical pricing model tells us which of these factors will win the race. The model says that if calls are purchased for less than theoretical value, the adjustments will win the race; if calls are purchased for more than theoretical value, loss in time premium will win the race. The conditions of the race are determined by the inputs to the theoretical pricing model.

How would our total profit and loss have been affected had the volatility of the futures contract turned out to be greater than 18.3%? Higher volatility means greater price fluctuations, resulting in more and larger adjustments. In our example more adjustments mean more profit. This is consistent with the principle that the value of all options increases as the volatility of the underlying market increases.

What about the reverse, if volatility turns out to be lower than 18.3%? If that happens the trader will have less chance to adjust. If volatility is low enough, the loss due to time decay will exactly offset the profits from adjustments, so that the trader just breaks even. This break even volatility is identical to the option's implied volatility at the trade price. Using the model, we find that the implied volatility of the 100 call at a purchase price of 3.25 is 14.6%. At that volatility, the race between the profits from adjustments and the loss in the option's time value will end in an exact tie. Above a volatility of 14.6% we expect the hedge (including adjustments) to make a profit; below 14.6% we expect the hedge to show a loss.

Since the trader needed to make adjustments in order to realize a profit, it may seem that every profitable hedge requires that the position be maintained for the full life of the option. In practice this might not be necessary. Suppose for example that immediately after the hedge was established the implied volatility in the option market began to increase. Suppose, that it increased immediately from 14.6% (the implied volatility) to 18.3% (our volatility estimate). In that case the price of the 100 call would rise to 3.88 (its theoretical value at a volatility of 18.3%). The trader could then sell his calls and immediately realize a profit of .63 per contract. Since futures contracts are not affected by changes in implied volatility, the price of the future would remain at 101.35. The trader could buy in all his futures at no profit or loss. His total profit of 63.00 would be immediate, and there would be no reason to hold the position for the full ten weeks.

Changes in implied volatility are usually less dramatic than this. Such changes are more often caused by a change in the volatility of the underlying futures contract, and these changes occur more gradually. Option traders are well aware of changes in the volatility of the underlying futures contract, and if that volatility begins to change, implied volatility can be expected to follow. In our example the marketplace would realize that the futures contract was moving at a volatility greater than 14.6%, and consequently implied volatility would probably begin to rise. If the implied volatility at some point reached 18.3%, we could simply sell out our calls and buy in our futures, thereby realizing a profit of approximately 63.00 points without having to wait the full ten weeks to expiration. Of course there is no guarantee that the marketplace will ever reevaluate implied volatility up to 18.3%. In that case we would have to hold our position and adjust over the full ten weeks in order to realize our profit.

In some cases the marketplace may even overreact to a change in the volatility of the futures contract. In such a case the implied volatilility may go above 18.3%. If we then sold our calls and bought back our futures we would find that we had realized a profit greater than the 63.00 points predicted by the model.

Every trader hopes for quick reevaluation of implied volatility towards his volatility forecast, not only because it enables him to realize his profit more quickly; but because closing out the position as quickly as possible eliminates the risk associated with holding a position for a long period of time.

What might have happened in our example if the underlying futures contract began to move upward at a volatility of 18.3%, but the marketplace insisted on keeping implied volatility well below 18.3%? While the market is rising we are showing a profit on our 100 calls and a loss on our futures. However, because of the different settlement procedures for the two contracts, we cannot offset the losses in our futures position with the profits on our option position. The profit on the calls, because they are settled like stock, is only on paper; while the loss on the futures side requires a daily outflow of cash. If we haven't sufficient capital to feed the futures position we may be caught in a cash squeeze and be forced to close out the position prior to expiration. If we do, there is no guarantee that we will make a profit since we are not able to adjust our position over the full ten weeks to expiration. Even if we do have sufficient capital to maintain the position for the full ten weeks, the outflow in cash will still result in an interest loss to our position. If this loss is great enough, it may reduce our profit significantly. New traders often fail to take into consideration the cash flow problems they might encounter when holding an option versus future position. When such problems do occur, a potential profit can quickly turn into a forced liquidation, and forced liquidations are never profitable.

Suppose that immediately after intitiating his hedge of 100 calls versus short futures the implied volatility in the 100 call which had been 14.6%, drops to 13.5%. In that case the 100 call would be trading at 3.06. Now there would be no cash flow problem because the 100 calls were already paid for; however, the position based on the current price of the 100 call would show a loss of $100 \times -.19 = -19.00$. Futures traders are told that it is unwise to add to a losing position, and that the best course is to cut one's losses as quickly as possible. Is the same advice valid for option traders? That depends on the trader's confidence in his volatility forecast and his margin for error in the forecast. If the recent volatility of the underlying futures contract has been low, and appears to be staying there, then the trader may indeed have a losing position. If so, perhaps he ought to close out the position and take his losses. On the other hand, if the historical volatility of the underlying contract is where he thinks it ought to be, and he sees no reason for a dramatic change, his position will eventually be a winner. If the trader has enough confidence in his volatility estimate and can accept the risk associated with a larger position, he might even consider increasing his position by purchasing additional 100 calls and hedging these against additional short futures. An option trader should never do a strategy in such large size that he cannot afford to do more of the same strategy if option prices move even further away from theoretical value.

In the example in Figure 5-1 we looked at one mispriced option, the 100 call. But in theory any mispriced option, if hedged properly against the underlying futures and adjusted over the life of the option, should yield a profit close to that predicted by the theoretical pricing model. As an example, suppose the 98 put is trading at 2.15. Using the same inputs as in our previous example (70 days to expiration, futures price = 101.35, volatility = 18.3%, interest rate = 8.00%) we can calculate a theoretical value for the 98 put of 1.76, with a delta of -.32. Note here that puts, because they move in the opposite direction of the underlying market, have negative deltas. Put deltas range from zero to -1.00, and like call deltas, change with changing market conditions. Again, we will adhere to the common convention of dropping the decimal point so that put deltas will range from zero to -100.

What will happen if we create a hedge by selling overpriced puts and hedging them against futures contracts? In the initial hedge if we sell 100 of the 98 puts we will have to sell 32 futures contracts:

Contract	Contract Delta	Delta Position
Sell 100 98 puts	–32	+3200
Sell 32 futures	100	–3200

Note that our put delta position is positive because we have sold puts. That is, a negative times a negative is a positive.

After one week, with futures at 102.26, the delta of the 98 put is -27. Now our delta position is:

Contract	Contract Delta	Delta Position
Short 100 98 puts	–27	+2700
Short 32 futures	100	–3200

Since we are short 500 deltas, we are forced to adjust by buying 5 futures contracts. Another week later with the futures at 99.07, our delta position is:

Contract	Contract Delta	Delta Position
Short 100 98 puts	− 42	+4200
Short 27 futures	100	− 2700

Now we are long 1500 deltas and must sell 15 futures contracts.

As theoretical traders, we follow this same procedure throughout the ten weeks to expiration. As in the previous example, at the end of ten weeks we intend to close out the position by letting any out-of-the money options expire worthless, by offsetting any in-the-money options at parity, and by buying in any short futures or selling out any long futures. The results of the hedge are shown in Figure 5-2. With the final futures price at 102.54, the 98 put is worthless, so we get to keep the whole 2.15 per contract. The futures we sold at 101.35 resulted in a loss of 1.19 per contract. Therefore, the total profit and loss from the original hedge is:

$$(+100 \times 2.19) - (32 \times 1.19) = +176.92$$

Week	Futures Price	Delta of 98 Put	Total Delta Position	Adjustment in Futures	Total Futures Adjustments
0	101.35	-32	0		
1	102.26	-27	-500	Buy 5	Long 5
2	99.07	-42	+1500	Sell 15	Short 10
3	100.39	-34	-800	Buy 8	Short 2
4	100.74	-31	-300	Buy 3	Long 1
5	103.59	-16	-1500	Buy 15	Long 16
6	99.26	-39	+2300	Sell 23	Short 7
7	98.28	-46	+700	Sell 7	Short 14
8	99.98	-28	-1800	Buy 18	Long 4
9	103.78	-1	-2700	Buy 27	Long 31
10	102.54			Sell 31	

Figure 5-2

Unfortunately, we don't get to keep all of this profit since we were forced to adjust in a manner just the opposite of that in Figure 5-1. In the present example, when the futures price goes up, our delta position becomes negative and we are forced to buy; when the futures price goes down our delta position becomes positive and we are forced to sell. In other words, we are forced to buy high and sell low which, as any trader will attest, is not a money making strategy. The losses resulting from the adjustments were 136.46 points. (Again, the reader may wish to confirm the profit and loss from the adjustments by adding up the results of all the adjustments in Figure 5-2).

What about interest considerations? The sale of the 98 puts resulted in a credit of $100 \times 2.15 = 215.00$ We were able to earn 8% on this amount for 70 days, for an additional profit of 3.30. The complete P & L is therefore:

Hedge	Adjustments	Interest
+176.92	-136.46	3.30

The total profit is +176.92 - 136.46 + 3.30 = +43.76 (total P & L).

versus a predicted profit of $100 \times +.39 = 39.00$. Here, the model was off by about 5 points.

6

Option Values and Changing Market Conditions

Because options are affected by many different forces in the marketplace, their prices and values can change in ways which may surprise even the most experienced trader. Since decisions must often be made quickly, and without the aid of a computer, the active trader must be aware of the effect of changing market conditions on both an individual option's value and the value of a complex option position. This is an important part of every trader's education.

First, it will be useful to summarize the general effects of changing market conditions on option values. These are given in Figure 6-1. Each input into the theoretical pricing model will cause an option to change its value, under some conditions only very slightly, while under other conditions quite dramatically. Without any useful tools, a trader may find that he must simply guess as to the changes which are taking place. Fortunately, theoretical pricing models, in addition to generating theoretical values, also generate several numbers which are useful tools in estimating both the direction and the magnitude of these changes.

**The Effect of Changing Market Conditions
on Theoretical Values of Options on Futures**

If...	Call Values will...	Put Values will...
The price of the underlying rises	rise	fall
The price of the underlying falls	fall	rise
Volatility rises	rise	rise
Volatility falls	fall	fall
Time passes	fall	fall
Interest rates rise	fall slightly	fall slightly
Interest rates fall	rise slightly	rise slightly

Figure 6-1

The Delta

We touched on the delta in the last chapter where we used it as a measure of the proper number of option contracts to futures contracts required to establish a neutral hedge. The delta also has several other interpretations, any of which may, from time to time, be useful to a trader.

Rate of Change

Figure 6-2 shows what happens to the theoretical value of a call as the underlying futures price changes. Under some conditions, when the call is very deeply in-the-money, its value changes at a rate almost identical to the underlying. If the underlying price goes up or down one point, the call will change by an equal amount. Under other conditions, when the call is far out-of-the-money, its value may change very little, even if the underlying contract makes a large move. The delta is a measure of how fast an option's value changes with respect to changes in the price of the underlying contract. In theory, an op-

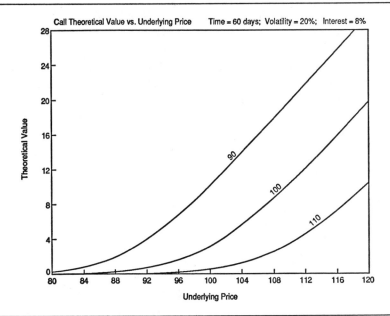

Figure 6-2

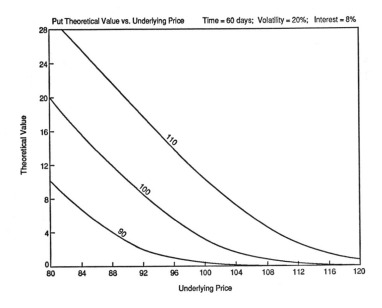

Figure 6-3

tion can never gain or lose value more quickly than the underlying futures contract, so the delta of a call always has an upper bound of 100. (Again, we will retain the common practice of writing the delta without the decimal point. A delta of 1.00 will be written as 100.) An option with a delta of 100 should move up or down one full point for each full point move up or down in the underlying. It is moving at 100% of the rate of the underlying. In theory, a call also cannot move in the opposite direction of the underlying, so the delta of a call has a lower bound of zero. A call with a delta of zero will move negligibly, even if the underlying futures contract makes a moderately large upward move.

Most calls, of course, will have deltas somewhere between zero and 100 and will move at a slower rate than the underlying. A call with a delta of 25 can be expected to rise or fall 1/4 point for each full point that the underlying rises or falls. It is moving at 25% of the rate of the underlying. A call with a delta of 75 can be expected to move at 75% of the rate of the underlying; a one point rise or fall in the underlying will cause the call to gain or lose 3/4 of a point. Call options which are at-the-money, i.e. which have exercise prices equal to the current price of the underlying, have delta values close to 50. They rise or fall in value at just about half the rate of the underlying.

Figure 6-3 shows what happens to put values as the price of the underlying changes. Puts have characteristics similar to calls, except that puts move in the opposite direction of the underlying futures contract. When the underlying moves up, puts lose value; when the underlying moves down, puts gain value. For this reason, puts have negative deltas, ranging from zero for far out-of-the-money puts to -100 for very deeply in-the-money puts. Again, the delta is a measure of the rate of change in a put's value with respect to the underlying, but the negative sign indicates the movement will be in the opposite direction of the underlying market. A put with a delta of -10 can be expected to move at 10% of the rate of the underlying, but in the opposite direction. If the underlying moves up .50, the put will move down .05. If the underlying moves down 1.20, the put will move up .12. An at-the-money put will have a delta of approximately -50, and will move at half the rate of the underlying, but in the opposite direction.

Hedge Ratio

This was our original definition of the delta in Chapter 5. If we wish to hedge an option position against the underlying futures contract, the delta tells us the proper ratio of options to futures contracts required to establish a neutral hedge. A futures contract always has a delta of 100, so the proper hedge ratio can be determined by dividing the option's delta into 100. An at-the-money call has a delta of 50, so the proper hedge ratio is 100/50, or 2/1. For every two options purchased we need to sell one futures contract to establish a neutral hedge. A call with a delta of 40 requires the sale of 2 futures for each five options purchased, since 100/40 = 5/2.

Since puts have negative deltas, a hedge including long puts will include long options, and a hedge including short puts will include short options. A put with a delta of -75 will require the purchase of three futures for each four puts purchased since 100/75 = 4/3.

Thus far all the hedges we have looked at have consisted of options versus futures. But any hedge, whether options vs. futures or options vs. options, is delta neutral as long as all the deltas in the hedge add up to zero. For example, suppose we buy four calls with a delta of 50 each, and ten puts with a delta of -20 each. Our delta position is neutral since $(+4 \times +50) + (+10 \times -20) = 0$. Indeed, a position can be highly complex, consisting of futures, calls, and puts, with different exercise prices and expiration dates. But as long as the deltas add up to approximately zero, we say that the position is delta neutral.

Theoretical or Equivalent Futures Position

If a trader is accustomed to evaluating his position in terms of the number of futures contracts which he is long or short, then he can use the delta to equate his option position with a futures position of similar size. Each 100 deltas represents a theoretical position equivalent to one futures contract. For example, a trader who owns an at-the-money call with a delta of 50 is long, or controls, 1/2 of a futures contract. If he owned ten such contracts he would be long 500 deltas or, in equivalent terms, five futures contracts. He would have a similar theoretical futures position if he were to sell 20 puts with a delta of -25 each, since $-20 \times -25 = +500$.

It is important to be aware of the theoretical aspect of an equivalent futures position since an option is not simply a surrogate for a futures position. An actual futures position is sensitive only to directional movement in the commodity. An option is sensitive to directional moves, but it is also sensitive to the passage of time and changes in volatility. An option trader who looks only at his delta position leaves himself at great risk from these other forces. He must realize that an option position is an equivalent futures position only under very narrowly defined market conditions.

The reader has perhaps already noted that our three interpretations of the delta—rate of change, hedge ratio, and theoretical futures positon—are all essentially the same. How a trader interprets his delta position depends primarily on his trading strategy at a particular time. For example, suppose a trader is preparing for the opening of the market and sees that he has a delta position of +500. This tells him that his position will gain or lose value at approximately five times the rate of the underlying futures contract (rate of change). If he wants to maintain a delta neutral position, he knows he must sell 500 deltas on the opening (hedge ratio). Finally, he may be bullish on the market and wish to maintain a long market position. In this case he knows that if he does nothing he is, in theory, long approximately five futures contracts (theoretical futures position). Even though a trader may make different uses of a delta figure, each interpretation is mathematically the same.

There is one other definition of the delta which is of less practical value to the trader but which may be of interest from a theoretical standpoint. If we assume that futures prices are lognormally distributed, then the delta of an option is approximately the probability that the option will finish in-the-money. A call or put with a delta of 25 or -25, respectively, has about a 25% chance of finishing in-the-money. An option with a delta of 100, or -100 in the case of puts, is almost certain to finish in-the-money. Finally, an option with a delta of zero has almost no chance to finish in-the-money. Since most option strategies depend not on the probability of an option finishing in-the-money, but rather on the total expected return, this definition will not be of much use to the serious trader. A trader who is courageous enough (or foolish enough) to simply sell naked options might perhaps use this probability concept to help assess risk.

The Gamma

In discussing the delta, we noted that under some circumstances, when the option is far out-of-the-money, its delta is close to zero. At other times, when the option is very deeply in-the-money, its delta is close to 100 (-100 for puts). Therefore, as the underlying futures contract moves up, call deltas must be moving towards 100 and put deltas towards zero. Conversely, as the underlying futures contract moves down, call deltas must be moving towards zero and put deltas towards -100. This effect is shown in Figures 6-4 and 6-5.

The gamma, sometimes referred to as the *curvature* of an option, is the rate at which an option gains or loses deltas as the underlying contract moves up or down. The gamma is given in deltas per point change in the underlying. For example, if an option has a gamma of 5, for each point increase in the price of the underlying futures contract the option will gain 5 deltas. If the option originally had a delta of 25, and the underlying moves up one full point, then the new delta of the option will be 30. If the underlying moves up another point, the option will have a delta of 35.

If the underlying moves down, we must subtract the gamma number from the old delta to obtain the new delta. In our example, if the underlying futures contract falls one full point from its original price, the delta of the option will be 20. If the underlying falls another point, the delta of the option will be 15.

Even though Figure 6-4 represents call deltas and Figure 6-5 represents put deltas, both sets of graphs look almost identical. This must mean that both calls and puts have similar curvature, and that as the price of the underlying rises the deltas of both calls and puts will increase. This may at first seem strange, but it becomes logical when we remember that zero is greater than -50 in the same way that -50 is greater than -100. Negative numbers become larger as one moves toward zero. This means that *both calls and puts have positive gammas.* This often confuses the new trader since, through his use of deltas, he is accustomed to associating positive numbers with calls and negative numbers with puts. But regardless of whether we are working with calls or puts, we always add the gamma number as the underlying rises and we always subtract the gamma number as the underlying falls. When a trader is long options, whether calls or puts,

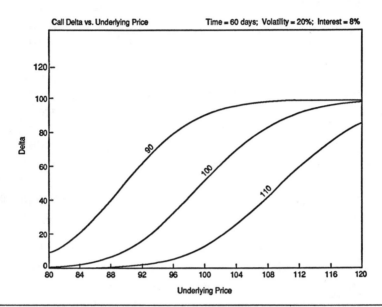

Figure 6-4

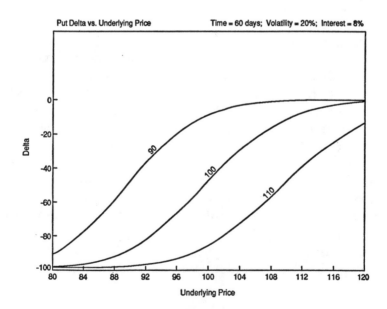

Figure 6-5

he has a long gamma position, and when he is short options, he has a short gamma position.

For example, suppose an at-the-money call, with a delta of 50, and an at-the-money put, with a delta of -50, both have a gamma value of 5. If the underlying moves up one point we add the gamma value (5) to the call delta (50) to get the new call delta (55). To calculate the new put delta we also *add* the gamma (5) to the put delta (-50) to get the new put delta (-45). This confirms our intuition that as the underlying moves up calls move into-the-money and puts move out-of-the-money.

Since the delta of a futures contract never changes, its gamma is always zero.

The gamma is a measurement of how fast an option is changing its market characteristics, acting more or less like an actual futures contract. In this sense the gamma is a useful indication of the risk associated with an option position in the same way that the delta is a useful indication of the risk associated with a futures position. A large gamma number, whether positive or negative, indicates a high degree of risk; a low gamma number indicates a low degree of risk. Every option trader must not only be aware of his market position (delta) at a particular moment, but also how the position will change if the underlying futures contract begins to move (gamma).

Suppose a trader sells 10 calls with a delta of 30 each. He is short 300 deltas, equivalent, in theory, to being short 3 futures contracts. If this trader is accustomed to dealing in lots of 5 futures contracts or less, he is for the moment within his normal risk limits. If the market rises 10 points, and if the trader only considers his original delta position of -300, he will assume that he is still short the same 3 futures contracts, and therefore within acceptable risk boundaries. But what if the initial gamma of each call was 5? Then, for each point rise in the underlying futures contract, each call will gain 5 deltas. Since the underlying rose 10 points each call will now have a delta of $30 + (10 \times 5) = 80$. Instead of a total delta position of -300, the trader's position will be -800, well beyond the risk he is used to accepting.

A large gamma can often overwhelm the inexperienced trader, turning a bad situation into a disastrous one. New traders are well-advised to avoid large gamma positions, particularly negative ones, because of the speed with which such positions can change. Even experienced traders sometimes take on gamma positions which, if they stopped to consider, are simply too risky. This was dramatically demonstrated in the collapse of Volume Investors on the COMEX in the spring of 1985. Several traders, all clearing their trades through the same firm, built up extremely large negative gamma positions by selling large numbers of out-of-the-money gold options. In the past this had been a profitable strategy since the gold market had been relatively quite with low volatility. But on this occassion the market made a violent upward move, and the traders, who were originally delta neutral, quickly found themselves short thousands of deltas in a rapidly rising market. The losses sustained by the traders not only led to the collapse of the clearing firm, but also to a crisis in the COMEX's Clearing Association. The incident might have been avoided had someone, either the traders themselves, the clearing firm, or the clearing association realized that the large negative gamma position represented an unacceptable risk. Many firms now have risk control managers responsible for identifying such dangerous positions. The trader to whom the position belongs is told to reduce the size to a risk acceptable to the clearing firm.

The gamma can also help a trader maintain a delta neutral position. Suppose a trader has a delta position of +500 prior to the opening of the market. If he wishes to be delta neutral he can sell 5 futures contracts on the opening. But suppose that his gamma position is +100 and the market is expected to open 2 points higher. If it does indeed open 2 points higher his delta position will no longer be +500, but +700 [+500 + (2 × +100)]. He will know that in order to be delta neutral he will have to sell 7 futures contracts. He can make this calculation without any computer assistance simply by knowing his delta and gamma positions prior to the opening of the market.

Like the delta, the gamma changes with changing market conditions. These changes are shown in Figures 6-6, 6-7, and 6-8. Figure 6-6 clearly demonstrates that the gamma of an option is always greatest when it is at-the-money, and becomes smaller as the option moves either out-of-the-money or into-the-money. Figures 6-7 and 6-8 show that the gamma of an at-the-money option can increase dramatically as expiration approaches, or as we decrease our volatility assumption about the underlying futures contract. This means that a trader's gamma position, which may have initially been small, can become

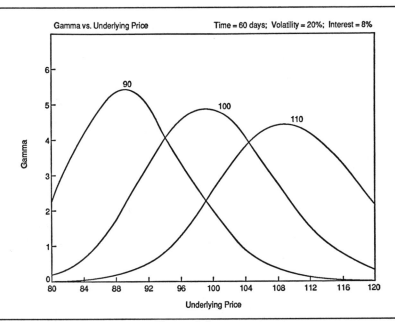

Figure 6-6

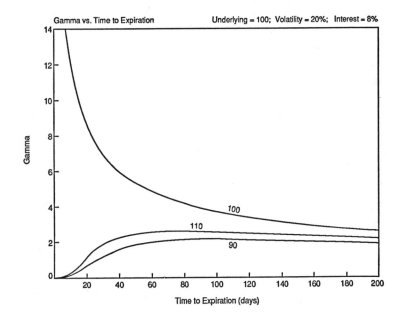

Figure 6-7

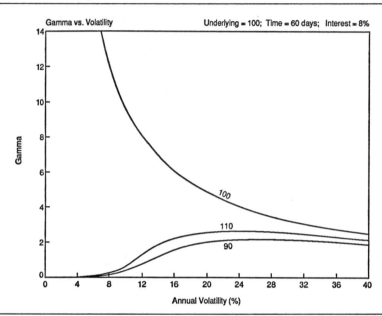

Figure 6-8

creasingly large simply through the passage of time or through changes in volatility. Even in a quiet market an option position must constantly be monitored to ensure that its risk characterisitics remain within acceptable limits.

The delta is subject to change from market conditions other than movement in the underlying futures contract. Figures 6-9 and 6-10 show the effect of changes in time to expiration on delta values; Figures 6-11 and 6-12 show the effect of changes in volatility. Note that all four sets of graphs have essentially the same shape. As we increase the time to expiration or increase volatility all options become more at-the-money, with call deltas approaching 50 and put deltas approaching -50. Conversely, as time to expiration grows shorter, or as volatility declines, all option deltas move away from 50 (-50 for puts). An option which is in-the-money will move further into-the-money, and an option which is out-of-the-money will move further out-of-the-money.

Just as a delta neutral option position can quickly become non-neutral through movement in the underlying contract (gamma effect), it can also become non-neutral through the passage of time or through changes in volatility. Traders who claim to always be delta neutral are actually fooling themselves. No one can say with any certainty exactly what delta neutral means. The delta value depends on the volatility assumption, and the volatility assumption is just that, an assumption, not a known. A trader who sells 4 calls with a delta of 25 each and buys one futures contract might say that he is delta neutral. But in order to arrive at a delta of 25 for the call the trader was required to feed some volatility into a theoretical pricing model. If he decides the next day that his original volatility assumption was too low, and he now raises it, Figure 6-11 clearly shows that the call's delta will move upwards towards 50. Using his new higher volatility estimate the call might now have a delta of 35. The trader is no longer delta neutral, but 40 deltas short. All he did to become non-neutral was to change his assumptions about market conditions.

Some traders prefer to calculate their delta position from the implied volatility of each option rather than from their own volatiliy

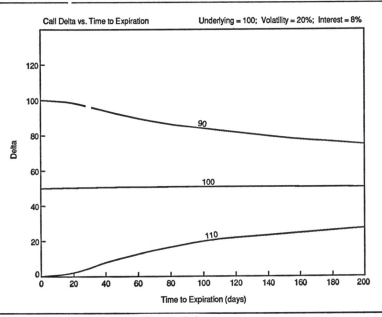

Figure 6-9

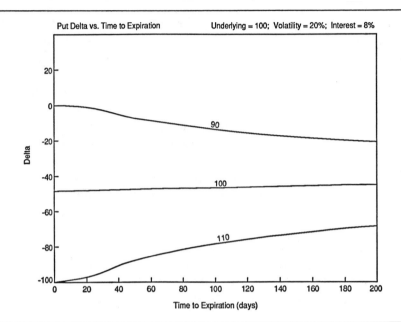

Figure 6-10

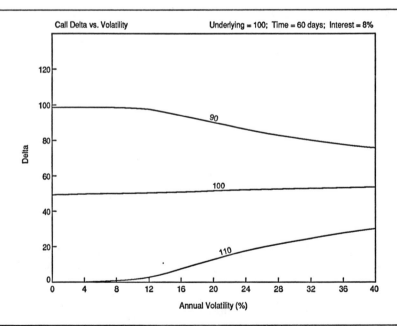

Figure 6-11

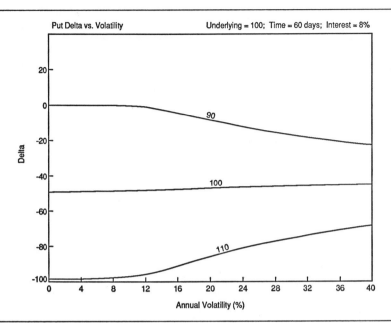

Figure 6-12

estimate. The delta value derived from this type of calculation is the *implied delta*, or price delta. If the trader knows the implied delta of an option, he can estimate how the price of the option, rather than its value, is likely to change as the underlying futures contract moves up or down. This is sometimes useful in assessing the short term risk associated with an option.

This does not mean that the concept of being delta neutral is not a useful one, particularly in assessing certain types of risk. It does mean that a delta neutral position depends on a trader's best guess about market conditions, but there is no guarantee that his guess will be correct. As he changes his assumptions about market conditions, he must constantly change his trading strategies to fit these new assumptions. Delta neutral trading is only one aspect of this principle.

The Theta

The effect of a change in time to expiration on the theoretical values of puts and calls is shown in Figures 6-13 and 6-14. Note that all op-

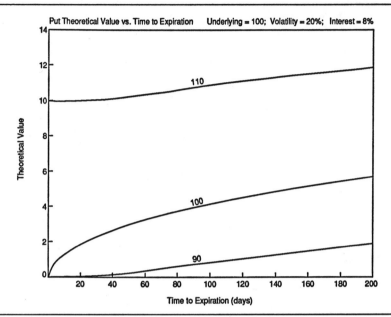

Figure 6-13

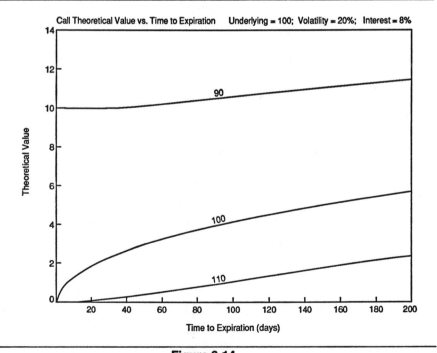

Figure 6-14

tions, both puts and calls, lose value as expiration approaches. The theta, sometimes referred to as the *time decay factor*, is the rate at which an option loses its value as time passes. The theta is usually given in points lost per day, so that an option with a theta of .25 will lose .25 in value for each day that passes with no change in other market conditions. If it is worth 2.75 today, then tomorrow, if there are no changes in other conditions, it will be worth 2.50. The day after that it will be worth 2.25.

Time runs in only one direction and, technically, the theta is a positive number. However, to simplify calculations, and to remind the reader that the theta is a loss in value, it will be written as a negative number. Therefore, the theta of an option which loses .25 per day will be written as -.25. Consequently, a long option position will always have a negative theta, and a short option position will always have a positive theta. Note that this is just the opposite of the gamma position, where a long option position has a positive gamma, and a short option position has a negative gamma. In fact, almost all option positions have a gamma and a theta which are of opposite signs.

Moreover, the size of the gamma position correlates to the size of the theta position. A large positive gamma position goes hand in hand with a large negative theta position, while a large negative gamma position goes hand in hand with a large positive theta position. This means that every option position is a tradeoff between market movement and time decay. If price movement in the underlying futures contract will help a trader's position (positive gamma), then passage of time will hurt it (negative theta), and vice versa. The trader can't have it both ways. Either he wants the market to move, or he wants it to sit still. This can be seen graphically by comparing Figures 6-15 (theta vs. time to expiration) and Figure 6-7 (gamma vs. time to expiration). As the theta becomes large, so does the gamma. Just as a large gamma indicates a high degree of risk with respect to market movement, a large theta indicates a high degree of risk with respect to the passage of time.

The reader may have noted the unusual squiggle in the theta of the 90 call in Figure 6-15. This seems to indicate that as expiration approaches the theta of the 90 call reverses itself. When options are subject to stock type settlement, as they are currently in the U.S., the carrying cost of an option (its interest component) can, under some

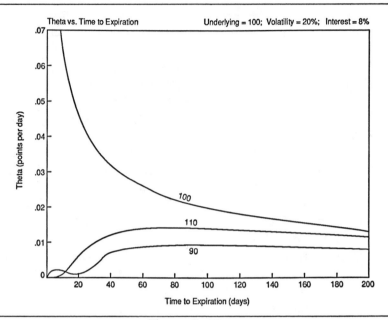

Figure 6- 15

conditions, be greater than the volatility component. If this happens, and the option is European (no early exercise permitted), it will have a theoretical value less than parity. As expiration approaches, the value of the option will slowly rise to parity. This effect is only possible when the option is deeply in-the-money with very little time remaining to expiration. We will discuss this phenomenon in greater detail when we look at early exercise in Chapter 12.

The Vega

Just as we are concerned with the effect on an option's theoretical value of movement in the underlying futures contract (delta), and the effect of the passage of time (theta), we are also concerned with the effect of a change in volatility. This effect is shown in Figures 6-16 and 6-17. While the terms delta, gamma, and theta are found in all books on option theory, there is no single commonly accepted term for this number. It is sometimes referred to as vega, kappa, omega, zeta, or sigma prime (sigma is the commonly used notation for volatility).

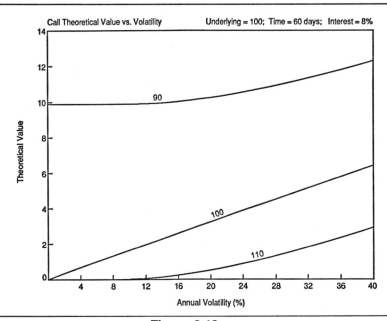

Figure 6-16

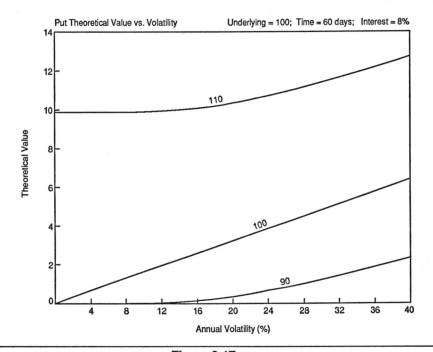

Figure 6-17

Because several computer services popular among traders use the term vega, we will also use this term to refer to an option's change in theoretical value with respect to a change in volatility.

The vega of an option is given in point change in theoretical value for each one percentage point change in volatility. Since all options gain value with rising volatility, the vega for both calls and puts is always a positive number. If an option has a vega of .50, for each percentage point increase in the volatility, the option will gain .50 in value. If it has a theoretical value of 5.25 at a volatility of 15%, then it will have a theoretical value of 5.75 at a volatility of 16%, and a theoretical value of 4.75 at a volatility of 14%.

Note in Figure 6-18 that the at-the-money option always has a greater vega than either the in-the-money or out-of-the-money option when all options have the same amount of time to expiration. This means that the at-the-money option is always the most sensitive in total points to any change in volatility. As a corollary, the out-of-the-money option is always the most sensitive in percent terms to a change in volatility. For example, suppose an at-the-money and an out-of-the-money option have theoretical values of 2.00 and .50, respectively, with a volatility assumption of 15%. If we raise the volatility assumption to 20%, the options might now have values of 3.00 and 1.00. The at-the-money option has shown the greater total point increase (1.00 vs .50), while the out-of-the-money option has shown the greater percent increase (50% vs.100%). Since many option strategies involve buying and selling unequal numbers of options, this latter characteristic will be important later.

Note also in Figure 6-18 that the vega of all options declines as time to expiration grows shorter. Therefore, a long-term option will always be more sensitive to a change in volatility than a short-term option with the same exercise price. A 4-month option will be more sensitive than a 1-month option to any change in our volatility assumption.

This last point illustrates an important principle of option evaluation, that time and volatility are closely interconnected. More time to expiration means more time for volatility to take effect, while less time to expiration may mean that any change in volatility will have only a negligible effect on an option's value. Moreover, changes in time to expiration and changes in volatility often have similar effects

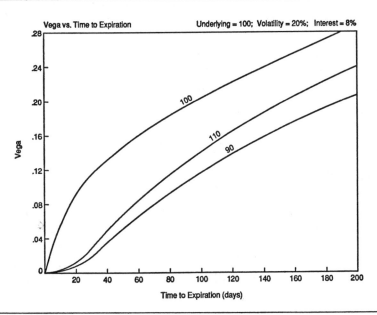

Figure 6-18

on an option's value. Decreasing volatility is similar to decreasing time to expiration. If a trader cannot remember what effect the passage of time will have on his position, he might instead consider what effect a reduction in volatility will have. This can be seen by comparing Figures 6-13 and 6-16 (theoretical values with respect to time and volatility), and Figures 6-9 and 6-11 (delta values with respect to time and volatility). In both cases the similar shapes of the graphs indicate the similar effects of time and volatility.

The Rho

The sensitivity of an option's theoretical value to a change in interest rates is given by its rho. All futures options will have a negative rho. An increase in interest rates will decrease the value of the option by increasing the carrying costs on the option position. However, this effect will be very small, and will be far outweighed by considerations of volatility, time to expiration, and price of the underlying contract.

For this reason, we will essentially ignore an option's rho in choosing viable option strategies and in managing risk.[1]

It is important for the active trader to be familiar with the delta, gamma, theta, and vega characteristics of options, since he may be called upon to make quick decisions about trading strategies and risk management. Such decisions could very well determine his financial fate. Let us therefore summarize the primary characteristics of these numbers:

Delta: Deltas range from zero for far out-of-the-money calls to 100 for deeply in-the-money calls, and from zero for far out-of-the-money puts to -100 for deeply in-the-money puts. At-the-money calls have deltas of approximately 50, and puts approximately -50. As time passes, or as we decrease our volatility assumption, all call deltas move away from 50, and puts away from -50. As we increase our volatility assumption all call deltas move towards 50, and put deltas towards -50.

Gamma: At-the-money options always have a greater gamma than either in-the-money or out-of-the-money options with the same expiration date. As time to expiration grows shorter, or as we decrease our volatility assumption, the gamma of at-the-money options can increase dramatically.

Theta: The theta of an at-the-money option always increases as expiration approaches, so that a short term at-the-money option will always decay more quickly than a long term at-the-money option. The at-the-money option always has a greater theta than either an in-the-money or out-of-the-money option with the same expiration date.

---

[1]This is not to say that the rho is of no use in option evaluation. Options on stocks, currencies, and physical commodities can in some situations be very sensitive to changes in interest rates. Here, however, we are concerned primarily with futures options.

Vega: The vega of all options decreases as time to expiration grows shorter, so that a long term option will always be more sensitive to a change in volatility than a short term option with the same exercise price. At-the-money options always have a greater vega than either in-the-money or out-of-the-money options with the same amount of time to expiration. Out-of-the-money options have the greatest vega as a percent of their theoretical value.

Figures 6-19A and B are reproductions of printouts from two popular computer pricing services used by option traders. The first is from the Schwarz-a-tron system by Reuters Information Services, and the second is from the TOG system by The Options Group. The printouts give the theoretical values, deltas, gammas, thetas, and vegas for options on May soybean futures traded on the Chicago Board of Trade at the close of trading on 28 January 1988. A volatility of 20% and an interest rate of 7.75% were used to make the calculations. Explanations of the symbols on these printouts are given in Figure 6-20 (page 140).

Knowing the total delta, gamma, theta, and vega associated with an option position can help a trader determine beforehand how the position is likely to react to changing market conditions. Since all these numbers are simply additive, the total delta, gamma, theta, and vega of the position can be calculated by adding up the delta, gamma, theta, and vega of all the individual options. For example, if a trader is long 5 options with a gamma of 2.5 each, and is short 2 options with a gamma of 4.0 each, his total gamma position is $(+5 \times 2.5) + (-2 \times 4.0) = +4.5$. Similarly, if he is long 5 options with a theta of -.08 each and short 2 options with a theta of -.03 each, his total theta position is $(+5 \times -.08) + (-2 \times -.04) = -.32$.

New traders sometimes have difficulty remembering whether a certain delta, gamma, theta, or vega position is long or short. The signs associated with these positions, either positive or negative, are given in Figure 6-21 (page 141). In addition, each positive or negative delta, gamma, theta, or vega position tells the trader which changes in market conditions will either help or hurt his position. The effect of changing market conditions on these positions is summarized in Figure 6-22 (page 141).

Reuters Information Services
Schwarz-a-tron (S-tron)

XSK[1] SIMULATION AT 615½[2] ON 1/28/88[3]   VOL   20[4]   20   20   INT   *   7.75[5]   7.75   7.75   7.75

U4/23/88[6]	Prc[10]	Thvl[11]	Dlt[12]	Gma[13]	Omg[15]	IV[16]	ID[17]	Bid[18]	BIF[19]	Ask[20]	AIV[21]	IDcy[14]	E/R[22]
	4/23/88				4/23/88					4/23/88			
8K[7] 475C[9]		140½	100	.0	-.00	.0			*****		*****	.00	*****
8A 500C	116	115½	100	.0	-.00	.0			*****		*****	.00	.50
8B 525C	91	91	96	.1	.28	19.9	96		*****		*****	1.26	-.02
8C 550C	68	68¼	88	.3	.64	19.5	88	75	30.6	78	35.3	3.27	-.33
8D 575C	47	48⅛	76	.51	.00	18.9	77	58	29.9	61	32.9	5.12	-1.44
8E 600C	29½	31⅜	61	.61	.11	18.2	62	34	22.3	37	25.0	5.29	-2.98
8F 625C	17¼	19⅜	45	.61	.20	18.2	45	33	31.3	34	32.2	6.24	-4.71
8G 650C	10	11⅛	30	.51	.07	18.9	29		*****		*****	5.83	-3.77
8H 675C	5½	5¾	19	.4	.73	19.7	18	15	32.7	16	34.1	4.12	-1.26
8I 700C	4½	2½	11	.3	.55	22.0	14	11	34.8	13	38.5	4.92	18.87
8J 725C	2¾	1 3+	5	.1	.38	24.2	9	9	40.8	11	46.1	2.63	30.07
8k 475P	¼	1+	-1	.0	.03	.0			*****		*****	.00	*****
8a 500P	½	5+	-4	.0	.11	21.9	-2	¼	19.7	½	21.9	.72	*****
8b 525P	¾	1⅛	-11	.1	.32	18.7	-4	⅞	19.1	1½	21.1	1.74	8.73
8c 550P	3½	3⅜	-23	.3	.66	20.1	-12	1½	17.1	2	17.8	3.82	-.60
8d 575P	6	8⅛	-37	.51	.01	17.9	-21	4	15.9	5	16.9	3.49	9.04
8e 600P	14½	16	-53	.61	.14	18.6	-37	29	31.3	32	33.0	5.48	3.97
8f 625P	25½	28¾	-69	.61	.20	17.3	-54	41	30.2	45	33.5	5.86	6.09
8g 650P	44	45¼	-80	.51	.07	18.9	-70	31	6.7	35	10.5	5.59	1.79
8h 675P	64	64⅝	-89	.4	.73	19.1	-82		*****		*****	3.69	.76
8i 700P		86¼	-95	.3	.49	.0			*****		*****	.00	****
8j 725P	109	110		.1	.30	.0			*****		*****	.00	1.00

Figure 6-19A

The Options Group (TOG)

Soybean Futures   Put/Call Simulation Scan   Page 2612   1/28/88 15:16
=) DATE 28 JAN 88;[3]   VOL. = 20.0%;[4]   INT. = 7.75%[5]

1 Exp Date	8 Days Exp	2 Future Last	9 Xer Prc	10 Call Last	11 Call Est Val	12 Call Hdg	13 Call Gam	14 C Prm Lost
MY88	85	615.50S	475	.00Y	140.50*	1.00	.000	.00
MY88	85	615.50S	500	*****S	115.50*	1.00	.000	.00
MY88	85	615.50S	525	91.00S	91.00	.96	.000	.20
MY88	85	615.50S	550	68.00S	68.25	.88	.003	.52
MY88	85	615.50S	575	47.00S	48.12	.77	.006	.89
MY88	85	615.50S	600	29.50S	31.50	.62	.007	1.17
MY88	85	615.50S	625	17.25S	19.13	.45	.007	1.24
MY88	85	615.50S	650	10.00S	10.75	.30	.006	1.09
MY88	85	615.50S	675	5.50S	5.50	.18	.004	.81
MY88	85	615.50S	700	4.50S	2.62	.10	.003	.53
MY88	85	615.50S	725	2.75S	1.12	.05	.001	.30

Spot: 605.75   MR88: 605.75S   MY88: 615.50S   JL88: 622.25S
AG88: 623.00S   SP88: 623.50S   NV88: 628.50S   JA89: 636.509

15 Call Vega	16 Call Impd	9 Xer Prc	10 Put Last	11 Put Est Val	12 Put Hdq	13 Put Gam	14 P Prm Lost	15 Put Vega	16 Put Impd
.00	N/A	475	.25S	.00	.00	.000	.03	.00	23.5
.00	25.6	500	.50S	.25	.01	.000	.10	.13	21.5
.25	19.9	525	.75S	1.12	.04	.000	.28	.25	18.4
.50	19.4	550	3.50S	3.37	.11	.003	.59	.50	20.1
.88	18.6	575	6.00S	8.00	.22	.006	.94	.88	17.5
1.12	18.0	600	14.50S	16.25	.37	.007	1.19	1.12	18.3
1.12	18.2	625	25.50S	28.50	.54	.007	1.23	1.12	17.3
1.00	19.2	650	44.00S	44.87	.69	.006	1.05	1.00	19.0
.75	19.8	675	64.00S	64.50	.81	.004	.75	.75	19.3
.50	23.1	700	.00Y	86.50	.90	.001	.45	.50	N/A
.25	23.9	725	*****S	109.87	.95	.000	.21	.25	N/A

Figure 6-19B

Explanation of Symbols on the S-tron and TOG Machine

1. *Expiration Month.*

2. *Underlying Futures Price.*

3. *Today's Date.*

4. *Volatility used for Theoretical Calculations.* Note that on the S-tron the user can enter three different volatilities. This machine was originally designed for stock options, which typically had three expiration months. The user was able to enter a different volatility for each month's expiration.

5. *Interest Rate Used for Theoretical Calculations.* As with volatility, the S-tron allowed the user to enter a different interest rate for each expiration month.

6. *Dividend Line.* On the S-tron the user is able to enter dividend amounts and payout dates for stock option evaluation.

7. *S-tron Computer Code.*

8. The Number of Days to Expiration (on the TOG machine.)

9. *Exercise Price,* including on the S-tron a C for call; and P for put.

10. *Option Last Trade Price.*

11. *Option Theoretical Value* (estimated value on the TOG machine).

12. *Option Delta.* Note thet the TOG machine gives delta values with the decimal point included, while the S-tron leaves the decimal out. The S-tron also includes the negative sign for put deltas.

13. *Option Gamma.* Again, the TOG machine includes the decimal, whole the S-tron leaves it out.

14. *Option Theta.* This is written as premium lost on the TOG machine, and the value given is the decay, in points over a 10-day period. The number is written as implied decay (IDcy) on the S-tron, and the value given is the dollar decay per day (one point in soybeans = $50).

15. *Option Vega.* This appears as the omega on the S-tron.

16. *Option Implied Volatility.* Based on the last trade price.

17. *Option Implied Delta.* On the S-tron only.

18. *Option Bid Price.* This, and items 19, 20, & 21, appear on the S-tron only. They are used on those marketplaces where both bids and offers are continuously posted.

19. *Bid Implied Volatility.*

20. *Option Ask Price.*

21. *Ask Implied Volatility*

22. *Equalized Ranking.* This is S-tron's proprietary method of ranking the extent to which an option of either undervalued (positive E/R) or overvalued (negative E/R).

Note that some values on the S-tron appear with a + (plus sign). This is the symbol for 16ths, and is necessary for stock options where 1/16 is the minimum increment for some prices.

Values from the two services may not be identical due to the fact the S-tron uses the Cox-Ross-Rubenstein Model, while the TOG machine uses the Black-Scholes Model.

Figure 6-20

If you are	Your Delta (Hedge Ratio) Position is	Your Gamma (Curvature) Position is	Your Theta (Time Decay) Position is	Your Vega (Volatility) Position is
Long Futures	Positive	0	0	0
Short Futures	Negative	0	0	0
Long Calls	Positive	Positive	Negative	Positive
Short Calls	Negative	Negative	Positive	Negative
Long Puts	Negative	Positive	Negative	Positive
Short Puts	Positive	Negative	Positive	Negative

Figure 6-21

If your Delta Position is:

	You want the Underlying Futures Contract to:
Positive	Rise in Price
Negative	Fall in Price

If your Gamma Position is:

	You want the Underlying Futures Contract to:
Positive	Make a big move
Negative	Sit still

If your Theta Position is:

	Passage of time will generally:
Positive	Help your position
Negative	Hurt your position

If your Vega Position is:

	You want Volatility to:
Positive	Rise
Negative	Fall

Figure 6-22

Futures price = 100.00; Time to expiration = 60 days; Volatility = 20%; Interest = 8.00%

C A L L S

Exercise Price	Price	Theoretical Value	Delta	Gamma	Theta	Vega
90	10.40	10.22	90	2.0	-.009	.07
95	6.31	6.18	74	3.9	-.020	.13
100	3.25	3.19	51	4.9	-.026	.16
105	1.31	1.38	28	4.1	-.022	.14
110	.44	.50	13	2.6	-.014	.08

P U T S

Price	Theoretical Value	Delta	Gamma	Theta	Vega
.46	.35	-9	2.0	-.011	.07
1.40	1.25	-25	3.9	-.021	.13
3.24	3.19	-48	4.9	-.026	.16
6.23	6.31	-70	4.1	-.021	.14
10.21	10.36	-86	2.6	-.012	.08

Position	Theoretical Edge	Delta Position	Gamma Position	Theta Position	Vega Position
1. long 20 futures short 27 95 calls	0 27 × + .13 +3.51	+20 × +100 -27 × + 74 + 2	0 -27 × 3.9 -105.3	0 -27 × -.020 +.540	0 -27 × .13 -3.51
2. long 25 110 calls short 10 105 calls	25 × + .06 10 × - .07 + .80	+25 × + 13 -10 × + 28 + 45	+25 × 2.6 -10 × 4.1 + 24.0	+25 × -.014 -10 × -.022 -.130	+25 × .08 -10 × .14 + .60

Figure 6-23

Position	Theoretical Edge	Delta Position	Gamma Position	Theta Position	Vega Position
3. short 10 95 puts short 10 105 calls	10 × + .15 10 × − .07 —— + .80	−10 × − 25 −10 × + 28 —— − 30	−10 × 3.9 −10 × 4.1 —— − 80.0	−10 × −.021 −10 × −.022 —— +.430	−10 × .13 −10 × .14 —— −2.70
4. long 10 110 puts short 10 105 puts	10 × + .15 10 × − .08 —— + .70	+10 × − 86 −10 × − 70 —— −160	+10 × 2.6 −10 × 4.1 —— − 15.0	+10 × −.012 −10 × −.021 —— +.090	+10 × .08 −10 × .14 —— − .60

5. long 10 90 puts
   short 20 95 calls
   long 10 100 puts
	10 × − .11
	20 × + .15
	10 × − .05
	——
	+1.40
		+10 × − 9
		−20 × − 25
		+10 × − 48
		——
		− 70
			+10 × 2.0
			−20 × 3.9
			+10 × 4.9
			——
			− 9.0
				+10 × −.011
				−20 × −.021
				+10 × −.026
				——
				+.050
					+10 × .07
					−20 × .13
					+10 × .16
					——
					− .30

6. short 10 90 calls
   long 10 90 puts
   short 6 95 calls
   long 9 100 puts
   long 15 105 calls
   long 20 110 calls
   long 13 futures
	10 × + .18
	10 × − .11
	6 × + .13
	9 × − .05
	15 × + .07
	20 × + .06
	0
	——
	+3.28
		−10 × + 90
		+10 × − 9
		− 6 × + 74
		+ 9 × − 48
		+15 × + 28
		+20 × + 13
		+13 × +100
		——
		+114
			−10 × 2.0
			+10 × 2.0
			− 6 × 3.9
			+ 9 × 4.9
			+15 × 4.1
			+20 × 2.6
			0
			——
			+134.2
				−10 × −.009
				+10 × −.011
				− 6 × −.020
				+ 9 × −.026
				+15 × −.022
				+20 × −.014
				0
				——
				−.744
					−10 × .07
					+10 × .07
					− 6 × .13
					+ 9 × .16
					+15 × .14
					+20 × .08
					0
					——
					+4.36

Figure 6-23 (continued)

Even though a trader can analyze the effect of changing market conditions on a position through its delta, gamma, theta, and vega characteristics, his first and primary concern is that the position be profitable. This means the position must have a positive theoretical edge. After all, if the trader is correct in his assumptions about market conditions, he ought to expect to make a profit.

The theoretical edge can be calculated in the same way as the delta, gamma, theta, and vega position. Simply multiply the theoretical edge of each individual option by the size of the position, and add up the theoretical edge of all the options involved. The amount of the positive (negative) theoretical edge is a reflection of the position's potential profit (loss).

Figure 6-23 gives trading prices, theoretical values, and delta, gamma, theta, and vega values for a hypothetical series of options. Below the table are several different positions showing the total theoretical edge, as well as the total delta, gamma, theta, and vega associated with each position. The reader should take a moment to see how these numbers where arrived at, and to analyze the risk characteristics associated with each position. Is each position likely to be profitable? What will help or hurt each position? These are questions an option trader must constantly ask himself.

One final word to the prospective option trader. All of the numbers we have discussed in this chapter, the theoretical value, the delta, gamma, theta, and vega, are constantly changing. This means that the strategies which are profitable, and the risk associated with these strategies, is constantly changing. The importance of analyzing risk in option trading cannot be over-emphasized. The great majority of traders who fail at option trading do so because they fail to fully understand risk, and do not plan beforehand how to manage risk under adverse conditions. But there is another type of trader, one who attempts to analyze every possible risk. When this happens, the trader invariably ends up with paralysis through analysis. A trader who is so concerned with risk that he is afraid to make a trade cannot profit, no matter how well he understands options. In order to win, you have to trade. When concern with risk overshadows everything else, that fact is sometimes forgotten.

7

Introduction to Spreading

The correct use of an option's theoretical value requires us to establish a hedge against the underlying futures contract. Whatever market position we take in options, we must take an opposing market position in the underlying futures contract. All spreading strategies are based on this type of hedge, where opposing market positions are taken in two different instruments. A spread trader makes the assumption that there is a well-defined price relationship between the two instruments; and although the trader may not know in which direction the general market will move, the price relationship between the two instruments should remain relatively constant. When the relationship appears to be temporarily mispriced, the spread trader will take either a long or short position in one instrument and an opposing position in the other instrument. The trader hopes to profit when the prices of the instruments return to their expected relationship.

Among futures traders the most common type of spread trades involve taking opposing positions in different delivery months for the same commodity. A trader might, for example, purchase October crude oil and sell November crude oil on the New York Mercantile Exchange; or he might buy July soybeans and sell May soybeans on the Chicago Board of Trade. The value of this type of intra-market spread depends on a wide variety of factors, usually involving the cost of carrying the physical commodity from one delivery month to another.

Suppose, for example, that May silver is trading for $8.00 per ounce. What should a July contract be trading for? A trader who takes delivery of silver in May at $8.00 per ounce and holds it until July will be incurring an $8.00 per ounce debit for a two month period. If interest rates are 9.00% annually, the cost of the two month carry will be 9.00%/6 × $8.00 per oz. = 12 cents per oz. Given the 12 cent carrying costs that the buyer of a July contract is saving, he ought to be willing to pay 12 cents more for the July contract than the May contract, or $8.12 per ounce

If the May contract is trading at $8.00, and the July contract is trading at $8.08, the trader knows that the spread is 4 cents too cheap. He can take advantage of this by buying the spread for 8 cents, i.e., buying the July contract for $8.08 and selling the May contract for $8.00. If the spread returns to its expected value of 12 cents, the trader can buy back his May silver and sell out his July silver, thereby realizing a profit of 4 cents.

Note that the above spread will be profitable, regardless of the general direction of the silver market, as long as the prices of the two delivery months return to their expected 12 cent spread. If May silver rises to $8.25 the trader will lose money on the May side of the spread because he is short that contract. But as long as July silver rises to $8.37, the gain in the value of the July contract will more than offset the loss on the May contract and result in the expected 4 cent profit.

With the savings on carrying costs, the price of the further out delivery month in our silver example will, in theory, always be greater than the price of the near-term delivery month. In a futures market this is known as a *contango* relationship, where distant delivery months trade at a greater price than near-term delivery months.

Factors other than the carrying costs can also affect the price relationship between different delivery months on the same commodity. The futures price of some agricultural commodities also includes the cost of storing and insuring the commodity for the period between delivery months. Any increases in these costs will increase the value of the futures contract. A trader who buys a stock index futures contract will save the carrying costs associated with owning the actual basket of stocks. But at the same time, he gives up the rights to any dividends he might receive if he actually owned the stocks. The savings in carrying costs add value to the futures contract, but the loss in dividend yield dilutes its value.

Matters can be further complicated if, as in the case of debt instruments, both long and short term interest rates play a role. The value of a treasury bond futures contract depends not only on the carrying costs saved by purchasing a futures contract instead of the bond (short term rate), but also on the interest lost by not actually owning the bond (long term rate). If short term interest rates are significantly less than long term rates, there may be an inverse relationship between delivery months, whereby the distant delivery month is trading at a lower price than the near term delivery month. This inverse relationship is sometimes referred to as *backwardation*. (See Figure 7-1).

Finally, foreign currency traders must take into consideration both the interest rate in the domestic currency, as well as the interest rate in the foreign currency. Depending on these rates, distant delivery months can be trading at either a premium or a discount to the nearby month.

Calculating the relationship between different delivery months can be a complex problem, and is covered more fully in books specifically on futures trading. The lesson here is that, in theory, there ought to be a well defined price relationship between different de-livery months. When that relationship is violated in the market-place, a profit opportunity exists by selling the overpriced delivery month and buying the underpriced.

Spreads need not be based solely on the relationship between different delivery months for the same commodity. They can also be based on an assumed price relationship between different, though related, commodities. The NOB (notes over bonds) spread traded on the Chicago Board of Trade is based on the assumption that there ought to be a well-defined relationship between the price of Treasury Bonds and Treasury Notes. When the spread between the prices of these two futures contracts is more or less than the expected spread, Treasury Notes at 95-16 and Treasury Bonds at 90-00, there is a 5-16 point spread between the two instruments. If a trader feels that the

U.S. TREASURY BONDS (CBT)
8%-$100,000 prin.; pts. and 32d's of 100%

Season High	Season Low		High	Low	Close	Chg.	Open Interest
100-26	67	Mar	95-2	93-17	94-28	+ 1-1	254,473
99-23	66-25	June	94-2	92-18	93-28	+ 1	46,360
99-12	74-20	Sep	93-3	91-23	92-31	+ 31	9,266
99-2	74-1	Dec	92-9	90-29	92-4	+ 30	3,013
95-10	73-20	Mar	91-15	90-6	91-11	+ 29	3,298
94-4	73-11	Jun	90-24	90	90-20	+ 28	2,108
93-16	72-26	Sep	90-4	89-21	89-31	+ 27	538

Est. sales 300,000, Mon.'s sales 247,147. -
Mon.'s open int 319,365, up 7,324

CRUDE OIL (NYM)
42,000 gallons; $ per barrel

Season High	Season Low		High	Low	Close	Chg.	Open Interest
21.20	14.70	Mar	17.02	16.90	16.94	+ .12	67,097
21.15	14.70	Apr	16.92	16.81	16.84	+ .11	66,520
21.20	14.70	May	16.83	16.74	16.75	+ .10	28,543
21.20	14.78	Jun	16.73	16.60	16.65	+ .10	17,168
20.17	14.85	Jul	16.63	16.55	16.55	+ .10	8,997
20.10	14.80	Aug	16.55	16.49	16.46	+ .10	4,515
19.72	14.95	Sep	16.40	16.40	16.37	+ .10	2,648
19.70	14.90	Oct	16.48	16.48	16.28	+ .10	1,448

Est. sales 41,961. Mon.'s sales 42,507.
Mon.'s open int 197,594, off 4,239.

CATTLE, Feeder (CME)
44,000 lb; ¢ per lb.

Season High	Season Low		High	Low	Close	Chg.	Open Interest
80.40	66.20	Mar	80.25	79.60	80.17	+ .25	7,957
79.60	67.20	Apr	79.20	78.40	79.17	+ .55	4,864
78.00	67.20	May	77.80	77.05	77.67	+ .60	3,627
76.85	68.30	Aug	76.75	76.15	76.62	+ .30	1,512
76.00	69.40	Sep	76.25	75.80	76.05	+ .25	590
75.50	69.70	Oct	75.90	75.30	75.90	+ .40	609
76.40	70.25	Nov	76.60	76.30	76.60	+ .20	68

Est. sales 2,482. Mon.'s sales 3,063.
Mon.'s open int 19,227, off 1,679.

Backwardation Markets

SOYBEANS (CBT) 5,000 bu.; $ per bu.

Season High	Season Low		High	Low	Close	Chg.	Open Interest
6.42½	4.74	Mar	6.08	5.96	5.97	-.11¼	42,656
6.51	4.76	May	6.17	6.05½	6.06¼	-10¾	24,803
6.57	4.88½	Jul	6.25½	6.13½	6.14¼	-.12	23,067
6.56	5.12	Aug	6.26½	6.15	6.15	-.11	3,282
6.53	5.03	Sep	6.23½	6.14	6.16	-.10	2,319
6.56	4.99¼	Nov	6.32½	6.21	6.21½	-.12	19,790
6.62	5.53	Jan	6.37	6.29½	6.29¾	-.11¼	602

Est. sales 38,000. Mon.'s sales 30,686.
Mon.'s open int 116,604, up 599.

GOLD (COMEX) 100 troy oz.; $ per troy oz.

Season High	Season Low		High	Low	Close	Chg.	Open Interest
510.50	371.50	Feb	457.50	453.70	453.90	-.20	7,483
488.80	451.50	Mar	458.20	458.20	455.50	-.10	4
514.00	378.00	Apr	461.90	458.10	458.30	-.10	76,187
523.00	399.00	Jun	466.70	463.00	463.10	-.10	17,575
527.00	425.00	Aug	471.00	469.00	468.10	-.10	8,342
533.50	429.00	Oct	476.50	474.00	473.40	-.10	9,581
546.00	430.80	Dec	482.00	478.50	478.70	-.10	11,320
549.50	480.00	Feb	487.50	486.60	484.30	-.10	5,200
550.00	487.50	Apr	.....	.....	490.20	-.10	6,341
570.00	493.30	Jun	498.50	498.00	496.20	-.10	6,227
575.00	501.00	Aug	504.60	504.60	502.50	-.10	2,413
575.50	504.70	Oct	.....	.....	509.00	-.10	1,798
.....	.....	Dec	.....	.....	515.50	-.10	700

Est. sales 32,000. Mon.'s sales 52,747.
Mon.'s open int 153,171, up 6,979.

WEST GERMAN MARK (IMM)
125,000 marks; $ per mark

Season High	Season Low		High	Low	Close	Chg.	Open Interest
.6426	.5350	Mar	.5973	.5938	.5967	+ 30	32,835
.6494	.5410	Jun	.6025	.5988	.6019	+ 30	3,877
.6555	.5609	Sep	.6075	.6060	.6074	+ 30	176
.6610	.5717	Dec	.....	.....	.6131	+ 30	79

Last spot .5943, up 33.
Est. sales 13,766. Mon.'s sales 20,740.
Mon.'s open int 36,967, up 351.

Contango Markets

Figure 7-1

spread between the Notes and Bonds ought to be 5 points, he can sell the spread at 5-16 (sell Notes at 95-16 and buy Bonds at 90-00).When the spread returns to its expected relationship of 5 points, the trader will buy in his short Notes and sell out his long Bonds, realizing a profit of 16/32.

Spreads can also be based on more complex relationships. Traders on the COMEX often follow the price relationship between silver and gold. However, with gold at $400 to $500 per ounce, and silver at $8 to $9 dollars per ounce, the relationship is more easily expressed as a ratio. A trader might define the spread between the two metals as 50 ounces of silver to 1 ounce of gold (a 50:1 ratio). Suppose silver is trading at $8. Given the 50:1 price ratio, gold should be at $400. If, instead, gold is at $425, the spread trader will sell 1 ounce of gold at $425 and buy 50 ounce of silver at $8. If the precious metals market drops so that gold is at $350 and silver at $7 the spreader will still make his expected $25 profit because the prices of gold and silver have returned to their expected 50:1 ratio. The trader will lose $50 on his long silver position, but he will gain $75 on his short gold position.

Another popular spread, using instruments on two different exchanges, involves futures on the New York Stock Exchange Composite Index traded on the New York Futures Exchange, and futures on the Standard & Poor's 500 Index traded on the Chicago Mercantile Exchange. If a trader believes the relationship between the two contracts should be 7 to 4 (7 NYSE = 4 S&P 500), and current prices do not reflect this relationship, he might take a short position in the overpriced contract and a long position in the underpriced contract, at a ratio of 7:4. He can expect to realize a profit anytime the spread between the two contracts returns to its expected 7 to 4 ratio.

Spread relationships need not involve just two instruments. Sometimes three, or even more, different instruments may define a spread relationship. For example, the price of a gold futures contract is determined by the spot price of gold and the carrying costs on gold to the delivery month. If interest rates rise, the carrying costs will rise, causing the spread between the spot price of gold and the price of the futures contract to widen. If a trader owns gold and is short a futures contract, and he feels that Eurodollar rates correlate closely to his cost of carry, he can sell Eurodollar futures to protect himself against a rise in interest rates. If interest rates do increase, he will lose on his spot/futures gold spread, but this will be offset by a gain in his Eurodollar position. There is a three-sided relationship between the spot price of gold, the price of a gold futures contract, and the price of Eurodollars.

Spreads between different delivery months on the same commodity, as well as price spreads between different instruments, are closely followed by professional traders. Buying or selling a mispriced spread can be just as profitable for a trader as an outright long or short market position.

In the foregoing spread examples, the price relationship between instruments was defined by the dollar prices of the individual instruments. In some cases, however, it might be easier to define a spread relationship in other than dollar terms. In our discussion of volatility in Chapter 4 we used the theoretical pricing model to determine an option's implied volatility. We noted that for an option trader the implied volatility might be a more accurate reflection of an option's price than its dollar price. Instead of defining a dollar price spread between two options, an option trader might define the spread in terms of the difference between the implied volatilites of the two options. An option with an implied volatility of 15% and an option with an implied volatility of 17% have a two-point volatility spread in their respective prices, regardless of the difference in their dollar prices. Here, the trader might establish a spread by purchasing the option with the 15% implied volatility and selling the option with the 17% implied volatility, hoping to profit if the spread between the implied volatilities narrows.

As we shall see, the situation is not quite so simple as selling high implied volatility options and buying low implied volatility options. Not only is the spread between the implied volatilities important, but also the general level of volatility. A two percentage point volatility spread may mean one thing if the implied volatilities are 6% and 8%, and quite something else if the implied volatilities are 16% and 18%.

In spite of the many factors affecting volatility relationships, these types of spreads form one of the most important classes of option trading strategies. Much of an option trader's education is spent defining these relationships, understanding their characteristics, and then learning to create the best risk versus reward positions based on mispriced volatility.

Why Traders Spread

Suppose an option trader estimates the volatility of a Deutschemark futures contract at 13%. Based on this estimate he is able to find a Deutschemark call on the Chicago Mercantile Exchange which is trading for 2.00 points, but which is only worth 1.50. If the call has a delta of 25, one possible strategy might be to sell four calls and buy one futures contract, resulting in a total theoretical edge of 2.00 points, or $2,500. Of course if the trader can make $2,500 with a 4 × 1 spread, he can make $25,000 by doing the same spread 40 × 10. Why stop now? He can make $250,000 by doing the spread 400 × 100.

Do you think this is likely to happen, that a trader will simply do whatever strategy he chooses as many times as possible in order to maximize his profit potential? At some point, the intelligent trader will have to consider not only his potential profit, but also the risk associated with his strategy. After all, his volatility estimate of 13% is just that, an estimate. What will happen if volatility actually turns out to be 18%? If the calls which he sold for 2.00 points turn out to be worth 2.50 points at a volatility of 18%, then his hoped-for profit of $250,000 will turn into a loss of $250,000. If the trader does not have sufficient capital to cover this loss, he will be out of business.

Option spreading strategies have two purposes. First, like some of the other spreading examples we have looked at, option spreads may offer better profit potential than outright purchases or sales of options. Secondly, spreading helps control the risk of a position by increasing the margin for error. If the trader in the foregoing example suspects that he might be wrong, and that volatility could actually turn out to be 18% (a 5-percentage point margin for error), then he might only be willing to do the spread 40 × 10. But if there were some way to increase his margin of safety to a volatility of 23% (a 10 percentage point margin for error) he might indeed be willing to do the spread 400 × 100. Option spreading strategies are designed primarily to give the trader the greatest possible margin for error in estimating the inputs to the theoretical pricing model.

How does spreading help control risk? Recall that in Chapter 3 we showed that roulette bets, which are only worth 92 cents, are sold in a casino for $1, resulting in an 8% theoretical edge to the casino. Suppose that you are the owner of a casino, and that one day a player walks in and asks if he can bet $2000 on one number. This may pose a problem for you. As the casino owner, you know that the odds are on your side, but there is always the chance that the player's number will come up. The casino's reward is likely to be the $2000 the player bets, but the risk is the $70,000 you will have to pay out if the player wins. If the loss of $70,000 will put you out of business, you may not be willing to accept the $2000 bet, even with an 8% theoretical edge.

While you are considering whether to let the first player make his bet, two more players come in who want to place $1000 bets each on the roulette table. They promise, however, to place their bets on different numbers. Whichever number one player bets on, the other player will bet on some other number.

As with the first player and his $2000 bet, your possible reward here is also $2000, if both players lose. But your risk now is only $34,000 because the bets are mutually exclusive. If one player wins, the other player must lose because the players promised to bet on different numbers. If you lose $35,000 to one player, you are assured of winning $1,000 from the other player.

Note that in neither case has the expected return changed. In the long run the casino can still expect to keep 8% of every dollar bet at the roulette table. Whether one player makes a $2,000 bet, or two players make $1,000 bets each, the casino's expected return is $160. However, in the latter case the risk to the casino is greatly reduced because the bets have been *spread* around the table. The ideal situation from the casino's point of view is for 38 players to place $1,000 bets each on 38 different numbers. Now the casino has a perfect spread position. One number will collect $35,000, but the casino will retain the $38,000 on the table, resulting in a sure profit of $3,000.

The option trader prefers to spread for exactly the same reason that the casino prefers the bets to be spread around the table: spreading maintains profit potential but reduces risk. There is no perfect spread for an option trader as there is for the casino. But the intelligent option trader learns to spread his risk off in as many different ways as possible so as to minimize the effects of bad luck. The situation can become quite complex since there is a risk associated with almost every input into a theoretical pricing model: market (directional) risk, volatility risk, time decay risk, and interest risk. If an option trader expects to become successful he must learn as many different ways as possible to spread off the risk associated with any trade he might make, regardless of whether the trade results in a simple naked option position, or a complex position consisting of many different options.

A beginning trader is often amazed at the size of the trades an experienced trader is prepared to make. For example, a floor trader in Treasury Bond options on the Chicago Board of Trade who buys 100 calls at 2-00 points ($2000) each has just taken a position worth $200,000. How can he afford to do this? His capital resources certainly have something to do with the risk he is willing to accept. But even more important, an experienced trader knows a variety of ways to spread off his risk, either with other options, with futures contracts, with cash bonds, or with some combination of these instruments. He may not be able to eliminate his risk completely, but he may be able to reduce it to such an extent that his risk is actually less than that of a much smaller trader who does not know how to spread.

8

Volatility Spreads

To take advantage of a theoretically mispriced option it is necessary to hedge the purchase or sale of the option with the underlying commodity. In previous examples the opposing position was always taken in the underlying futures contract. But it is also possible to hedge an option position with other options which are theoretically equivalent to the opposing futures position. For example, suppose a certain call with a delta of 50 is underpriced in the marketplace. If we buy 10 calls, giving us a delta position of +500, we can hedge our position in any of the following ways:

1. Sell 5 futures contracts.

2. Buy puts with a total delta of -500.

3. Sell different calls with a total delta of +500.

With many different puts and calls available, there are many different ways of spreading off the risk associated with our ten calls. Regardless of which method we choose, each spread will have certain features in common:

1. Each spread will initially be delta neutral.

2. Each spread will be sensitive to price changes in the underlying futures contract.

3. Each spread will be sensitive to changes in implied volatility.

4. Each spread will be sensitive to the passage of time.

Spreads with these characteristics fall under the general heading of volatility spreads.

In this chapter we will define the basic types of volatility spreads and look at each spread's characteristics, initially by examining each spread's value at expiration, then later by looking at the delta, gamma, theta, and vega associated with each spread.

Backspread

A backspread always consists of more long (purchased) contracts than short (sold) contracts, where all contracts expire at the same time. In order for a call backspread to be delta neutral, it will require the purchase of calls with a higher exercise price and the sale of calls with a lower exercise price. A put backspread will require the purchase of puts with a lower exercise price and the sale of puts with a higher exercise price. Figures 8-1 and 8-2 are typical call and put backspreads. (In these and the following examples, delta values are given in parentheses.)

The primary characteristics of a call or put backspread are shown in the graphs of each spread's value at expiration. In each case, a move away from the long (purchased) option's exercise price will increase the value of the spread. Depending on the type of backspread, movement in one direction may be preferable to movement in the other direction. In a call backspread the upside potential is unlimited; in a put backspread the downside potential is unlimited. But above all, the backspreader needs movement. If the market sits still, a backspread is likely to be a losing strategy.

A backspread is almost always done for a cash credit. That is, the amount of money taken in for the options which are sold will exceed the amount paid out for the options which are purchased. This is done to ensure that a backspread will be profitable if the market makes a big move in either direction. If the market collapses in the case of a call backspread, or explodes in the case of a put backspread, all options will expire worthless and the trader will get to keep the credit from the initial transaction.

A trader will tend to choose the type of backspread which reflects his opinion about market direction. If he foresees a market with great upside potential, he will tend to choose a call backspread; if he

Call Backspread

long 25 April 105 calls (26)
short 15 April 100 calls (44)

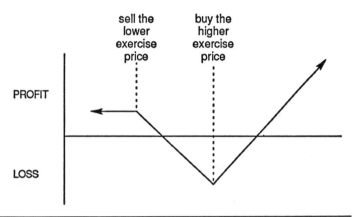

Figure 8-1

Put Backspread

long 20 June 95 puts (-33)
short 10 June 105 puts (-61)

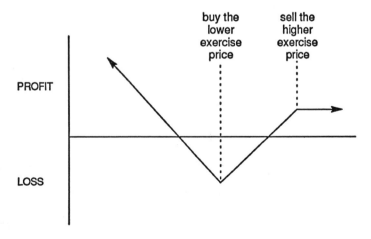

Figure 8-2

Call Ratio Vertical Spread

long 15 June 100 calls (50)
short 20 June 105 calls (37)

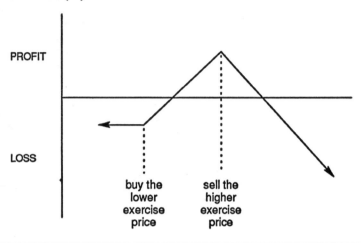

Figure 8-3

Put Ratio Vertical Spread

long 10 April 105 puts (-73)
short 20 April 95 puts (-34)

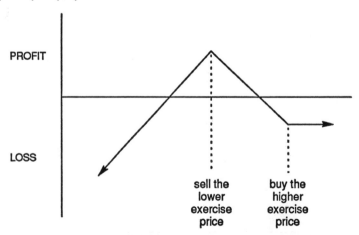

Figure 8-4

foresees great downside potential he will tend to choose a put back-spread. He will avoid backspreads in quiet markets since then the underlying futures contract is unlikely to move very far away from the short exercise price.

Ratio Vertical Spread

Some traders refer to the opposite of a backspread as either a ratio spread or a vertical spread. However, these terms can also be applied to other types of spreads. In order to avoid later confusion we will define the opposite of a backspread as a ratio vertical spread.[1] This position consists of more short (sold) contracts than long (purchased) contracts, with all contracts expiring in the same month. Figures 8-3 and 8-4 are typical call and put ratio vertical spreads.

In Figures 8-3 and 8-4 we see that a ratio vertical spread will realize its maximum profit at expiration when the underlying futures contract finishes at the short (sold) option's exercise price. The value of the position will decrease if the underlying contract moves away from this exercise price. Since the ratio vertical spreader assumes the opposite risks of the backspreader, his risk is unlimited on the upside in a call ratio vertical spread, and unlimited on the downside in a put ratio vertical spread. While the ratio vertical spreader expects the market to remain quiet, he will tend to choose either a call or put ratio vertical spread depending on his concerns of a large move in the underlying market.

Straddle

A straddle consists of either a long call and a long put, or a short call and a short put, where both options have the same exercise price and expire at the same time. If both the call and put are purchased, the trader is long the straddle; if both the call and put are sold, the trader is short the straddle. Figure 8-15 is a long June 100 straddle; Figure 8-6 is a short April 100 straddle.

---

[1]Some older traders may occasionally refer to a ratio vertical spread as a frontspread. This description makes considerable sense, but seems to have gone out of style.

Long Straddle

long 10 June 100 calls (50)
long 10 June 100 puts (-47)

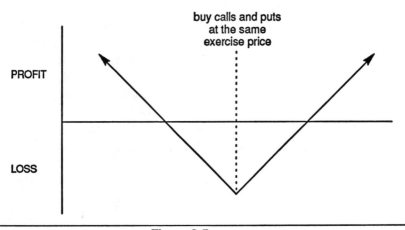

Figure 8-5

Short Straddle

short 25 April 100 calls (44)
short 20 April 100 puts (-55)

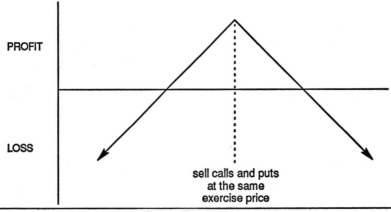

Figure 8-6

In Figure 8-6 the number of long market contracts (either long calls or short puts) and the number of short market contracts (either short calls or long puts) are not equal. Any spread where the number of such contracts is unequal is a *ratio spread*. The most common types of ratio spreads are backspreads and ratio vertical spreads. But any spread, including straddles, strangles, and time spreads, can be ratioed. This is usually done to ensure that the spread is delta neutral.

A long straddle (Figure 8-5) has many of the same characteristics as a backspread. Like a backspread, a long straddle has limited risk and unlimited profit potential. With a long straddle, however, the trader's profit potential is unlimited in either direction. If the market moves sharply up or down he will realize ever increasing profits as long as the market continues to move in the same direction

A short straddle (Figure 8-12) has many of the same characteristics as a ratio vertical spread. The spread will realize its maximum profit if the market stays close to the call and put exercise price. The spread also has limited profit, and unlimited risk if the market moves violently in either direction.

The beginning trader often finds long straddles attractive because strategies with limited risk and unlimited profit potential seem to have great appeal. However, if the hoped for large movement fails to materialize, he soon finds that losing money little by little, even a limited amount, can also be a painful experience. This is not an endorsement of either long or short straddles. Under the right conditions either strategy may be sensible. But the serious trader's primary concern must be the total expected return. If the strategy with the greatest expected return also entails unlimited risk, a trader may have to accept that risk as a part of doing business.

Strangle

Like a straddle, a strangle consists of a long call and a long put, or a short call and a short put, where both options expire at the same time. In a strangle, however, the options have different exercise prices. If both the call and put are purchased, the trader is long the strangle; if both options are sold, the trader is short the strangle. Figure 8-7 is a long June 95/105 strangle; Figure 8-8 is a short April 95/100 strangle.

Long Strangle

long 10 June 105 calls (-33)
long 10 June 95 puts (-37)

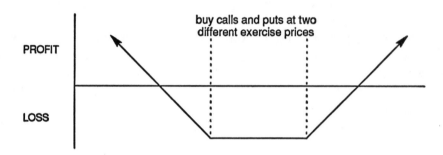

Figure 8-7

Short Strangle

Example A:
short 15 April 100 calls (44)
short 20 April 95 puts (-34)

Example B (guts):
short 10 June 95 calls (64)
short 10 June 105 puts (-61)

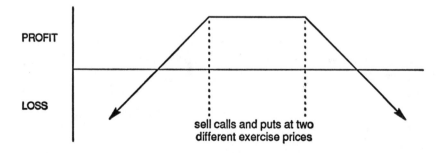

Figure 8-8

Long and short strangles have characteristics similar to long and short straddles, and therefore similar to backspreads and ratio vertical spreads. Like a long straddle, a long strangle needs movement to be profitable (compare Figure 8-7 to Figure 8-5), and has unlimited profit potential should such movement occur. And like a short straddle, a short strangle has unlimited risk, but will show a profit if the market remains in a narrow trading range (compare Figure 8-6 to Figure 8-8).

If a trader refers to a strangle simply by its expiration month and exercise prices, there may be some confusion as to the specific options involved. A June 95/105 strangle might consist of either a June 95 put and 105 call, or a June 95 call and 105 put. Both these combinations are consistent with our definition of a strangle. To avoid confusion, a strangle is commonly assumed to include out-of-the-money options. When both options are in-the-money the position is sometimes referred to as a *guts*. Figure 8-8, Example B is an in-the-money strangle, or guts.

If we ignore the unlimited reward characteristics of backspreads, long straddles, and long strangles, these spreads differ essentially in degree of desired movement. A backspreader needs some movement to make a profit, a long straddler needs more movement, and a long strangler needs very large movement.

The same considerations of degree are also true for ratio vertical spreads, short straddles, and short strangles. The ratio vertical spreader, the short straddler and the short strangler all hope for the market to remain in a narrow range. We shall see later that this fact is reflected in the gamma, theta, and vega characteristics of each spread.

Based on these similar characteristics, it will be convenient to classify long straddles and strangles as special types of backspreads. This follows logically from the definition of a backspread: long more contracts than short, with all contracts expiring in the same month. A long straddle or strangle consists of only long contracts (long calls and long puts) with all contracts expiring at the same time, so the position must be a backspread. (Even though the owner of a put has a short market position, he is still long the put because he has purchased it.)

The same reasoning enables us to classify short straddles and strangles as special types of ratio vertical spreads. Short straddles and strangles consist of only short contracts, so these positions must be ratio vertical spreads.

If we define a contract to be either a call, a put, or an underlying futures contract, we can now include hedges consisting of long calls versus short futures, or long puts versus long futures, in the backspread category. When delta neutral, such hedges will always be long more contracts than short and will therefore have the same characteristics as a backspread: they will have limited risk and unlimited profit potential, and they will be profitable only if the underlying market makes a large enough move away from the long (purchased) exercise price.

Conversely, we can place hedges consisting of short calls vs. long futures, or short puts vs. short futures into the ratio vertical spread category. When delta neutral, such hedges will always be short more contracts than long, and will therefore have the same characteristics as ratio vertical spreads: they will have limited profit potential and unlimited risk, and will be most profitable when the market remains close to the short (sold) exercise price. We shall see later that delta neutral spreads consisting of options versus futures have characteristics very similar to straddles. These types of spreads are referred to as *synthetic* straddles.

Butterfly

Thus far we have looked at spreads which involve buying or selling two different contracts. However, we do no have to restrict ourselves to two-sided spreads. We can also construct spreads consisting of three, four, or even more different contracts. One of the most common volatility spreads of this type is the butterfly. A butterfly consists of three consecutive exercise prices with all options of the same type (either all calls or all puts) and expiring at the same time. In a long butterfly the top and bottom exercise prices are purchased and the middle exercise price is sold, and vice versa for a short butterfly.[2]

---

[2]The inside exercise price is sometimes referred to as the *body* of the butterfly, while the outside exercise prices are referred to as the *wings*.

Long Butterfly

Example A: long 10 April 95 calls (64)
short 20 April 100 calls (44)
long 10 April 105 calls (26)

Example B: long 10 June 95 puts (-33)
short 20 June 100 puts (-47)
long 10 June 105 puts (-61)

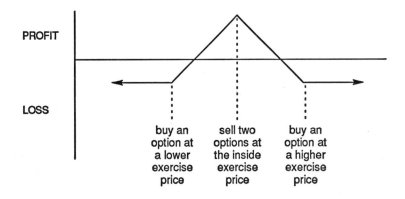

Figure 8-9

Short Butterfly

Example A: short 10 June 95 calls (64)
long 20 June 100 calls (50)
short 10 June 105 calls (37)

Example B: short 10 April 95 puts (-34)
long 20 April 100 puts (-55)
short 10 April 105 puts (-73)

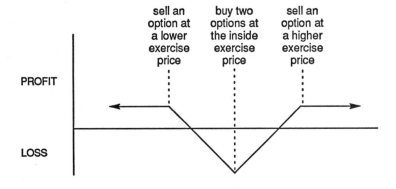

Figure 8-10

Moreover, the ratio of a butterfly never varies: it is always $1 \times 2 \times 1$. If the ratio is other than this, the spread is no longer a butterfly. Figure 8-9 (Parts A and B) are long butterflies; Figure 8-10 (Parts A and B) are short butterflies.

Since a butterfly consists of equal numbers of long and short contracts, it does not seem to fit conveniently into either the backspread or ratio vertical spread category. In fact, a long butterfly tends to act like a ratio vertical spread, and a short butterfly tends to act like a backspread. To see why, consider the trader who buys the 95/100/105 call butterfly (long a 95 call, short two 100 calls, long a 105 call). What will this position be worth at expiration? If the futures contract finishes at 95 or below, all options will be worthless, so the entire position will be worthless. If the futures contracts finishes at 105 or above, the value of the 95 call and 105 call together will be identical to the value of the two 100 calls. Again, the entire position will be worthless. Now suppose the futures contract finishes somewhere between the extreme exercise prices, specifically, right at the inside exercise price of 100. The 95 call will be worth 5 points, while the 100 and 105 calls will be worth zero. Therefore the position will be worth 5 points. At expiration a butterfly will always have a value somewhere between zero and the amount between consecutive exercise prices. It will be worth zero if the underlying futures contract finishes below the lowest exercise price or above the highest exercise price. It will be worth its maximum if the underlying futures contract finishes right at the inside exercise price.

Since a butterfly has a value between zero and the amount between exercise prices (5 points in our example), a trader should be willing to pay between zero and 5 points for the position. Exactly how much depends on the likelihood of the position expiring right at the inside exercise price. If there is a high probability of this, a trader might be willing to pay close to 5 points for the position. If there is a low probability of this, and consequently a high probability that the underlying market will finish outside the extreme exercise prices, a trader will want to pay a much lower price for the position.

Now we can see why a long butterfly tends to act like a ratio vertical spread. If a trader feels the underlying market will trade within a narrow range, he can go long a butterfly where the inside exercise price is at-the-money. If he is right, and the market does sit still, the butterfly will eventually widen to its maximum value. Figure 8-9, the value of a long butterfly at expiration, illustrates this principle.

In contrast, the trader who is short a butterfly will want the market to move as far as possible from the inside exercise price so that the position will expire with the underlying futures contract outside the extreme exercise prices. In that case, he will get to keep the full sale amount of the butterfly. A short butterfly therefore tends to act like a backspread since it wants movement in the underlying market. This principle is illustrated in Figure 8-10.

Why is a long butterfly a "long" position? The common practice is to refer to any spread which requires an outlay of capital as a long, or purchased spread. When a trader buys the outside exercise prices of a butterfly and sells the inside exercise price, the position can never be worth less than zero at expiration. The trader should, in theory, have to lay out some amount for the position when he initiates it. When he does this, the trader is long, or has purchased, the butterfly. (If a trader can initiate a long butterfly for a credit he should do it as many times as the law will allow; he can't lose.) Since all butterflies will be worth their maximum when they expire with the underlying futures contract right at the inside exercise price, both a call and a put butterfly with the same exercise prices and expiration dates want exactly the same outcome, and therefore have indentical characteristics. Both the April 95/100/105 call butterfly and the April 95/100/105 put butterfly will be worth their maximum of 5 points right at 100, and zero anywhere below 95 and above 105. If both butterflies are not trading at the same price there is a sure profit available by selling the more expensive and buying the cheaper.

If a trader foresees a quiet market, why might he choose a long butterfly over some other type of strategy, a short straddle for example? An important characteristic of the butterfly is its limited risk. A trader who feels that the market will trade within a narrow range may still not like the unlimited risk associated with a short straddle, and might choose a long butterfly as a more appropriate strategy. Because of their limited risk characteristics, butterflies are usually traded in much greater quantity than other types of volatility spreads. The same trader who is willing to sell 25 straddles might be willing to buy 100 butterflies ($100 \times 200 \times 100$). While 100 spreads sounds riskier than 25 spreads, 100 butterflies may in fact be much less risky than 25 straddles because of the butterfly's limited risk exposure.

Time Spreads

If all options in a spread expire at the same time, the value of the spread at expiration is simply a function of the price of the underlying market at expiration. If, however, we establish a spread with options expiring on two different dates, then the value of the spread cannot be determined exactly until both options expire. The spread's final value depends not only on where the underlying market is when the short term option expires, but also on what will happen between that time and any later option expiration. A position, where a trader holds one option position expiring in one month and an opposing option position expiring in a different month, is known as a time spread, also referred to as a calendar spread or horizontal spread.[3]

The most common type of time spread consists of opposing positions in a long term option and a short term option of the same type (either both calls or both puts) with the same exercise price. When the long term option is purchased and the short term option is sold, the trader is said to be long the time spread. When the short term option is purchased and the long term option is sold, the trader is said to be short the time spread. Since a long term option will have more time value, and hence a higher price than a short term option, this is consistent with our practice of referring to any spread which is initiated for a debit (credit) as a long (short) spread position.

Although time spreads are most commonly done one to one (one contract purchased for each contract sold), a trader may ratio a time spread to reflect a bullish, bearish, or neutral market sentiment. For the present, we will assume that all time spreads will be ratioed delta neutral. Figure 8-11 (Examples A and B) are long time spreads; Figure 8-12 (Examples A and B) are short time spreads.

The value of a spread where all options expire at the same time is determined primarily by movement in the underlying market. The

---

[3]Expiration months were originally listed horizontally on exchange price boards. Hence the term horizontal spread.

Long Time Spread

Example A:

long 10 June 95 calls (64)

short 10 April 95 calls (64)

Example B:

long 25 June 100 puts (-47)

short 20 April 100 puts (-55)

Figure 8-11

Short Time Spread

Example A:

long 15 April 105 calls (26)

short 10 June 105 calls (37)

Example B:

long 10 April 95 puts (-34)

short 10 June 95 puts (-33)

Figure 8-12

value of a time spread, however, depends not only on movement in the underlying market, but also on traders' expectations about the future as reflected in implied volatility. Because of this, it may not be immediately apparent what market conditions will help or hurt a time spread.

A long time spread always wants the underlying market to sit still. Recall that an important characteristic of an option's theta (time decay) is its tendency to get larger as expiration approaches. As time passes, a short term option will generally lose value more quickly than a long term option. (Note the value of at-the-money options in Figures 6-13 and 6-14, and the theta values in Figure 6-15.) This principle has an important effect on time spreads.

As an example, suppose an at-the-money call with 3 months to expiration and an at-the-money call with 6 months to expiration have values of 6 and 7 1/2 points, respectively. The value of the spread between the two options is therefore 1 1/2 points. If one month passes and the underlying market is unchanged, both options will lose value. But the short term option, with its greater theta, will lose a greater dollar amount. If the long term option loses 1/4 point, the short term option may lose a full point. Now the options will be worth 5 and 7 1/4, respectively, and the spread will have widened to 2 1/4 points. If another month passes and the underlying market is still unchanged, both options will continue to decay. But, again, the short term option, with less time to expiration, will lose more dollar value. If the long term option loses 1/2 point, the short term option may lose 2 points. Now the options will be worth 3 and 6 3/4, and the spread will have increased in value to 3 3/4 points. Finally, if at expiration the market is still unchanged, the short term option, since it is still at-the-money, will be worthless. The long term option will retain some value, perhaps 6 points. The spread will therefore be worth 6 points (see Figure 8-13).

What will happen if the underlying market makes a violent move? Assume, as before, that both options are at-the-money with values of 6 and 7 1/2. Assume also that the underlying market for both options is 100. (This may not be a realistic assumption since different delivery months for the same commodity often trade at different prices. Here, however, such an assumption will make it easier to understand the characteristics of the spread.) If the market makes a violent move upward both options will begin to lose their time

---

The Effect of Time Passage on Time Spreads

Time to Expriration

Short Term Option	3 months	→	2 months	→	1 months	→	none
Long Term Option	6 months		5 months		4 months		3 months

Option Value

Short Term Option	6	→	5	→	3	→	0
Long Term Option	7 1/2		7 1/4		6 3/4		6

Spread Value

Spread Value	1/2	→	2 1/4	→	3 3/4	→	6

Figure 8-13

value. If the upward move is large enough, it won't make any difference that the long term option has three months more to go to expiration. Both options will eventually lose all time value. (See Figures 6-2 and 6-3 for a graphic representation of this effect.) If the market moves up to 150 and both options trade at parity (intrinsic value), or 50 points each, the spread will be worth zero. Even if the long term option retains as much as 1/4 point in time value, the spread will still have collapsed to 1/4.

What about a downward move in the market? The situation here is almost identical to an upward move. As an option moves further and further out-of-the-money its time value also begins to shrink. Here, however, neither option will have any intrinsic value, so that if the market moves down far enough both options will be worth zero. If, as above, the long term option retains 1/4 point in value, the spread will also have collapsed to 1/4 on the downside.

Since a short term option decays more quickly than a long term option, regardless of whether the options are calls or puts, both a long call or a long put time spread want the underlying market to sit still. Ideally, both spreads would like the short term option to expire at-the-money so that the long term option will retain as much value as possible while the short term option becomes worthless.

Given the fact that both a call and put time spread want identical outcomes, the reader might suspect that there is a relationship between the value of a call time spread and a put time spread with the same exercise prices, in the same way that there is a relationship between a call butterfly and a put butterfly. Such a relationship does in fact exist which, when violated, represents an arbitrage opportunity. We shall discuss this relationship in detail in Chapter 11 when we look at synthetic positions.

If a trader with a long time spread wants the market to sit still, then logically the trader with a short time spread wants the market to move enough so that eventually both options will lose all time value. When this happens the spread will collapse to zero on the downside, and to the difference between underlying futures prices on the upside.

It may seem from the foregoing discussion that, as with back-spreads and ratio vertical spreads, the major consideration in deciding whether to initiate a time spread is the likelihood of movement in the underlying market. Certainly time spreads are sensitive to price movement. But they are also very sensitive to changes in implied volatility.

Look again at Figure 6-18, the relationship between an option's vega (sensitivity to changes in volatility) and the time to expiration. As the amount of time to expiration increases the vega of all options also increases. This means that the theoretical value of a long term option is always more sensitive in total dollars to a change in volatility than the theoretical value of a short term option with the same exercise price.

For example, suppose again that a 100 call time spread is worth 1 1/2 points (short term and long term options worth 6 and 7 1/2 points, respectively). Assume also that the value of the spread is based on a volatility estimate of 20%. What will happen to the value of the spread if we raise our volatility estimate to 25%? Both options will increase in value since an increase in volatility increases the value of all options. But the long term option, with more time remaining to expiration, and therefore a higher vega, will gain more dollar value as a result of the rise in volatility. If the short term option gains 1/2 point, the long term option may gain 1 full point. Now the options will be worth 6 1/2 and 8 1/2, respectively, and the spread will have widened from 1 1/2 points to 2 points (see Figure 8-14).

The Effect of Volatility on Time Spreads

Volatility	15%	←	20%	→	25%
Option Value					
Short Term Option	5 1/2	←	6	→	6 1/2
Long Term Option	6 1/2		7 1/2		8 1/2
Spread Value	1	←	1 1/2	→	2

Figure 8-14

Conversely, if we decrease the volatility estimate to 15%, both options will lose value. But, again, the long term option, with more time remaining to expiration, will be more sensitive to the change in volatility and will lose a greater dollar amount. The new option values might be 5 1/2 and 6 1/2 points, causing the spread to narrow to 1 point.

The effects of volatility on the value of a time spread become especially evident when there is a change in implied volatility in the marketplace. When implied volatility rises, time spreads tend to widen; when implied volatility falls, time spreads tend to narrow. This volatility effect on time spreads can often be great enough to offset a favorable or unfavorable move in the underlying market. A trader who is long a time spread expects to lose money if the market makes a swift move in either direction. He knows that such movement tends to cause a time spread to collapse. But if this movement is accompanied by a sufficient increase in implied volatility, the increase in the spread's value due to volatility may actually be greater than the loss due to market movement. In the case, the trader may find that his spread has actually widened. Conversely, if the market sits still, the trader with a long time spread expects to make money because of the short term option's greater time decay. But if, at the same time, there is also a collapse in implied volatility, the loss in the spread's value due to the lower volatility may more than offset any gain from the passage of time. If this happens, the trader may find that the spread has narrowed. An example of these effects in treasury bond options are shown in Figure 8-15.

These two opposing forces, the decay in an option's value due to the passage of time and the change in an option's value due to changes in volatility, give time spreads their unique characteristics. When a trader either buys or sells a time spread he is not only attempting to forecast movement in the underlying market. He is also trying to forecast implied volatility. The trader would like to be able to forecast both inputs accurately. But often an error in one input can be offset by an accurate forecast for the other input.

Ideally, the trader who is long a time spread wants two apparently contradictory conditions in the marketplace. First, he wants the underlying market to sit still so that time decay will have a beneficial effect on the spread. Second, he wants everyone to think the market

Expanding and Contracting Time Spreads

Date	Underlying Price	Option Price	Implied Volatility
27 March 1988	June Treasury Bonds at 99-22	June 100 call at 1-00	8.0
	September Treasury Bonds at 98-22	September 100 call at 1-28	8.6
		Spread Price = 28	
10 April 1988 (2 weeks later)	June Treasury Bonds at 94-22	June 100 call at 13	15.2
	September Treasury Bonds at 93-22	September 100 call at 50	14.2
		Spread Price = 37	

The rapidly expanding implied volatility has more than offsett the effects of a large market move.

Date	Underlying Price	Option Price	Implied Volatility
12 June 1988	September Treasury Bonds at 92-14	September 94 call at 1-25	13.3
	December Treasury Bonds at 91-17	December 94 call at 1-57	12.5
		Spread Price = 32	
19 June 1988 (1 week later)	September Treasury Bonds at 92-15	September 94 call at 1-14	12.8
	December Treasury Bonds at 91-18	December 94 call at 1-40	12.0
		Spread Price = 26	

Even a small decline in implied volatility has more than offset the effects of time decay.

Figure 8-15

is going to move because this will cause implied volatility to remain high. This may seem an impossible scenario, the market sitting still but everyone thinking it will move. In fact, it happens quite often because traders' expectations about the future, as reflected in implied volatility, may be based on events which do not immediately affect the underlying market.

Assume, for example, that an announcement is made that the finance ministers of the major industrialized countries will meet to discuss foreign exchange rates. If no one knows what the outcome of the meeting will be, there is unlikely to be any significant change in rates when the the initial announcement is made. On the other hand, all traders will assume that major changes in foreign exchange rates could result from the meeting. This possibility will immediately be reflected in an increase in the implied volatility of currency options. The lack of movement in the underlying market, together with an increase in implied volatility, will cause all time spreads to widen.

Suppose that, as a result of the meeting, the finance ministers decide to maintain the status quo. Now expectations of a major change in exchange rates will disappear, implied volatility will fall, and as a result, all time spreads will narrow. (The reader who has access to such information may wish to compare the implied volatility of currency options just prior to and just after G-5 meetings. He will see just such an effect as we have described.)

Scenarios with similar consequences are possible in debt options when a policy statement is expected from the Federal Reserve, or in stock options when a company's earnings are due to be reported. These events are unlikely to have an effect on the market before the fact, but after the fact they could have significant repercussions.

The effect of implied volatility is what separates time spreads from the other spreads we have discussed. Backspreads and ratio vertical spreads (including short and long butterflies) want real volatility (price movement in the underlying market) and implied volatility (a reflection of expectations about future price movement) to either *both* rise or *both* fall. A swift move in the underlying market or an increase in implied volatility will help a backspread. A stagnant market, or a decrease in implied volatility, will help a ratio vertical spread. With time spreads, however, real volatility and implied volatility have opposite effects. A big move in the underlying market, or a decrease in implied volatility, will help a short time spread, while a stagnant market, or an increase in implied volatility, will help a long time spread. This opposite effect of real and implied volatility is what gives time spreads their unique characteristics.

Diagonal Spreads

It is also possible to construct spreads involving options which not only expire in different months but which have different exercise prices (Figures 8-16A and 8-16B). These diagonal spreads do not fit easily into any one category. Under some conditions, such spreads may act like time spreads. Under other conditions, they may act like either backspreads or ratio vertical spreads. It is usually best not to make any prior assumptions about diagonal spreads, but to analyze each spread individually.

---

long 20 April 105 calls (26)

short 10 June 100 calls (50)

Figure 8-16A

---

long 25 June 95 puts (-33)

short 15 April puts (-55)

Figure 8-16B

Classification of Volatility Spreads

Just as every individual option has a unique delta, gamma, theta, and vega associated with it; every spread position also has a unique delta, gamma, theta, and vega. These numbers can help a trader determine beforehand how changing market conditions are likely to affect a spread. Before going further, the reader may want to review Figure

6-22 which summarizes the market conditions which will help or hurt each type position.

A trader who initiates a volatility spread is primarily interested in the magnitude of movements in the underlying market, and only secondarily in the direction of movement. Therefore, the delta of all volatility spreads will be approximately zero. Some volatility spreads may prefer movement in one direction rather than another. But, the primary consideration is still whether movement of any type will occur. If a trader has a large positive or negative delta, such that the directional considerations become more important than the volatility considerations, then the position can no longer be considered a volatility spread.

All spreads which are helped by movement in the underlying market have a positive gamma. These include backspreads, long straddles and strangles, short butterflies, and short time spreads. All spreads which are hurt by movement in the underlying market have a negative gamma. These include ratio vertical spreads, short straddles and strangles, long butterflies, and long time spreads. A trader with a positive gamma is hoping for significant movement in the underlying contract and is *long premium*; a trader with a negative gamma position is hoping for a quiet market and is *short premium*.

Since the effect of market movement and the effect of time decay are always working in opposite directions, any spread with a positive gamma will necessarily have a negative theta. Any spread with a negative gamma will necessarily have a positive theta. If market movement helps, the passage of time hurts. If market movement hurts, the passage of time helps. A trader can't have it both ways.

Spreads which are helped by a rise in volatility have a positive vega. These include backspreads, long straddles and strangles, short butterflies, and long time spreads. Spreads which are helped by a decline in volatility have a negative vega. These include ratio vertical spreads, short straddles and strangles, long butterflies, and short time spreads.

The delta, gamma, theta, and vega associated with each of the spreads we have so far discussed are summarized in Figure 8-17. Since the delta of a volatility spread is assumed to be approximately zero, and the theta is always the opposite of the gamma, we can place every volatility spread into one of four categories based on its gamma and vega characteristics, shown below.

Category	Gamma	Vega
Backspread	Positive	Positive
Ratio Vertical Spread	Negative	Negative
Long Time Spread	Negative	Positive
Short Time Spread	Positive	Negative

No matter how complex a position is, even if it includes options at many different exercise prices in several different expiration months; a trader can tell generally which of these four categories his strategies fall into simply by looking at the sign of his gamma and vega position. The extent to which he is pursuing one of these strategies will be determined by the magnitude of these numbers. A trader with a gamma of -100 and a vega of +200 will be long time spread, but not nearly as much so as a trader with a gamma of -500 and a vega of +1000.

Characteristics of Volatility Spreads

Spread Type	Delta Position	Gamma Position	Theta Position	Vega Position
Call Backspread	0	+	-	+
Put Backspread	0	+	-	+
Long Straddle	0	+	-	+
Long Strangle	0	+	-	+
Short Butterfly	0	+	-	+
Call Ratio Vertical Spread	0	-	+	-
Put Ratio Vertical Spread	0	-	+	-
Short Straddle	0	-	+	-
Short Strangle	0	-	+	-
Long Butterfly	0	-	+	-
Long Time Spread	0	-	+	+
Short Time Spread	0	+	-	-

Figure 8-17

Figure 8-18 is an evaluation matrix giving the theoretical values, delta, gamma, theta, and vega of several different options. Following this are volatility spreads constructed from the matrix, along with the delta, gamma, theta, and vega position of each spread. The reader will see that each spread does indeed have the characteristics summarized in Figure 8-17.

Note that no market price is given for any of the individual options in Figure 8-18, and therefore no theoretical edge is given for any of the spreads. The prices at which a spread is done may be favorable or unfavorable, resulting in a positive or negative theoretical edge. But once the spread is established, the market conditions which will help or hurt the spread are determined by its type, not by the initial prices.

Choosing an Appropriate Strategy

Which types of spreading strategies are likely to be profitable under which market conditions? First and foremost our goal should be to choose spreads with a positive theoretical edge. Ideally, we would like to buy undervalued options and sell overvalued options. If we do this, we will not have to focus on a particular category of spreads. The resulting spread, whatever its type, will always have a positive theoretical edge.

More often, however, our opinion about volatility will make all options in a market appear either undervalued or overvalued. When this happens, it will be impossible to both buy undervalued and sell overvalued options. Such a market can be easily identified simply by comparing our volatility estimate to the implied volatility in the option marketplace. If implied volatility is generally lower than the estimate, all options will be undervalued. If implied volatility is generally higher than the estimate, all options will be overvalued.

If all options appear undervalued (low implied volatility), look for spreads with a positive vega. This includes strategies in the backspread or long time spread category. *If all options appear overvalued (high implied volatility), look for spreads with a negative vega.* This includes strategies in the ratio vertical spread or short time spread category.

It may seem at first glance that if one encounters a market of either of these types, where everything is too cheap or everything is too

April Futures at 98.25; Volatility = 25%; Time = 8 weeks; Interest = 9.00%

Exercise Price	CALLS					PUTS				
	Theoretical Value	Delta	Gamma	Theta	Vega	Theoretical Value	Delta	Gamma	Theta	Vega
95	5.54	64	3.8	−.030	.140	2.34	−34	3.8	−.031	.140
100	3.02	44	4.1	−.033	.150	4.74	−55	4.1	−.032	.150
105	1.45	26	3.4	−.027	.124	8.11	−73	3.4	−.026	.124

June Futures at 99.60; Volatility = 25%; Time = 16 weeks; Interest = 9.00%

Exercise Price	CALLS					PUTS				
	Theoretical Value	Delta	Gamma	Theta	Vega	Theoretical Value	Delta	Gamma	Theta	Vega
95	7.76	64	2.6	−.020	.197	3.29	−33	2.6	−.021	.197
100	5.17	50	2.8	−.023	.214	5.56	−47	2.8	−.023	.214
105	3.26	37	2.7	−.022	.204	8.51	−61	2.7	−.021	.204

BACK SPREAD: Long more contracts than short; all contracts expiring in the same month

	Delta Position	Gamma Position	Theta Position	Vega Position
Long 25 Apr 105 calls	+25 × 26	+25 × 3.4	+25 × −.027	+25 × .124
Short 15 Apr 100 calls	−15 × 44	−15 × 4.1	−15 × −.033	−15 × .150
	−10	+23.5	−.180	+.850
Long 20 Jun 95 puts	+20 × −33	+20 × 2.6	+20 × −.021	+20 × .197
Short 10 Jun 105 puts	−10 × −61	−10 × 2.7	−10 × −.021	−10 × .204
	−50	+25.0	−.210	+1.900

RATIO VERTICAL SPREAD: Short more contracts than long; all contracts expiring in the same month

	Delta Position	Gamma Position	Theta Position	Vega Position
Long 15 Jun 100 calls	+15 × 50	+15 × 2.8	+15 × −.023	+15 × .214
Short 20 Jun 105 calls	−20 × 37	−20 × 2.7	−20 × −.022	−20 × .204
	+10	−12.0	+.095	−.870
Long 10 Apr 105 puts	+10 × −73	+10 × 3.4	+10 × −.026	+10 × .124
Short 20 Apr 95 puts	−20 × −34	−20 × 3.8	−20 × −.031	−20 × .140
	−50	−42.0	+.360	−1.560

Figure 8-18

LONG BUTTERFLY: Short two options with the same exercise price, and long one option with an immediately higher exercise price and one option with an immediately lower exercise price. All options must be of the same type and expire in the same month.

	Delta Position	Gamma Position	Theta Position	Vega Position
Long 10 Apr 95 calls	+10 × 64	+10 × 3.8	+10 × −.030	+10 × .140
Short 20 Apr 100 calls	−20 × 44	−20 × 4.1	−20 × −.033	−20 × .150
Long 10 Apr 105 calls	+10 × 26	+10 × 3.4	+10 × −.027	+10 × .124
	+20	−10.0	+.090	−.360
Long 10 Jun 95 puts	+10 × −33	+10 × 2.6	+10 × −.021	+10 × .197
Short 20 Jun 100 puts	−20 × −47	−20 × 2.8	−20 × −.023	−20 × .214
Long 10 Jun 105 puts	+10 × −61	+10 × 2.7	+10 × −.021	+10 × .204
	00	−3.0	+.040	−.270

SHORT BUTTERFLY: Long two options with the same exercise price, and short one option with an immediately higher exercise price and one option with an immediately lower exercise price. All options must be of the same type and expire in the same month.

	Delta Position	Gamma Position	Theta Position	Vega Position
Short 10 Jun 95 calls	−10 × 64	−10 × 2.6	−10 × −.020	−10 × .197
Long 20 Jun 100 calls	+20 × 50	+20 × 2.8	+20 × −.023	+20 × .214
Short 10 Jun 105 calls	−10 × 37	−10 × 2.7	−10 × −.022	−10 × +.204
	−10	+3.0	−.040	+.270
Short 10 Apr 95 puts	−10 × −34	−10 × 3.8	−10 × −.031	−10 × .140
Long 20 Apr 100 puts	+20 × −55	+20 × 4.1	+20 × −.032	+20 × .150
Short 10 Apr 105 puts	−10 × −73	−10 × 3.4	−10 × −.026	−10 × .124
	−30	+10.0	−.070	+.360

LONG TIME SPREAD: Long a long term option and short a short term option, where both options have the same exercise price. Both option must be of the same type.

	Delta Position	Gamma Position	Theta Position	Vega Position
Long 10 Jun 95 calls	+10 × 64	+10 × 2.6	+10 × −.020	+10 × .197
Short 10 Apr 95 calls	−10 × 64	−10 × 3.8	−10 × −.030	−10 × .140
	00	−12.0	+.100	+.570
Long 25 Jun 100 puts	+25 × −47	+25 × 2.8	+25 × −.023	+25 × .214
Short 20 Apr 100 puts	−20 × −55	−20 × 4.1	−20 × −.032	−20 × .150
	−75	−12.0	+.065	+2.350

SHORT TIME SPREAD: Long a short term option and short a long term option, where both options have the same exercise price. Both options must be of the same type.

	Delta Position	Gamma Position	Theta Position	Vega Position
Long 15 Apr 105 calls	+15 × 26	+15 × 3.4	+15 × −.027	+15 × .124
Short 10 Jun 105 calls	−10 × 37	−10 × 2.7	−10 × −.022	−10 × .204
	+20	+24.0	−.185	−.180
Long 10 Apr 95 puts	+10 × −34	+10 × 3.8	+10 × −.031	+10 × .140
Short 10 Jun 95 puts	−10 × −33	−10 × 2.6	−10 × −.021	−10 × .197
	−10	+12.0	−.100	−.570

Figure 8-18 (continued)

LONG STRADDLE: Long calls and puts at the same exercise price; all options expiring in the same month

	Delta Position	Gamma Position	Theta Position	Vega Position
Long 10 Jun 100 calls	+10 × 50	+10 × 2.8	+10 × −.023	+10 × .214
Long 10 Jun 100 puts	+10 × −47	+10 × 2.8	+10 × −.023	+10 × .214
	+30	+56.0	−.460	+4.280
Long 10 Apr 95 calls	+10 × 64	+10 × 3.8	+10 × −.030	+10 × .140
Long 20 Apr 95 puts	+20 × −34	+20 × 3.8	+20 × −.031	+20 × .140
	−40	+114.0	−.920	+4.200

SHORT STRADDLE: Short calls and puts at the same exercise price; all options expiring in the same month

	Delta Position	Gamma Position	Theta Position	Vega Position
Short 25 Apr 100 calls	−25 × 44	−25 × 4.1	−25 × −.033	−25 × .150
Short 20 Apr 100 puts	−20 × −55	−20 × 4.1	−20 × −.032	−20 × .150
	00	−184.5	+1.465	−6.750
Short 25 Jun 105 calls	−25 × 37	−25 × 2.7	−25 × −.022	−25 × .204
Short 15 Jun 105 puts	−15 × −61	−15 × 2.7	−15 × −.021	−15 × .204
	−10	−108.0	+.865	−8.160

LONG STRANGLE: Long calls and puts at different exercise prices; all options expiring in the same month

	Delta Position	Gamma Position	Theta Position	Vega Position
Long 10 Jun 105 calls	+10 × 37	+10 × 2.7	+10 × −.022	+10 × .204
Long 10 Jun 95 puts	+10 × −33	+10 × 2.6	+10 × −.021	+10 × .197
	+40	+53.0	−.430	+4.010
Long 20 Apr 105 calls	+20 × 26	+20 × 3.4	+20 × −.027	+20 × .124
Long 10 Apr 100 puts	+10 × −55	+10 × 4.1	+10 × −.032	+10 × .150
	−30	+109.0	−.860	+3.980

SHORT STRANGLE: Short calls and puts at different exercise prices; all options expiring in the same month

	Delta Position	Gamma Position	Theta Position	Vega Position
Short 15 Apr 100 calls	−15 × 44	−15 × 4.1	−15 × −.033	−15 × .150
Short 20 Apr 95 puts	−20 × −34	−20 × 3.8	−20 × −.031	−20 × .140
	+20	−137.5	+1.115	−5.050
Short 10 Jun 95 calls	−10 × 64	−10 × 2.6	−10 × −.020	−10 × .197
Short 10 Jun 105 puts	−10 × −61	−10 × 2.7	−10 × −.021	−10 × .204
	−30	−53.0	+.410	−4.010

Figure 8-18 (concluded)

expensive, the sensible strategies are either long straddles and strangles, or short straddles and strangles. Such strategies allow us to pick up theoretical edge on both sides of our spread. These are certainly possible strategies according to our positive or negative vega criteria, but we will see in the next chapter that straddles and strangles, while often having large positive theoretical edge, can also be among the riskiest of all strategies. For this reason, we will often want to consider other types of spreads in either the backspread or ratio vertical spread category, even if such spreads entail buying some overpriced options or selling some underpriced options.

The theoretical values and deltas in Figure 8-19 are the same as those in Figure 8-18, but now we have added option prices reflecting an implied volatility of 22%. As a result, every option now appears to be undervalued. The reader will find that in this environment only spreads with a positive vega will be profitable:

1. Call and put backspreads

2. Long straddles and strangles

3. Short butterflies

4. Long time spreads.

Figure 8-20 uses the same theoretical values and deltas, but now all option prices reflect an implied volatility of 28%. As a result, all options appear overvalued. Here the reader will find that only spreads with a negative vega will be profitable:

1. Call and put ratio vertical spreads

2. Short straddles and strangles

3. Long butterflies

4. Short time spreads

One of the assumptions in theoretical pricing models is that the volatility of an underlying contract is constant throughout the life of the option. In real life, however, volatility is usually either rising or falling, and very often implied volatility is either rising or falling along with it. Since time spreads are particularly sensitive to changes in implied volatility, whether volatility is rising or falling can be an

IMPLIED VOLATILITY = 22%

April Futures at 98.25; Volatility = 25%; Time = 8 weeks; Interest = 9.00%

Exercise Price	CALLS			PUTS		
	Price	Theoretical Value	Delta	Price	Theoretical Value	Delta
95	5.12	5.54	64	1.92	2.34	−34
100	2.57	3.02	44	4.29	4.74	−55
105	1.09	1.45	26	7.75	8.11	−73

June Futures at 99.60; Volatility = 25%; Time = 16 weeks; Interest = 9.00%

Exercise Price	CALLS			PUTS		
	Price	Theoretical Value	Delta	Price	Theoretical Value	Delta
95	7.18	7.76	64	2.70	3.29	−33
100	4.53	5.17	50	4.92	5.56	−47
105	2.65	3.26	37	7.91	8.51	−61

Figure 8-19

IMPLIED VOLATILITY = 28%

April Futures at 98.25;   Volatility = 25%;   Time = 8 weeks;   Interest = 9.00%

Exercise Price		CALLS Theoretical Value	Delta		PUTS Theoretical Value	Delta
	Price			Price		
95	5.96	5.54	64	2.76	2.34	−34
100	3.47	3.02	44	5.19	4.74	−55
105	1.83	1.45	26	8.49	8.11	−73

June Futures at 99.60;   Volatility = 25%;   Time = 16 weeks;   Interest = 9.00%

Exercise Price		CALLS Theoretical Value	Delta		PUTS Theoretical Value	Delta
	Price			Price		
95	8.36	7.76	64	3.88	3.29	−33
100	5.81	5.17	50	6.20	5.56	−47
105	3.88	3.26	37	9.13	8.51	−61

Figure 8-20

important consideration in time spreads. Consequently, we can add a corollary to our spread guidelines:

Long time spreads are most likely to be profitable when implied volatility is low, but is expected to rise. Short time spreads are most likely to be profitable when implied volatility is high, but is expected to fall.

Recall that a long time spread position has a negative gamma. This means any movement in the underlying market will, in theory, reduce the value of the position. The trader with a long time spread would therefore like to avoid any big moves in the market up to the time the near term option expires. After that, however, any increased volatility in the underlying market will make the long term option, which he owns, all the more valuable. This is another way of stating the principle that a long time spreader wants the market to sit still, but he wants the marketplace to think that a big move is coming.

By contrast, the trader with a short time spread wants just the opposite. Volatility which occurs prior to the expiration of the near term option will make that option more valuable. If volatility later declines, it will depress the value of the long term option. This is another way of saying that a short time spreader wants the market to move, but he wants everyone in the marketplace to think that the move will be short-lived.

Adjustments

Every volatility spread will have a gamma which is either positive or negative, causing the delta position of the spread to change as the underlying futures contract moves up or down. Moreover, changes in volatility and in time to expiration can also change the delta position of a spread. A spread which is delta neutral today may not, indeed, probably will not be delta neutral tomorrow. Since the correct use of a theoretical pricing model requires a trader to remain essentially delta neutral, some thought should be given to when a trader should adjust. Essentially, there are three possibilities:

1. *Adjust at Regular Intervals*—Since volatility is a continuous measure of the speed of a market, theoretical pricing models assume that adjustments are being made continuously throughout the life of an option. In real life, however, such continous ad-

justments are physically impossible and, if commission costs are high, may not even be desirable. Since volatility is calculated from price changes over regular intervals, the next best solution might be to make adjustments at these same intervals. If the volatility estimate is based on daily price changes, adjust daily. If the volatility estimate is based on weekly price changes, adjust weekly.

2. *Adjust when the position becomes a predetermined number of deltas long or short*—A trader's delta position is a reflection of his market (directional) risk. Many option traders, having originally traded the underlying futures contract, equate their risk with number of futures contracts they are willing to hold. If, in the futures market, the trader was accustomed to holding positions no larger than 10 contracts he should not be willing to hold a delta position more than 1000 deltas long or short.

3. *Adjust by Feel*—This suggestion is not made facetiously. Some traders have good market feel. They can sense when a market is about to move in one direction or another. If a trader has this ability, there is no reason why he should not make use of it. Suppose, for example, that a trader has a gamma position of -200, and is delta neutral with the underlying futures market presently at 50.00. If the market falls to 48.00, the trader can estimate that he is now 400 deltas long. If 400 deltas is the limit of the risk he is willing to take, he might decide to adjust at this point. Suppose, however, he is also aware that 48.00 represents strong support for this market. If the trader has confidence in his technical analysis skills, he might wait and see whether the market does in fact bounce off the support. If he is right, he will have avoided an unprofitable adjustment. Of course if the market continues downward through the support he will regret not having adjusted. But if he is right more often than not, he should certainly take advantage of this skill.

There is no one right answer to the question of when to adjust, and traders probably make use of all three methods from time to time. The important consideration is that the trader learn to be disciplined in his adjustments. In theory, the best method is perhaps to adjust at regular intervals because this corresponds most closely to the mechanics of the theoretical pricing model. Most professional traders probably lean towards this method. An active trader may adjust several times throughout the day; at the very least he will try to go home delta neutral at the end of the day. If a trader does decide to sit with a large positive or negative delta position, he should certainly decide beforehand just how large he is willing to let the position become. If it exceeds that limit, he should adjust.

Graphing Spreads

Rather than looking at raw numbers, it may be easier to understand the characteristics of an option position by looking at a graph of its theoretical profit and loss as a function of the underlying futures price. This graph must necessarily be a theoretical one, since the true value of the position cannot be determined until expiration.

The general characteristics of any theoretical graph are determined initially by the trader's theoretical edge, his delta position, and his gamma position. Using, as before, a grid where the vertical axis (y-axis) represents profit or loss, and the horizontal axis (x-axis) represents movement in the underlying futures contract, we can interpret the theoretical edge, delta, and gamma as follows:

1. *Theoretical Edge*—The graph of a position with a positive theoretical edge will be above the x-axis at the current futures price. This is the first thing a trader should look for. If a position does not have positive theoretical edge, the position will be a losing one, even if the trader is right about future market conditions.

2. *Delta*—A positive delta reflects a theoretically long futures position. The graph of this position will, like an actual long futures position, cross the current futures price moving from the lower left to the upper right. The graph of a negative delta, or theoretically short futures position, will cross the current futures price moving from the upper left to the lower right. The exact slope of the graph as it crosses this price is determined by the magnitude of the delta position. A severely angled graph indicates a large non-neutral position; a generally horizontal graph reflects an approximately neutral delta position.

3. *Gamma*—A positive gamma position will theoretically increase in value if there is movement in either direction in an underlying

contract. The graph of such a position will be convex (a smile). A negative gamma position will theoretically decrease in value with movement in the underlying contract. The graph of such a position will be concave (a frown) (see Figure 8-21).

In order to complete the graph we also need to know what the tails of the graph look like, i.e., what effect a very big upward or downward move in the market will have on the position's value. We can determine this by adding up the *lot position*. This is a measure of how many contracts a position will be naked long or short if either all calls or all puts go so deeply into-the-money that they begin to act like futures contracts.

On the upside, all puts will eventually be worth zero, so we need only worry about the call position. The graph of a position which is long more calls than short will continue up and to the right indefinitely (unlimited upside profit). The graph of a position which is short more calls than long will continue down and to the right indefinitely (unlimited upside risk). If the number of long and short calls are equal, or if the position consists only of puts, the graph will eventually flatten out on the upside.

On the downside, all calls will eventually be worth zero, so we need only worry about the put position. The graph of a position which is long more puts than short puts will continue up and to the left indefinitely (unlimited downside profit). The graph of a position which is short more puts than long will continue down and to the left indefinitely (unlimited downside risk). If the number of long puts and short puts are equal, or if the position consists only of calls, the graph will eventually flatten out on the downside.

As an example of graphing a spread position, suppose that, using the theoretical values in Figure 8-18, we are able to initiate a put ratio vertical spread by purchasing 10 April 105 puts at 8.40 each and selling 20 April 95 puts at 2.70 each. What will the theoretical graph of this position look like?

First we need to calculate the theoretical edge. The 105 puts are worth 8.11 and the 95 puts are worth 2.34, so the total edge is:

$$(10 \times -.29) + (20 \times +.36) = +4.30$$

This is where the graph will cross the current futures price.

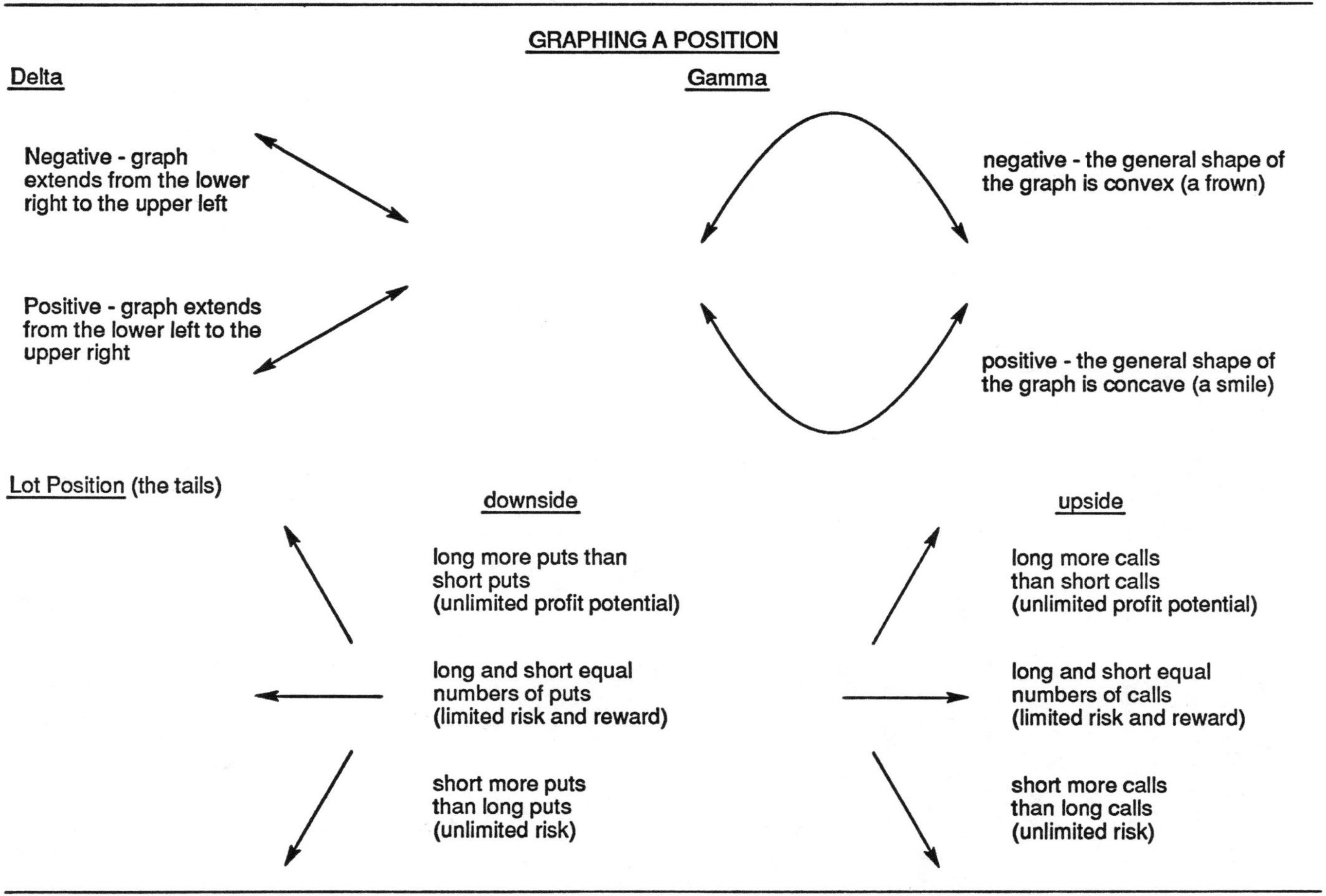

GRAPHING A POSITION

Delta

Negative - graph extends from the lower right to the upper left

Positive - graph extends from the lower left to the upper right

Gamma

negative - the general shape of the graph is convex (a frown)

positive - the general shape of the graph is concave (a smile)

Lot Position (the tails)

downside

long more puts than short puts (unlimited profit potential)

long and short equal numbers of puts (limited risk and reward)

short more puts than long puts (unlimited risk)

upside

long more calls than short calls (unlimited profit potential)

long and short equal numbers of calls (limited risk and reward)

short more calls than long calls (unlimited risk)

Figure 8-21

Second, the delta of -50 tells us that the spread is currently a slightly short position and will increase in value if there is a decline in the market. The graph should therefore cross the current futures price, at +4.30, sloping from the lower right to the upper left.

Third, we know from the gamma of -42 that large movement in either direction is likely to decrease the value of the position. The general shape of the graph must therefore be convex, or a frown.

Finally, we can determine the maximum upside and downside risk or reward by adding up the lot position. This spread involves only puts, so that if the market moves up far enough all options will eventually be worthless. The profit or loss will therefore be limited to the credit or debit from the original trade. The original cash flow was:

$$(10 \times -8.40) + (20 \times +2.70) = -30.00$$

On the upside this position cannot lose more than 30.00 points.

If the market moves down far enough all puts will go into-the-money and eventually start acting like short futures contracts. When this happens, the spread will essentially be naked short 10 puts (long 10 April 105 puts, short 20 April 95 puts), and the graph will have the same slope as a position which is long 10 futures contracts. The risk on the downside is unlimited (see Figure 8-22).

We can also determine how the passage of time or a change in volatility will affect the graph of a spread by looking at its theta and vega position. The passage of time will increase the value of a position with a positive vega, shifting the graph upward. Conversely, the passage of time will decrease the value of a spread with a negative theta, shifting the graph downward.

While time only moves in one direction, volatility can either increase or decrease. The graph of a spread with a positive vega will be shifted upward (increased value) if volatility increases, and downward (decreased value) if volatility decreases. The graph of a spread with a negative vega will be shifted downward (decreased value) if volatility rises, and upward (increased value) if volatility falls (see Figure 8-23).

The theta position of our spread is +.36, so each day that passes with no change in the underlying market will shift the graph upward by .36. Our vega position is -1.56, so each percentage point increase (decrease) in volatility will shift the graph downward (upward) by 1.56 points (see Figure 8-24).

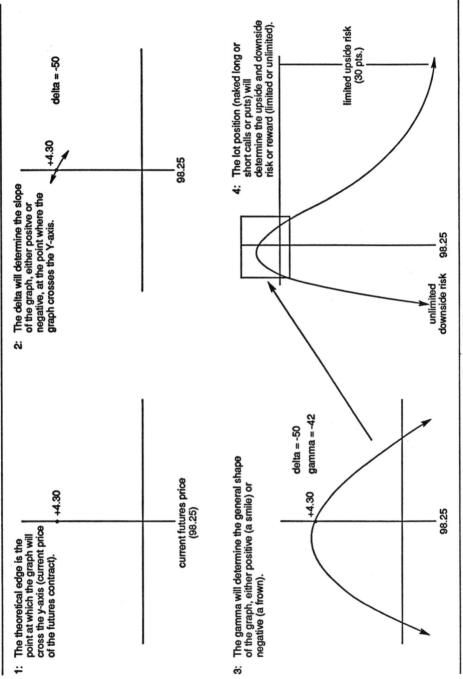

Figure 8-22

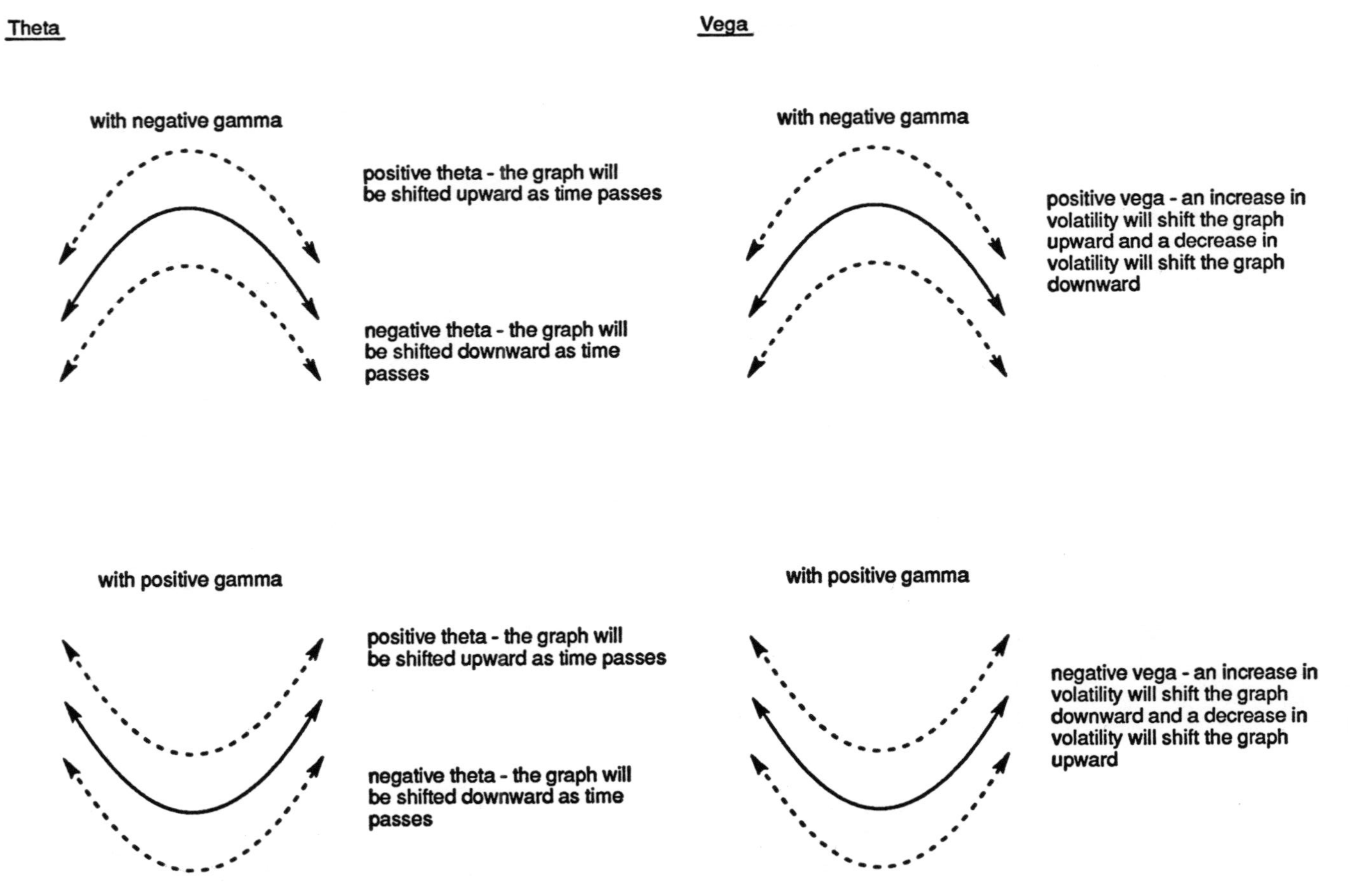
Theta
Vega
with negative gamma
positive theta - the graph will be shifted upward as time passes
negative theta - the graph will be shifted downward as time passes
with negative gamma
positive vega - an increase in volatility will shift the graph upward and a decrease in volatility will shift the graph downward
with positive gamma
positive theta - the graph will be shifted upward as time passes
negative theta - the graph will be shifted downward as time passes
with positive gamma
negative vega - an increase in volatility will shift the graph downward and a decrease in volatility will shift the graph upward

Figure 8-23

5: The passage of time will shift the graph either upward (positive theta) or downward (negative theta) for each day that passes without any movement in the underlying contract.

6: A positive (negative) vega will shift the graph upward (downward) if volatility increases and downward (upward) if volatility decreases.

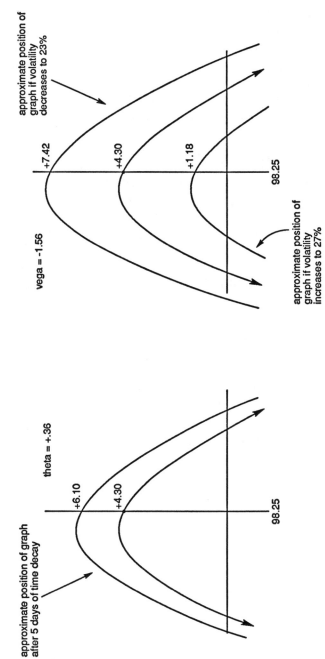

approximate position of graph after 5 days of time decay

theta = +.36

+6.10

+4.30

98.25

vega = -1.56

+7.42

+4.30

+1.18

98.25

approximate position of graph if volatility decreases to 23%

approximate position of graph if volatility increases to 27%

Figure 8-24

Note that this position will be helped by a downward movement in the market (delta = -50) but the graph has a generally convex shape (gamma = -42). We might therefore ask, how far down can the market go before the position begins to lose value? In other words, where is the apex of the graph, the point where it just turns over? We can calculate an approximate answer by ignoring positive or negative signs and dividing the delta by the gamma:

$$50 / 42 = 1.19$$

The apex of the graph must be approximately 1.19 points lower than the current futures price of 98.25, or approximately 97.06. At this price, given current market conditions, the spread should have its greatest theoretical value, and a delta of zero.

Finally, we can ask at what prices of the underlying market will this spread theoretically break even, that is, where does the graph cross the X-axis? None of the numbers we have at our disposal can tell us this, and the solution will probably require a computer. In our example, the numbers are approximately 94 and 102.

Every active trader ought to have some idea of what the theoretical profit and loss graph of his position looks like given his current theoretical edge, delta, gamma, theta, vega, and lot position. Many option software vendors offer plotting capabilities along with their theoretical evaluation services. Clearing firms for professional traders very often supply plots to traders each morning, although an experienced trader can probably visualize the general characteristics of such graphs in his head. A useful exercise for a new trader is to actually sit down and sketch his graph on a piece of paper. Doing so will enable him to objectively analyze his strategies, and understand the risks to which he is exposed.

Spread Order Entry

Before concluding this section, a word about spread orders will perhaps be worthwhile. Spreads are traded in sophisticated options markets in the same way that individual options are traded. This means that a spread will be quoted with a single bid and a single offer price. For example, suppose a trader is interested in buying a certain straddle and is quoted a price for the straddle of 3.45 - 3.55.

This means that market-makers or locals are willing to buy the straddle at 3.45 and sell it at 3.55. If the trader decides that he is willing to pay 3.55, neither he nor the market maker from whom he is purchasing the straddle really care whether he pays 1.75 for the call and 1.80 for the put, or 1.65 for the call and 1.90 for the put, or some other combination of put and call prices. The only real consideration is the total spread price of 3.55.

No matter how complex a spread, if a quote is requested in the marketplace, market makers will endeavor to give one price for the whole spread. When the spread involves only two or three options, a bid and offer will usually be given very quickly. If the spread is complex, involving several different options in unusual ratios, it may take a market maker several minutes to give his best bid and offer. But, regardless of the type of spread, active market makers will usually make an effort to give the best 2-sided market (bid and offer) they can.

Spread orders, like individual option orders, can also be submitted with qualifying instructions. The most common types are market orders (orders to be filled at the current price) and limit orders (orders to be filled at a specified price). A broker handling a spread order is fully responsible for adhering to any instructions which accompany the order. Unless a trader knows exactly what current market conditions are, or has a great deal of confidence in the broker who will be handling the order, it is always a good practice to give specific written instructions with the order so that there is no misunderstanding about how the order is to be executed. The following contingency orders are defined in Appendix A.

All or none
Fill or kill
Immediate or cancel
Market if touched
Market on close
One cancels the other
Stop limit order
Stop loss order

Figures 8-25A and 8-25B are typical spread orders submitted with their contingencies.

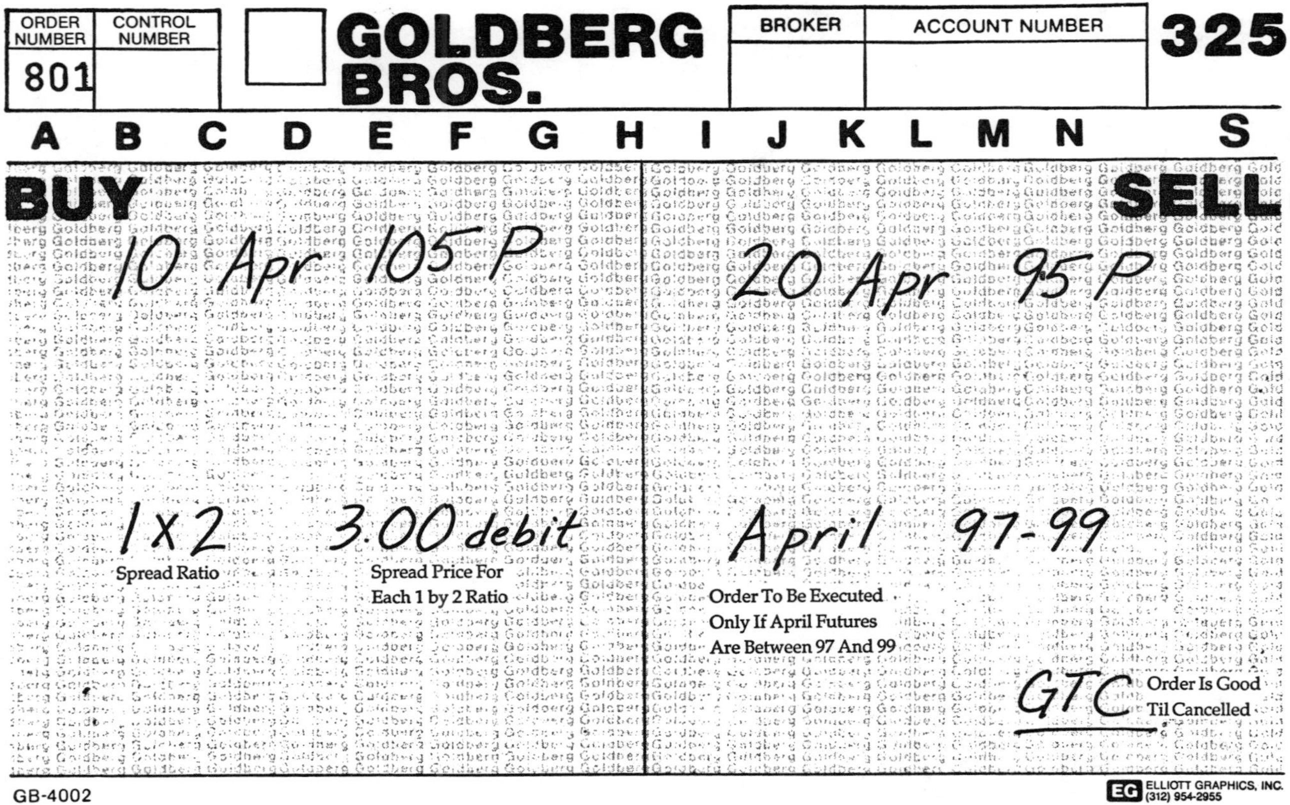

ORDER NUMBER 801

CONTROL NUMBER

☐ GOLDBERG BROS.

BROKER

ACCOUNT NUMBER

325

A B C D E F G H I J K L M N S

BUY 10 Apr 105 P 20 Apr 95 P **SELL**

1 x 2   3.00 debit   April 97-99

Spread Ratio   Spread Price For   Order To Be Executed
Each 1 by 2 Ratio   Only If April Futures
Are Between 97 And 99

GTC Order Is Good
Til Cancelled

GB-4002

EG ELLIOTT GRAPHICS, INC.
(312) 954-2955

Figure 8-25A

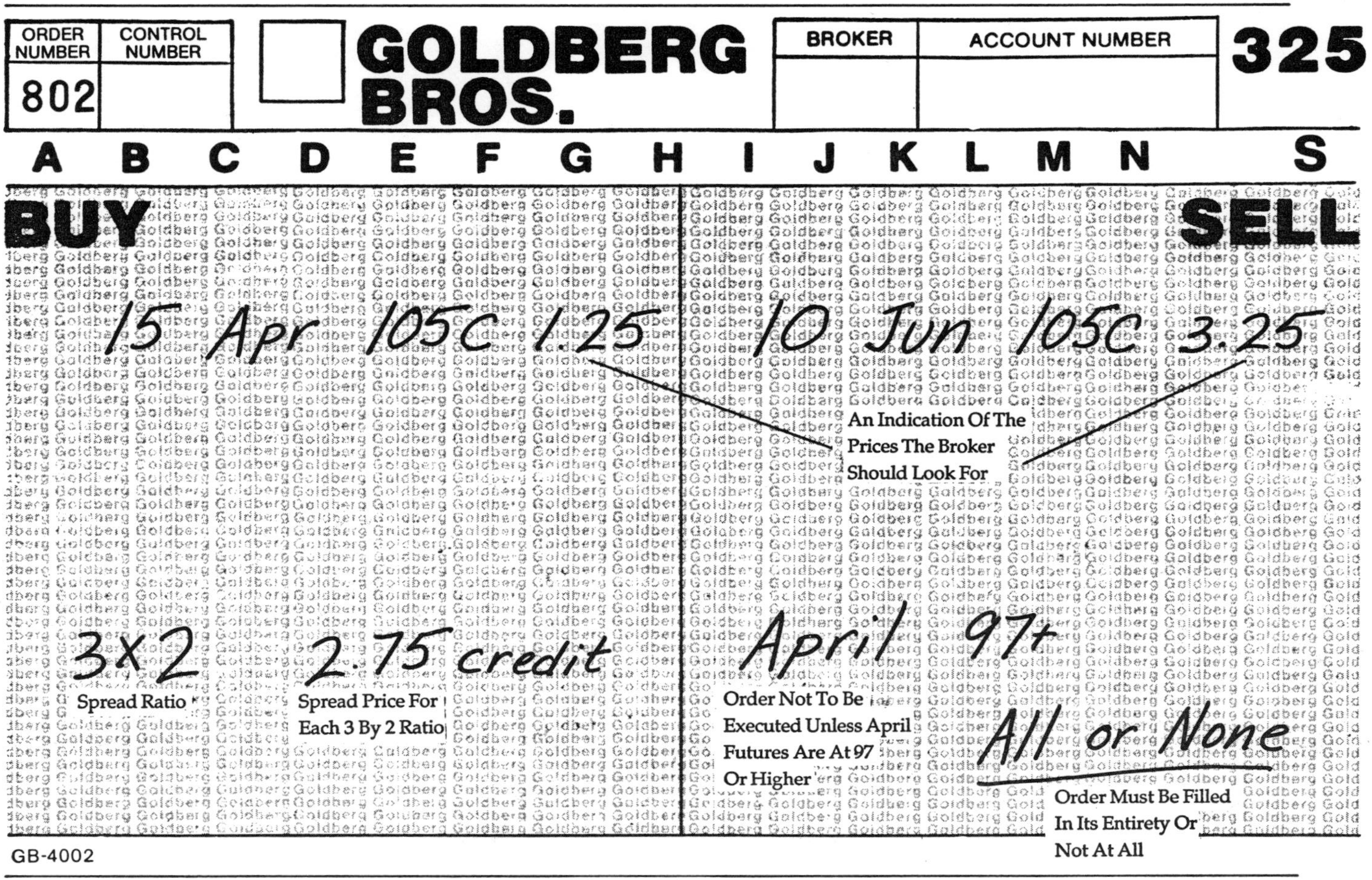
ORDER NUMBER
802
CONTROL NUMBER
GOLDBERG BROS.
BROKER
ACCOUNT NUMBER
325
A B C D E F G H I J K L M N S
BUY
SELL
15 Apr 105C 1.25
10 Jun 105C 3.25
An Indication Of The Prices The Broker Should Look For
3X2
Spread Ratio
2.75 credit
Spread Price For Each 3 By 2 Ratio
April 97+
Order Not To Be Executed Unless April Futures Are At 97 Or Higher
All or None
Order Must Be Filled In Its Entirety Or Not At All
GB-4002

Figure 8-25B

9

Risk
Considerations

$\mathbf{S}$uppose we are faced with the prices and theoretical values in Figure 9-1. Which categories of volatility spreads might be profitable, and within each of these categories which specific spread might be best? It is immediately apparent, by looking at either the actual prices of the options or by looking at the implied volatilities, that all options are undervalued. We will therefore want to concentrate on spreads with a positive vega:

1. Call and Put Backspreads

2. Long Straddles and Strangles

3. Short Butterflies

4. Long Time Spreads.

Choosing the Best Spread

For the moment, let's restrict ourselves to April options only. Now we will have to look for spreads specifically in the backspread category (positive gamma, positive vega). Even with only six different options (three calls and three puts), it is still possible to construct a wide variety of spreads which fall into this category. How can

April Futures at 98.25; Volatility = 25%; Time = 8 weeks; Interest = 9.00%

Exercise Price	CALLS							PUTS						
	Price	Theoretical Value	Delta	Gamma	Theta	Vega	Imp. Vol.	Price	Theoretical Value	Delta	Gamma	Theta	Vega	Imp. Vol.
95	5.45	5.54	64	3.8	−.030	.140	24.3	2.15	2.34	−34	3.8	−.031	.140	23.7
100	2.65	3.02	44	4.1	−.033	.150	22.6	4.40	4.74	−55	4.1	−.032	.150	22.7
105	1.25	1.45	26	3.4	−.027	.124	23.3	7.90	8.11	−73	3.4	−.026	.124	23.3

June Futures at 99.60; Volatility = 25%; Time = 16 weeks; Interest = 9.00%

Exercise Price	CALLS							PUTS						
	Price	Theoretical Value	Delta	Gamma	Theta	Vega	Imp. Vol.	Price	Theoretical Value	Delta	Gamma	Theta	Vega	Imp. Vol.
95	7.27	7.76	64	2.6	−.020	.197	22.5	2.75	3.29	−33	2.6	−.021	.197	22.3
100	4.42	5.17	50	2.8	−.023	.214	21.5	2.66	5.56	−47	2.8	−.023	.214	21.8
105	2.85	3.26	37	2.7	−.022	.204	23.0	7.93	8.51	−61	2.7	−.021	.204	22.1

we make an intelligent decision about which spread might prove to be the best? Suppose we choose three possible strategies and try to analyze them. The three strategies are spreads 9-2, 9-3, and 9-4 (see page 206). Each of these spreads fits into the backspread category: spread 9-2 is a long straddle, 9-3 is a call backspread, and 9-4 is a short put butterfly. How can we evaluate the relative merits of each spread?

At first glance it appears that 9-2 is best since it has the greatest theoretical edge. If the volatility estimate of 25% turns out to be correct, 9-2 will show a profit of 9.63, while 9-3 will show a profit of 4.65, and 9-4 will show a profit of only 2.80.

Is theoretical edge our only concern? If that is true, we can simply do a spread in bigger and bigger size to increase the theoretical edge as much as we want. Instead of doing spread 9-3 15 by 10 we might increase the size fivefold to 75 by 50. Now the theoretical edge is 5 × 4.65, or 23.25. This ostensibly makes it a better strategy than 9-2 with its theoretical edge of only 9.63. Clearly, theoretical edge can't be the only consideration.

Theoretical edge is only an indication of what we expect to earn if we are right about market conditions. Since there is no guarantee that we will be right, we must give at least as much consideration to the question of risk. If we are wrong about market conditions, how badly might we be hurt?

In order to focus on the risk considerations, let's change the size of spreads 9-3 and 9-4 so that their theoretical edge is approximately equal to the theoretical edge of spread 9-2. We can do this by doubling the size of 9-3 to 30 by 20, and by increasing the size of 9-4 3 1/2 times to 35 by 70 by 35. The new spreads, 9-2, 9-3′, and 9-4′, and their sensitivity factors are shown on page 207.

With all three spreads having approximately the same theoretical edge, we can now focus on the risks associated with each spread.

As with all volatility spreads, we will certainly have to consider the possibility of an incorrect volatility estimate. Since each spread has a positive vega, an underestimate of volatility will not be a problem. If 25% turns out to be too low, the value of the spread will increase, and we will end up with a greater profit than we had originally expected. On the other hand, if we have overestimated volatility and 25% turns out to be too high, this could present a problem. What will happen if volatility turns ot be 23%, or 21%,

	Theoretical Edge	Delta Position

Spread 9-2:

Long 15 April 100 calls @ 2.65
Long 12 April 100 puts @ 4.40

	Theoretical Edge	Delta Position
15 April 100 calls	15 × +.37	+15 × +44
12 April 100 puts	12 × +.34	+12 × -55
	+9.63	00

Spread 9-3:

Long 15 April 100 calls @ 2.65
Short 10 April 95 calls @ 5.45

	Theoretical Edge	Delta Position
	15 × +.37	+15 × +44
	12 × -.09	-10 × +64
	+4.65	+20

Spread 9-4:

Short 10 April 95 puts @ 2.15
Long 20 April 100 puts @ 4.40
Short 10 April 105 puts @ 7.90

	Theoretical Edge	Delta Position
	10 × -.19	-10 × -34
	20 × +.34	+20 × -55
	10 × -.21	-10 × -73
	+2.80	-30

	Theoretical Edge	Delta Position	Gamma Position	Theta Position	Vega Position
Spread 9-2:					
Long 15 April 100 calls @ 2.65	15 × +.37	+15 × +44	+15 × 4.1	+15 × −.033	+15 × .150
Long 12 April 100 puts @ 4.40	12 × +.34	+12 × −55	+12 × 4.1	+12 × −.032	+12 × .150
	+9.63	00	+110.7	−.879	+4.050
Spread 9-3!:					
Long 30 April 100 calls @ 2.65	30 × +.37	+30 × +44	+30 × 4.1	+30 × −.033	+30 × .150
Short 20 April 95 calls @ 5.45	20 × −.09	−20 × +64	−20 × 3.8	−20 × −.030	−20 × .140
	+9.30	+40	+47.0	−.390	+1.700
Spread 9-4!:					
Short 35 April 95 puts @ 2.15	35 × −.19	−35 × −34	−35 × 3.8	−35 × −.031	−35 × .140
Long 70 April 100 puts @ 4.40	70 × +.34	+70 × −55	+70 × 4.1	+70 × −.032	+70 × .150
Short 35 April 105 puts @ 7.90	35 × −.21	−35 × −73	−35 × 3.4	−35 × −.026	−35 × .124
	+9.80	−105***	+35.0	−.245	+1.260

***While somewhat delta long this is still the at-the-money butterfly, and therefore as close to delta neutral as possible.

or some lower figure? How badly will we be hurt? One way to find out is to use a theoretical pricing model to simulate the value of each spread as volatility declines. From this we can construct a graph of each spread's theoretical edge versus volatility (see Figure 9-2).

As a result of our size adjustments each spread has approximately the same theoretical edge, so we can now focus on the volatility risk of each spread. Looking at Figure 9-1 we see that the graph of spread 9-2 has a much more severe slope than the graphs of spreads 9-3' and 9-4'. If we are wrong, and volatility starts to decline, spread 9-2 will lose its theoretical edge very quickly compared to spreads 9-3' and 9-4'.

The volatility at which a spread just breaks even (zero theoretical edge) is the implied volatility of the spread. This is a logical extension of the general definition of implied volatility: the volatility we must feed into our pricing model to yield a theoretical value for the option (spread) equal to the price of the option (spread) in the marketplace. The implied volatilities of spreads 9-2, 9-3', and 9-4' are approximately 22.6%, 19.8%, and 18.8%, respectively.

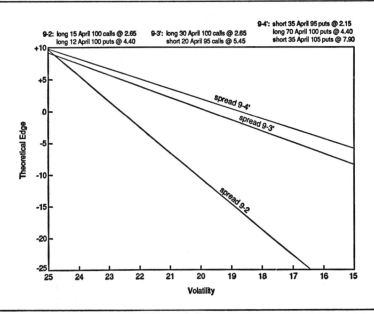

Figure 9-2

At a low enough volatility all spreads will eventually lose money, but this won't happen until the actual volatility falls below the implied volatility of each spread. Since the implied volatilities of spreads 9-3' and 9-4' (19.8% and 18.8%, respectively) are much lower than the implied volatility of spread 9-2 (22.6%), there is a much greater margin for error in spreads 9-3' or 9-4'. Moreover, if we have greatly overestimated volatility, so that each spread results in a loss, spreads 9-3' and 9-4' result in smaller losses then spread 9-2. At a volatility of 17% spreads 9-3' and 9-4' lose approximately 4.90 and 2.60 points, respectively, while spread 9-2 loses 22.60 points. If we are really wrong, spread 9-2 could turn into a disaster.

Viewing each of these spreads purely from the standpoint of volatility risk, spread 9-4' has to be the winner. Its implied volatility of approximately 18.8% means that we can be wrong by as much as 6.2 points in our volatility estimate and still not lose money. Spread 9-3', with its implied volatility of approximately 19.8%, has a slightly smaller margin for error (5.2 volatility points). Finally, spread 9-2, with its implied volatility of approximately 19.8%, has only a very small margin for error (2.4 volatility points).

Even though it was helpful to construct a graph of the theoretical edge of each spread at increasingly lower volatilities, there is an easier way to compare these spreads. In any strategy, we would like to maximize our reward with respect to our risk. If we think of the theoretical edge as the reward of the spread, and the vega as the volatility risk of the spread, we can divide the initial theoretical edge of each spread by its vega to yield a risk/reward ratio for each spread. The spread which yields the highest ratio will be the optimal spread with respect to volatility risk. Using the vega values for each spread we have:

Spread	Theoretical Edge/Vega
9-2	9.63 / 4.05 = 2.38
9-3'	9.30 / 1.70 = 5.47
9-4'	9.80 / 1.26 = 7.78

Note that this technique of dividing the reward (theoretical edge) by the risk (vega) will yield the same number regardless of the size of the spread. Changing the size will change the theoretical edge and the vega, but the ratio of the two numbers will remain the same.

Since volatility is not quite linear, this method will not tell us the exact implied volatiliy of each spread. But, in relative terms, the resulting values confirm that spread 9-4' has the greatest margin for error in estimating volatility, while spread 9-2 has the least margin for error. Consequently, from a volatility standpoint, spread 9-4' is the least risky, while spread 9-2 is the most risky.[1]

Why are we so concerned with our volatility estimate being too high? A trader might take the view that he is just as likely to under-estimate as overestimate volatility. If volatility turns out to be greater than 25%, there is no denying that spread 9-2, with its greater vega, will do best. If a volatility of 25% defines the average expected return, why worry about whether 25% turns out to be too high? After all, for each time the estimate turns out to be too high, there will also be times when the estimate turns out to be too low. In the long run, the big losers should be offset by the big winners.

The problem with certain types of spreads is that a serious error in estimating an input may result in the trader being wiped out. In that case he has no chance to reach the "long run." Suppose in our example volatility actually turns out to be 17%. Going back to Figure 9-2, we see that if we choose spread 9-2 we will lose approximately 22.60 points. In the long run, this should be offset by the times when volatility turns out to be very high, say 33%, and we profit by an equal amount. Unfortunately, if a loss of 22.60 points results in our going out of business, we won't be around for the long run. We won't ever have the chance to see volatility go to 33%. *An intelligent volatility estimate will maximize our long-run expected return. An intelligent assessment of the risk characteristics of a spread will serve to ensure that we do, indeed, survive to reach the long run.*

An incorrect volatility estimate is not the only risk about which a trader must be concerned. Every input represents a risk to the trader

---

[1]It is true that if volatility goes to zero (the market never moves from 98.25) spread 9-3' will lose less than spread 9-4'. In real life, however, it is impossible to take into consideration every extreme outcome.

since any incorrect input will alter an option's theoretical value. These risks are reflected in the delta, gamma, theta, and vega numbers associated with a spread. We can define them as follows:

1. **Delta (Directional) Risk**—The risk that the market will move in one direction rather than another. A volatility spread wants the underlying market to either move (positive gamma) or sit still (negative gamma). When we ratio a spread so that we are delta neutral, we are trying to ensure that, initially, the spread has no special preference for the direction in which the market will move, and that, consequently, there is no directional risk.

2. **Gamma (Curvature) Risk**—The risk of a large move in the underlying contract. Theoretical pricing models assume a normal distribution of price changes, which means that there is some probability associated with every price change. As the price change becomes larger and larger, the corresponding probability becomes smaller and smaller. However at no time does the probability become zero. There is always some chance, even a very remote one, that a large move will occur. The gamma position is essentially a measure of how sensitive the spread will be to such large moves. Positive gamma positions do not really have gamma risk since such positions, in theory, increase in value with movement in the underlying contract. Negative gamma positions, however, can quickly lose their theoretical edge with a large move in the underlying. The effect of such a move must always be a consideration when a trader contemplates a spread with a negative gamma.

3. **Theta (Time Decay) Risk**—The risk that time will pass with no movement in the underlying contract. This is the opposite side of gamma risk. Positive gamma spreads have no gamma risk because the spread cannot be hurt by a large move in the underlying contract. But if movement helps, then the passage of time hurts. Positive gamma and negative theta always go hand in hand. A trader with a negative theta position will want to assess his risk in terms of how much time can pass before the spread's theoretical edge disappears. The position wants movement, but if the movement doesn't occur by tommorow, or by next week, or by next month will the spread still, in theory, be profitable?

4. **Vega (Volatility) Risk**—The risk that the volatility we enter into a theoretical pricing model will be incorrect. If we enter an incorrect volatility, we will be using a normal distribution curve with incorrect probabilities associated with the possible price outcomes of the underlying contract. This is the risk we tried to quantify in spreads 9-2, 9-3, and 9-4.

Unlike gamma and theta risk, which may not always be a consideration, vega risk is a concern to every trader. A trader with a positive vega must worry about a decline in volatility; a trader with a negative vega must worry about an increase in volatility.

Each of the delta, gamma, theta, and vega numbers associated with a spread position can represent a risk to the trader. The trader will therefore want to give some consideration to estimating the relative risks of spreads, in much the same way as we looked at the volatility risks associated with spreads 9-2, 9-3, and 9-4. Since we have made the assumption that all volatility spreads are initially delta neutral, delta risk will not be a concern. A negative gamma position will be at risk from a large move in the underlying contract. Will the risk be greater or less than the gamma risk to a different negative gamma position? The same questions can be asked of negative theta positions with respect to the passage of time. Finally, what about the volatility risk to either a positive or negative vega position?

The size of the gamma, theta, or vega numbers may not be an accurate reflection of the risk simply because spreads done in larger size tend to have larger numbers associated with them. We can always keep our risk low by keeping the size of our spreads small. What we want is a way to evaluate not just risk, but risk versus reward.

We have already compared the vega (volatility) risks of spreads 9-2, 9-3, and 9-4, and come to the conclusion that spread 9-2 was the most risky, and 9-4 was the least risky. Each of these spreads has a negative theta, so we will also have to be concerned with theta risk. How badly will we be hurt if there is no immediate movement in the underlying futures contract? We can use essentially the same method to analyze this risk as we did to analyze vega risk.

In order to focus on the theta risk characteristics of each spread, we will again equalize the theoretical edge by looking at spreads 9-2, 9-3', and 9-4' instead of our original spreads 9-2, 9-3, and 9-4.

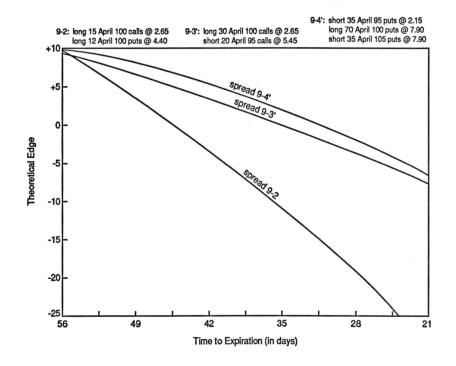

Figure 9-3

Figure 9-3 shows in graph form what happens to the value of each spread as we decrease time to expiration. Spread 9-2 loses all its theoretical edge in about 1 1/2 weeks, spread 9-3' in about 3 weeks, and spread 9-4' in about 3 1/2 weeks.

Alternatively, we can, as with vega, estimate risk versus reward of each spread by dividing the theoretical edge by the theta. Using the theoretical edges and theta values of each spread we have:

Spread	Theoretical Edge / Theta
9-2	9.63 / .879 = 10.96
9-3'	9.30 / .390 = 23.85
9-4'	9.80 / .245 = 40.00

Theta is even less linear than vega (the theta can become very large as we get close to expiration), so this method will not tell us the exact date on which the spread will theoretically break even. But, in relative terms, these numbers still enable us to compare the theta risks of the three spreads. The larger the number, the greater the margin for error, and, therefore, the less risk associated with each spread.

Again, no matter which of these methods we use, all roads lead to the same conclusion: spread 9-4 is the least risky and spread 9-2 is the most risky.

Practical Considerations

Based on our risk analysis of volatility and time decay, it certainly appears that spread 10-4 has the best risk/reward characteristics. Does this mean that a trader will invest his capital in spread 9-4, and essentially ignore spreads 9-2 and 9-3? In theory the answer is yes. As long as a spread has positive theoretical edge, one should always choose the spread with the greatest margin for error in estimating inputs to the theoretical pricing model. In the real world, however, practical trading considerations may also play a role a trader's decision.

For example, spread 9-4 is a 3-sided spread, while 9-2 and 9-3 are 2-sided spreads. A 3-sided spread will always be more difficult to execute than a 2-sided spread and is therefore likely to carry a higher price in the marketplace. If a trader decides not to execute all three sides simultaneously, and instead tries to execute one side at a time, he is at risk from an adverse market move until the entire spread has been executed.

Additionally, there is the consideration of market liquidity. In order to attain a theoretical edge approximately equal to spreads 9-2 and 9-3', it was necessary to increase the size of spread 9-4 3 1/2 times, to $35 \times 70 \times 35$. If there is not enough liquidity in the April 95, 100, and 105 puts to support this size, it may not be possible to do the butterfly in the size required to meet our profit goals. Alternatively, we may be able to execute part of the spread at favorable prices, but as we increase the size of the spread, the prices may become less favorable.

If trading considerations make spread 9-4 impractical, we may have to choose between spreads 9-2 and 9-3. If that happens, spread

9-3 is the clear winner. It allows for a much greater margin for error in volatility (5.2 points versus 2.4 points), as well as a greater margin for error in time decay (3 weeks versus 1 1/2 weeks). A trader who is given the choice of putting his capital into either of these spreads will strongly prefer spread 9-3.

The choice of spreads may not always be as obvious as in our previous example. The superiority of spread 9-4, at least from a theoretical point of view, was clear-cut. Sometimes, however, one spread may be superior with respect to one type of risk, but inferior with respect to another type of risk.

Suppose we go back to Figure 9-1 and now also consider the June options. Since all options are underpriced, we still want to concentrate on spreads with a positive vega. Now, however, we can also look at time spreads.

Consider spreads 9-7 and 9-8 on the next page. Since both spreads have approximately equal theoretical edge (8.75 versus 9.15), we can immediately focus on their risk characteristics. Both spreads have a positive vega so they will be at risk from a decline in volatlity. We can, as before, graph the theoretical edge of each spread vs. a change in volatility (Figure 9-4). But, again, by simply dividing each spread's theoretical edge by its vega, we can quickly establish the relative volatility risk associated with each spread.

Spread	Theoretical Edge / Vega
9-7	8.75 / 1.425 = 6.14
9-8	9.15 / 1.278 = 7.16

From these figures, we can see that spread 9-8 has a slightly better risk vs. reward ratio, and is therefore slightly less risky, with respect to volatility, than spread 9-7.

What about time decay? Both these spreads have a positive theta, so the passage of time can only help them. Time decay is not a problem.

What about market movement? Here we do have something to worry about because long time spreads have a negative gamma. Any

	Theoretical Edge	Delta Position	Gamma Position	Theta Position	Vega Position
Spread 9-7:					
Long 25 June 95 puts @ 2.75	+25 × +.54	+25 × −33	+25 × 2.6	+25 × −.021	+25 × .197
Short 25 April 95 puts @ 2.15	−25 × −.19	−25 × −34	−25 × 3.8	−25 × −.031	−25 × .140
	+8.75	+25	−30.0	+.250	+1.425
Spread 9-8:					
Long 27 June 100 calls @ 4.42	+27 × +.75	+27 × +50	+27 × 2.8	+27 × −.023	+27 × .214
Short 30 April 100 calls @ 2.65	−30 × −.37	−30 × +44	−30 × 4.1	−30 × −.033	−30 × .150
	+9.15	+30	−47.4	+.369	+1.278

Spreads 9-7 and 9-8

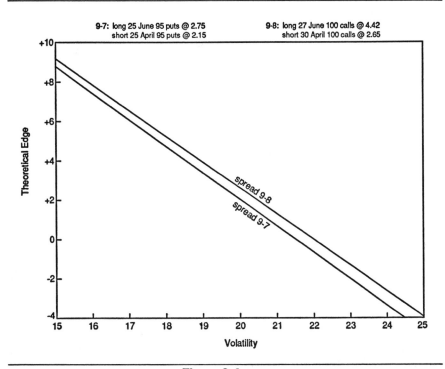

Figure 9-4

significant movement in the underlying market will have an adverse effect on these spreads. Since pricing models measure movement in standard deviations, it will be practical to look at price changes in the same terms. A one standard deviation daily price change will be approximately:

$$\text{April: } 98.25 \times .25/16 = 1.54$$
$$\text{June: } 99.60 \times .25/16 = 1.56$$

We can now graph the theoretical edge of each spread versus underlying price movement in standard deviations (Figure 9-5). Note that the graph of spread 9-8 is more severely convex than the graph of spread 9-7. This greater convexity means that spread 9-8 has greater gamma (curvature) risk; it will lose its theoretical edge more quickly if the underlying futures contracts begin to move either up or down.

We might ask where the break even prices are for each of these spreads in terms of standard deviation price movement. The downside break even point can be determined from Figure 9-5; the upside break even points, while off the graph, can be determined using a computer:

Spread	Downside	Upside
9-7	-4.6 std. dev.	+7 std.dev.
9-8	-3.7 std. dev.	+5 std. dev.

We can see that spread 9-7 is at less risk from a big move in the market. On the downside, a 4.6 std. dev. move is less likely than a 3.7 std. dev. move, and on the upside a 7 std. dev. move is less likely than a 5 std. dev. move. Based on the risk from market movement, we will want to choose spread 9-7.

Instead of going through the effort of graphing both spreads, we can again simplify the comparison process by dividing the theoretical edge by the risk factor, in this case gamma. Using this method we have:

Spread	Theoretical Edge / Gamma
9-7	8.75 / 30 = .29
9-8	9.15 / 47.4 = .19

In relative terms, spread 9-7 has a better risk versus reward ratio so that, with respect to gamma (curvature) risk, it is less risky than spread 9-8.

We now have a situation which we did not have before, risk considerations that are pulling in opposite directions. From a volatility standpoint spread 9-8 is less risky, while from a market movement standpoint spread 9-7 is less risky. Which spread should we choose?

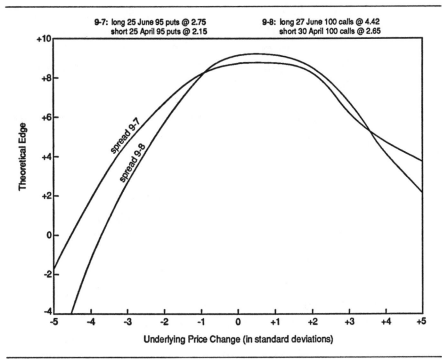

Figure 9-5

Here the situation is not clear-cut, and the answer will probably depend on the experience of the individual option trader. If the trader feels that a collapse in volatility is more likely than a large move in the underlying market, he will probably choose spread 9-8. If he feels that a large move in the underlying futures contract is more likely, he will probably choose spread 9-7. The science of options can only help point the trader in the right direction. There will always be a place for individual judgement in option trading which no amount of science can replace.

In our previous examples we were able to use an option's sensitivity factors (gamma, theta, vega) to carefully analyze a spread's risk characteristics. Sometimes, however, markets are moving so fast that one simply doesn't have time to sit down with a computer and carefully analyze each spread. If a trader were to do that, all the good trades might disappear by the time he was ready to make a decision. In such cases, a trader will have to rely on his instincts to find the best spread. While there is no substitute for experience, most traders eventually learn one important rule: *straddles and strangles are the riskiest of all spreads*. Speculators often like these strategies because they offer the possiblity of "hitting a home run." If volatility explodes or collapses, a trader who is on the right side of the volatility market can reap large profits with straddles and strangles. But an experienced trader knows that these strategies offer the least margin for error, and he will therefore try to avoid them.

How Much Margin for Error?

Beginning traders often ask what is a reasonable margin for error in assessing the inputs into a theoretical pricing model. A more logical approach is to ask what is the correct size in which to do a spread given a known margin for error. Practical trading considerations aside, a trader should always choose the spread with the best risk/reward characteristics. But even the best spread may have a very small margin for error, and consequently entail great risk. In such cases, the trader, if he insists on making a trade, will do so only in very small size. If, however, a trader can do a spread with a very large margin for error, then he will not hesitate to do the spread in much larger size.

Suppose, for example, a trader's best estimate about volatility in a certain market is 15%. Suppose implied volatility is higher than this number, and he starts to look for spreads with a negative vega. If the best negative vega spread he can find is a 1 × 2 ratio vertical spread with an implied volatility of 17% (only a 2-percentage point margin for error), he will almost certainly limit the size of the spread, perhaps executing the spread only 5 × 10. If, however, he can execute the same spread at an implied volatility of 25% (a 10-percentage point margin for error), and the market has never exhibited a volatility that high, he may have the confidence to do the spread in much larger size, perhaps 50 × 100. Margin for error and size are always counterbalancing considerations.

Net short contracts

Up to now we have attempted to analyze risk by analyzing the sensitivity factors (gamma, theta, vega) of a spread. Sometimes, however, it will be useful for a trader to consider the limited/unlimited risk charactersitics of a spread. We have tended to de-emphasize this approach in earlier chapters, choosing instead to place our emphasis on the total expected return. Sometimes, however, a market may act in a way which seems totally at odds with the theoretical pricing model. This occurs especially when a market makes a move of several standard deviations, a move which, according to the assumptions of a normal distribution, is virtually impossible. When this happens any spread which is net short contracts (short more contracts than long) can turn into a serious, perhaps fatal, situation.

Experienced traders who wish to take short premium (negative gamma) positions, but who are sensitive to the possibility of a larger than expected move in the market, often choose spreads based on their fears of such movement. A trader who is particularly worried about a large downward move will tend to avoid put ratio vertical spreads, with their unlimited downside risk. A trader who is especially concerned about a large upward move will tend to avoid call ratio vertical spreads, with their unlimited upside risk. The trader who is unwilling to accept the risk of a large move in either direction will tend to choose long butterflies, with the risk in either direction limited to the initial debit.

A trader who is willing to do a ratio vertical spread which is net short options may also want to give some thought to the size of the ratio. Some traders will not do any ratio spread where the ratio is greater than 2 to 1 (short 2 contracts for each long contract). They feel that any larger ratio is just too risky, regardless of the gamma and vega risk of the spreads. Experienced traders know that as the ratio of a spread approaches 1 to 1, it almost always becomes less risky.

The dangers of ratio vertical spreads were dramatically demonstrated in the wake of the October 1987 collapse in the stock market, and the accompanying drop in interest rates. Any trader who was net short puts in the stock index market, or net short calls in the debt market (treasury bonds, treasury notes, Eurodollars), was immediately devastated. Due to the accompanying explosion in implied volatility, even those with positions which were net short calls in the stock market, or net short puts in the debt market, were in danger of being forced out of business if they could not meet huge margin calls.

The painful experience of October 1987 led many option clearing firms to significantly tighten their risk control procedures, prohibiting traders from initiating any types of spreads with a large number of net short options. Even if a trader was able to meet margin requirements, as established by the option clearinghouses, clearing firms were simply unwilling to risk a re-enactment of the painful events of October 19th.

What is a Good Spread?

Option traders, being human, would rather recount their successes in the marketplace than their disasters. If one were to eavesdrop on conversations in a trading pit, one would sometimes think that no one ever made a losing trade. Disasters, when they do occur, only happen to other traders. The fact is that every successful option trader has had his share of disasters. What separates the successful trader from the unsuccessful one is the ability to survive disasters.

Consider the trader who initiates a spread with good theoretical edge and a large margin for error in almost every risk department. If something goes wrong and the trader loses money, this does not necessarily mean that the spread was a poor choice. Maybe a similar spread, but one with less margin for error, would have resulted in an even larger loss, perhaps a loss from which the trader could not recover.

It is impossible to take into consideration every possible risk; a spread which passed every risk test would probably have so little theoretical edge that it wouldn't be worth doing. But the trader who allows himself the greatest margin for error will find that even his losses will not lead to financial ruin. A good spread is not necessarily the one on which a trader makes the most money if things go well; it may be the one on which he loses the least when things go wrong. Winning trades always seem to take care of themselves. Losing trades, which don't give back all the profits from the winning trades, are just as important.

Offsetting Spreads

We noted previously that straddles and strangles are the riskiest of all strategies, and that experienced traders will usually try to avoid them. This doesn't mean a trader will not trade a straddle or a strangle. A market maker will often have to make a trade which he would rather not, just to maintain good relations with other traders or customers. Of course if the price of the straddle or strangle is greatly inflated or depressed, the risk may be worth accepting. But the trader will know that he has left himself little margin for error. Realizing this, he will often try to take protective measures.

Going back to Figure 9-1, suppose a trader has purchased 10 April 100 straddles at 7.05 each (long 10 calls at 2.65, long 10 puts at 4.40). The theoretical edge and sensitivity factors associated with this position are:

> total theoretical edge +7.10
> total delta -110
> total gamma +82
> total theta -.65
> total vega +3.00

While the position has significant theoretical edge, it is still risky because straddles have so little margin for error. How should the trader deal with the situation? The simple solution is to sell out the straddles for a profit, or, if the trader is really worried, scratch the trade by selling them out at the same price he purchased them, 7.05 each. But perhaps, as often seems to happen, there is no further interest in these options. Should the trader then simply hold the position and hope that the underlying futures market starts to move?

An experienced trader knows that "hope" is never the best strategy. Since his long straddles leave him with a large positive gamma, perhaps he can offest this with a negative gamma strategy. One possible offsetting strategy might be to sell strangles. Then, if the market sits still, his losses from the long straddles will be at least partially offset by the profits from his short strangles. Ideally, the trader will want to sell expensive, overvalued strangles so that he can add to his theoretical edge. Even if he must sell the strangles at exactly theoretical value, the strategy is still sensible. He won't be adding to his theoretical edge, but he will be reducing his risk. Reducing risk is always a worthwhile goal.

Unfortunately, in our example situation (Figure 9-1) the strangles, like the straddles, are also undervalued. If he sells the strangles he will be reducing his risk, but he will also be giving up some of the theoretical edge he gained when he purchased the straddles. If he gives up all the theoretical edge, his potential profit will disappear.

This is a situation that every floor trader is familiar with, and there is no right answer. Every trader has to decided how much risk he is willing to live with. In our example, the trader may decide that he can temporarily live with the risk, in which case he will sell no strangles; or he may decide to sell just a few strangles to partially offset the risk associated with his short straddles. If he is totally averse to risk, he may sell enough strangles to completely offset his risk, provided, of course that he doesn't give up all his theoretical edge.

Suppose the trader decides to sell 10 April 95/105 strangles at 3.40 each (sell 95 puts at 2.15, sell 105 calls at 1.25). The theoretical edge and sensitivity factors of this trade are:

> theoretical edge -3.90
> delta +80
> gamma -72
> theta +.58
> vega -2.64

This trade does give up some theoretical edge, but, at the same time, it has the very desirable effect of reducing each of the delta, gamma, theta, and vega risks associated with the long straddle position. Now the total theoretical edge and sensitivity factors of the 10 long straddles and 10 short strangles taken together are:

> theoretical edge +3.20
> delta -30
> gamma +10
> theta -.07
> vega +.36

The potential profit, as reflected in the theoretical edge, is now smaller, but as the sensitivity factors are also reduced, this potential profit becomes more secure. A trader who is risk averse might very well be satisfied with a smaller but more secure profit, rather than a larger but riskier profit.

This type of exercise is common to all active traders: get an edge, reduce risk; get an edge, reduce risk. If a trader can't immediately make a profit from a trade, he should at least try to reduce the risk associated with the trade by spreading off the risk. In the case of individual options, he reduces the risk by taking opposing positions in other options. In the case of spreads, he reduces the risk by taking opposing positions in other spreads.

Some spreads offer very good hedges against other spreads because they have almost identical offsetting risk characteristics. Straddles and strangles, for example, make good opposing positions because they both have gammas, thetas, and vegas which are similarly signed, as well as similar unlimited risk/reward characteristics. The particular strategy discussed above, where a straddle is offset with a strangle, is known as an *iron butterfly*. The reader will find that a long iron butterfly (long a straddle, short a strangle) has exactly the same characteristics as a short butterfly using the same exercise prices.

Another similar strategy is to offset a strangle position with a different strangle. For example, if a trader purchases an April 95/100 strangle (buy a 95 put, buy a 100 call), he might consider selling an April 90/105 strangle (sell a 90 put, sell a 105 call). The 90/105 strangle will partially offset each of the risks associated with the 95/100 strangle. If the new position has a positive theoretical edge, even though a reduced one, the strategy may be sensible because the profit is more secure.

While an iron butterfly has the same characteristics as a true butterfly, the foregoing position, where a long strangle is offset by a short strangle, has the same characteristics as a *condor*. A condor consists of options at four consecutive exercise prices where all options are of the same type. Either the outside exercise prices are purchased and the inside exercise prices are sold (long condor) or vice versa (short condor). Like a butterfly, a condor has limited risk and limited profit. At expiration it will have a value somewhere between zero and the amount between consecutive exercise prices, in our example 5 points.

Some spreads offer only a partial hedge against other spreads, reducing some risks, leaving some unchanged, and perhaps increasing other risks. A trader who has done call ratio vertical spreads has a negative gamma, positive theta, and negative vega position. If he sells a time spread, with its positive gamma and negative theta, he will partially offset his gamma and theta risk. But a short time spread also has a negative vega, which means that, when combined with a call ratio vertical spread, the vega risk will increase rather than decrease. Additionally, the trader will still have unlimited upside risk because he will be net short calls.

Ideally, a trader will want to look for spreads which exactly offset the risks of the spreads he already has. In a perfect world, he will be able to do both spreads for a positive theoretical edge. Or at least he will be able to do the offsetting spread at no worse than its theoretical value. In the real world however, he may have to do some spreads at worse than theoretical value. Whether this is worthwhile depends on how much theoretical edge remains, as well as the amount of protection the second spread offers. If the second spread completely eliminates his risk, it may be worth doing even if it only leaves a small theoretical edge. On the other hand, if the offsetting spread only slightly reduces his risk while greatly reducing his theoretical edge, it may not be worth doing at all. Moreover, the trader may have to consider which risk he is most worried about, and decide how much of his theoretical edge he is willing to give up to reduce that particular risk.

An active option trader's total position at any one time really consists of a collection of offsetting smaller positions. Every trade is made with the intention of either increasing theoretical edge or decreasing risk. Moreover, a trader can't worry about the prices at which a trade was initially made. He must concentrate on the here and now. What can he do to make the best of the current situation, either by protecting what he has, or by looking for new profit opportunities? A new trader will want to spend some time studying the characteristics of the most common volatility spreads, listed in Appendix D. By familiarizing himself with these characteristics, a trader, when he does a spread, will know immediately which types of risk he must be concerned with and, at the same time, which other spreads will best offset these risks.

How to Adjust

In the last chapter we looked at the question of when to adjust. But equally important when considering risk is the question of how to adjust. An adjustment to a trader's position may reduce his delta (directional) risk but if, in so doing, it also changes his gamma, theta, and vega risk he may simply be trading in one type of risk for another.

An adjustment made with the underlying futures contract is essentially a risk neutral adjustment. Of all our sensitivity factors, the only one associated with a futures contract is the delta. Futures have no gamma, theta, or vega. Therefore, if a trader wants to make a delta adjustment without changing any of the other risks associated with the spread, he can do so by adjusting with the underlying futures contract.

An adjustment made with options will reduce the delta risk, but will, at the same time change the gamma, theta, and vega risk of the position. Every option, in addition to having a delta, also has a gamma, theta, and vega. When an option is either added to or subtracted from a position, the gamma, theta, and vega, of the position change. New traders sometimes forget this.

Suppose that all options in a certain market are overvalued (high implied volatility), and that, with the underlying futures contract at 99.50, a trader has decided to sell April 95 / 105 strangles. If the delta of the April 95 put is -30 and the delta of the April 105 call is +30, the proper delta neutral ratio is 1 to 1. Suppose the trader sells this strangle 20 times.

Several days later the market has dropped to 97.50, with the new delta values of the 95 put and 105 call -35 and +25, respectively. The trader's delta position is now:

$$(-20 \times -35) + (-20 \times +25) \; = \; +200$$

If the trader wants to adjust, he has, essentially, three choices:

1. Sell futures.

2. Sell calls.

3. Buy puts.

Which method is best?

If possible, a trader will always try to reduce risk. Here he can do so by purchasing puts. Ideally, he would like to purchase undervalued puts in order to add to his theoretical edge. At worst he would like to pay no more than theoretical value, so that he would at least not be reducing his theoretical edge.

Unfortunately, in the real world implied volatility tends to fall slowly. If all options were originally overvalued, it is very probable that implied volatility is still high and that all options are still overvalued. A trader will not want to adjust by purchasing puts, since that will entail purchasing overpriced options. On the other hand, if all options are indeed overpriced, the trader can add to his theoretical edge by selling some overpriced calls. Suppose he sells eight more 105 calls. Now he is short 20 April 95 puts and short 28 April 105 calls, and is again delta neutral:

$$(-20 \times -35) + (-28 \times +25) = 0$$

Several more days pass and the market has rebounded to 101, with the deltas of the 95 put and 105 call now at -20 and +30, respectively. The trader's new delta position is:

$$(-20 \times -20) + (-28 \times 30) = -440$$

If the trader wants to adjust, he is again faced with the problem of how—buy futures, buy calls, or sell puts? If implied volatility is still high, and the trader is still only concerned with adding to his theoretical edge, then he might very well sell more puts. He might for example, sell 22 April 95 puts. Again, he is delta neutral:

$$(-42 \times -20) + (-28 \times +30) = 0$$

We can continue in this manner as long as we want, always having the trader make whatever adjustments are necessary by selling more overpriced calls or overpriced puts. This method of adjustment may indeed turn out to be best. However, notice what is happening. The spread, which the trader originally thought should be done 20 × 20, has increased in size to 42 × 28. If the market now makes a violent move in either direction, the negative consequences will be greatly magnified. Unfortunately, the new trader, overly concerned with always increasing his theoretical edge, often finds himself in just such a position. If the market does make a swift move, the trader is no longer in business.

No trader can afford to ignore the effect his adjustments will have on his total position. If he has a positive (negative) gamma position, buying (selling) any additional options will increase his gamma risk. The same is true for theta and vega risk.

A trader cannot continue to sell what he thinks are overpriced options and buy what he thinks are underpriced options *ad infinitum*. At some point the size of the position will simply become too large, and risk considerations will have to take a back seat to any additional theoretical edge. When that happens there are only two choices:

1. Decrease the size of the spread.

2. Adjust in the underlying futures market.

An intelligent trader knows that sometimes, because of risk considerations, the best course is to reduce the size of the position, even if it means giving up some theoretical edge. This is analogous to reducing the risk of a spread by looking for an offsetting spread, even if that offsetting spread gives back some theoretical edge. This may be hard on the trader's ego, especially if he must personally go back into the market and either buy back options he originally sold, or sell out options he originally bought. However, if a trader is not willing to swallow his pride from time to time, his trading carreer is certain to be short.

Some traders cannot stand the thought of giving up any theoretical edge. If an adjustment with options entails either giving up some theoretical edge or increasing the size of the spread, the only choice such a trader has is to go into the futures market and make his adjustments there. Futures have no gamma, theta, or vega, so the risks of the spread will remain essentially the same.

A new trader, who is unfamiliar with all the subtleties of an option market, should avoid making adjustments which will increase the size of a spread. If he decides not to decrease the size of the spread, then the only alternative is to go into the underlying futures market and make the adjustments there. This will at least leave the size of the spread essentially unchanged.

Style Considerations

An option trader who trades from a theoretcal pricing model should not make any prior assumption about the likelihood of the market moving in one direction rather than another. If price movement is random, as theoretical pricing models assume, there is no such thing as strength, weakness, support, resistance, or trends.

In practice, however, many option traders begin their trading careers in the underlying futures market where direction of movement is the overriding consideration. Many traders develop a style which calls for either trading with or against the general trend of the market. Such traders subscribe to either the "trend is your friend" philosophy, or "buy weakness, sell strength" philosophy. If a trader wants to continue this trading style, he will have to take this into consideration in choosing his option strategies.

Suppose a trader is doing ratio vertical spreads which are initially delta neutral. Such spreads have a negative gamma, so that, as the market moves up, the trader's position is becoming shorter (delta negative). If this trader likes to trade against the trend, he will find it very difficult to take an additional short position into strength. Doing so will increase the size of his delta position. By virtue of having chosen a ratio vertical spread, the trader is automatically trading against the trend. If the market moves in either direction, the trader always wants a retracement of this movement.

The opposite is true of a backspreader. He has a positive gamma position so that, as the market moves up, his delta position is getting longer. If he likes to trade with the trend, he will find it difficult to take any additional long position in the market because doing so will greatly increase his delta risk. The characteristics of the backspread mean that he is always trading with the trend. If he were also to make adjustments with the trend, it would be similar to increasing the size of the spread.

The trader with a negative gamma is always adjusting with the trend. The trader with a positive gamma is always adjusting against the trend. If a trader wants to adjust with or against the trend, he should choose spreads with an appropriate gamma. A trader with a negative gamma position is always trading against the trend, as long as he does not adjust. A trader with a positive gamma position is always trading with the trend, as long as he does not adjust. The highly disciplined theoretical trader will not have to worry about this, because for him there is no such thing as a trend. However for most traders, old habits, such as trading with or against the trend, die hard.

Market Liquidity

As long as a trader has an option position in his account it represents a risk. The risk may be limited to the current value of the options.

However, by leaving the position in his account, the trader is still risking that value. If a trader wants to eliminate the risk of a position, he must eliminate the position from his account. Sometimes this can be done through early exercise of an option. More often, however, a trader will have to trade out of a position in order to get rid or it.

An important consideration in deciding whether to enter into a trade is often the ease with which the trader can reverse the trade. Liquid options, for which there are many buyers or sellers, are much less risky than illiquid options, for which there may be no buyers or sellers. In the same way, a spread which consists only of liquid options is much less risky than a spread which consists of one or more illiquid options.

When a trader enters into a spread with an illiquid option he must often ask himself whether he is willing to live with the position until expiration. That may be the only time at which he will be able to get out of the position at anything resembling a fair price. If the option is long term, for example 9 months, the trader may be married to that option for better or worse, in sickness and in health, for the next 9 months. If he is unwilling to commit his capital for that period of time, perhaps he should avoid such positions. If he is willing to make the commitment, he should expect a greater theoretical edge for his long-term risk.

A new trader is often advised, and sensibly so, to begin trading in liquid markets. If he does make a losing trade, he will be able to keep the loss to a minimum because he will be able to reverse the trade with relative ease. An experienced trader, on the other hand, often prefers to trade in illiquid options. There is less activity in such markets, but the bid and ask spread is also much wider, resulting in a greater theoretical edge each time a trade is made. Of course any mistake will be a problem the trader may have to live with for a long time. However, an experienced trader is expected to keep his mistakes to a minimum.

The most liquid options in any market are those which are near term, and which are either at-the-money, or slightly out-of-money. Such options always have a narrow bid/ask spread, and there are usually traders willing to buy and sell large numbers of these options. As options become more and more in-the-money, or become longer term, the spread between the bid and ask widens, and the options become less and less liquid. While at-the-money short-term options are constantly traded, deeply in-the-money long-term options may not trade for weeks at a time.

Examples of the bid/ask spread in Deutschemark futures options on the Chicago Mercantile Exchange on February 19, 1988 are given in Figure 9-6. Note the wider bid/ask spread for September options versus March and June options, as well as the wider spread for in-the-money versus at-the-money and out-of-the-money options.

Option	MARCH OPTION (MARCH DEUTSCHEMARKS AT 58.65) Bid/Ask		JUNE OPTIONS (JUNE DEUTSCHEMARKS AT 59.15) Bid/Ask		SEPTEMBER OPTIONS (SEPTEMBER DEUTSCHEMARKS AT 59.68) Bid/Ask	
57 call	1.64	1.70	2.77	2.83	3.78	3.85
58 call	.83	.87	2.12	2.16	3.02	3.12
59 call	.25	.26	1.53	1.56	2.52	2.59
60 call	.06	.08	1.12	1.13	2.00	2.05
61 call ·	.02	.03	.77	.81	1.60	1.66
57 put	.04	.06	.65	.69	1.07	1.17
58 put	.14	.15	.97	.99	1.36	1.43
59 put	.56	.59	1.40	1.43	1.79	1.82
60 put	1.37	1.43	1.94	1.97	2.29	2.37
61 put	2.38	2.40	2.49	2.54	2.65	2.75

Figure 9-6

Bid/Ask Spread for Deutschemark Options February 19, 1988

10

Bull and Bear Spreads

While delta neutral strategies are perhaps the most popular among active option traders, a trader need not restrict himself to these strategies. Many successful option traders prefer to trade with a bullish or bearish perspective, rather than a neutral one. What separates these traders from outright long or short futures traders is their ability to integrate option pricing theory into their bull or bear strategies in order to also take advantage of theoretically mispriced options.

Since the delta is a theoretical measure of a position's bullishness or bearishness, we can begin by looking at methods of creating option positions which are either delta positive or negative.

Naked Positions

Since the purchase of calls or the sale of puts will create a delta long position, and the sale of calls or the purchase of puts will create a delta short position, we can take a bull or bear position simply by taking an appropriate naked position in either calls or puts. If all options are overvalued (high implied volatility), we can sell puts (a bull position), or sell calls (a bear position). If all options are undervalued (low implied volatility), we can buy calls (a bear position) or buy puts (a bear position).

The problem with this approach is that, as with all non-hedged positions, there is very little margin for error. If we buy options, we will lose not only if the market moves in wrong direction, but also if the market sits still; for then time decay will erode the value of our position. If we sell options, we leave ourselves open to the risk of un-limited loss if the market makes a swift move in the wrong direction. An experienced trader will always try to reduce his risk by looking for strategies with the greatest possible margin for error. This philosophy applies no less to bull and bear spreads than to delta neutral volatility spreads. For this reason, we will concentrate on bull and bear spreads, rather than on outright naked long or short positions.

Ratioing a Spread Bullish or Bearish

Suppose a trader believes that implied volatility is too high. If he prefers delta neutral strategies, he can look for spreads with a negative vega. For example, if a July 100 call has a delta of 50 and a July 110 call has a delta of 25, a neutral spreader can:

buy 1 July 100 call (50)

sell 2 July 110 calls (25)

This ratio vertical spread is initially delta neutral, and has no special preference for upward or downward movement in the market. Now suppose the same trader likes this particular ratio vertical spread, but is also bullish on the market. No law requires him to do this spread delta neutral. If he wants the spread to reflect his bullish sentiment, he can:

buy 2 July 100 calls (50)

sell 3 July 110 calls (25)

As long as the spread in the new ratio still has a positive theoretical edge, the trader has essentially the same ratio vertical spread, but with a bullish bias. This is reflected in the fact that the position is now 25 deltas long.

There is an important drawback to this type of strategy. Even though the trader is initially bullish, this spread is still essentially a ratio vertical spread. As such, it has a negative gamma. If the trader has mis-estimated volatility, and the market moves up too fast, the spread can invert from a positive to a negative delta. If all options go so deeply into-the-money that they start to act like futures contracts, the trader will eventually be naked short one extra futures contract, and his delta position will be -100. The trader correctly predicted market direction, but volatility was still the primary determinant of whether the spread was profitable or not.

The same type of delta inversion is also possible with a backspread. Unlike a negative gamma position, where the inversion can be caused by price movement which is more volatile than expected, the backspread can invert when price movement is less volatile than expected. For example, suppose a trader believes that implied volatility is too low, and that the spread in the last example is a good backspread. He can, if he is a delta neutral trader:

buy 2 July 110 calls (25)
sell 1 July 100 call (50)

If he is bullish on the market, he can, as in the last example, ratio the spread so that it reflects his bullish sentiment:

buy 3 July 110 calls (25)
sell 1 July 100 call (50)

Now he is 25 deltas long.

However, we know from Chapter 6 that as volatility declines, or as time passes, all delta values move away from 50. If three weeks pass with no movement in the underlying futures contract, the delta of the July 100 call will remain at 50, but the delta of the July 110 call may drop to 10. When that happens, the spread will no longer be 25 deltas long, but 20 deltas short. Since this spread is essentially a volatility spread, the overriding concern (as before) is the volatility of the market, and only secondarily its direction. If the trader overestimates volatility, such that the market moves only very slowly, the spread can invert its delta characteristics.

Bull and Bear Butterflies and Time Spreads

Butterflies and one-to-one (non-ratioed) time spreads can also be done to reflect a trader's bullish or bearish sentiment. Like ratioed volatility spreads, however, their delta characteristics can invert as market conditions change.

For example, with high implied volatility and the underlying futures contract at 100, a delta neutral trader might buy the 95/100/105 butterfly. He hopes that the market will sit right at 100 until expiration, and the butterfly will widen to its maximum of 5 points. If, however, a trader wants to buy a butterfly, but is also bullish on the market, he can choose a butterfly where the inside exercise price is above the current futures price, for example the 105/110/115 butterfly. This trader will want the underlying futures contract, which is now at 100, to rise to 110 by expiration. His preference for an upward move in the futures market will be reflected in the 105/110/115 butterfly having a positive delta.

Unfortunately, if the market moves up too far and too fast the delta position of this butterfly will invert. If the market goes to 120, the trader will want it to fall back to 110, since a long butterfly is always worth its maximum when the position expires with the underlying futures contract right at the inside exercise price. This will be reflected in the delta of the butterfly changing from positive to negative as the underlying futures contract moves upward and passes through the inside exercise price.

Conversely, a bearish trader can buy a butterfly where the inside exercise price is below the current futures price. With the futures contract at 100, the 85/90/95 butterfly will be delta negative, and therefore a bearish position. The trader who is long this butterfly will want the market to decline to 90 by expiration. If, however, the market falls to 80, the butterfly will become bullish because the trader will want the market to rise back to 90 by expiration. The butterfly, which was originally delta negative, will become delta positive as the futures contract moves downward and passes through the inside exercise price.

Similarly, time spreads can be chosen so that they are either bullish or bearish. A long time spread always wants the near term contract to expire right at-the-money. A time spreader can ensure that a spread is initially bullish by buying a spread where the exercise price of the time spread is above the current price of the underlying commodity.[1] With the market at 100, the July/May 110 call time spread will be bullish, since the trader will want the underlying market to rise to 110 by May expiration. The July/May 90 call time spread will be bearish, since the trader will want the underlying market to fall to 90 by May expiration. However, like a butterfly, a long time spread has a negative gamma and can invert its bull or bear characteristics. If the underlying market is at 100, the July/May 110 call time spread will be bullish. But if the market starts to rise, and passes through 110, the spread will then become bearish. The trader will want the market to fall back to 110. This will be reflected in the spread changing its delta from positive to negative as the market passes through 110.

Vertical Spreads

While any volatility spread can be done bullish or bearish, either by ratioing a spread to reflect that sentiment or by choosing appropriate exercise prices for a butterfly or time spread, in each of these spreads volatility is still the primary concern. The trader can be right about market direction, but if he is wrong about volatility, the spread may no longer have the bullish or bearish characteristics that the trader originally intended.

A true bull or bear spreader would like to find a a spread where market direction is the primary concern, and volatility only of secondary importance. Moreover, he would like to know that the spread, if it is initially bullish or bearish, will remain so no matter how market conditions change. He will want a spread which cannot invert, so that a bull spread will remain delta positive and a bear spread will remain delta negative under all possible market conditions.

The class of spreads which meet the above requirements are known as *vertical spreads*. A vertical spread always consists of one long (purchased) option and one short (sold) option, where both op-

---

[1]The situation may be complicated by the fact that different futures contracts on the same commodity can trade at different prices. When that happens, the trader may have to choose a diagonal spread to ensure that his delta position is positive.

tions are of the same type (either both calls or both puts) and expire at the same time. The options are distinguished only by their different exercise prices. Typical vertical spreads might be:

long 1 May 100 call
short 1 May 105 call
OR
long 1 July 105 put
short 1 July 95 put

Vertical spreads are not only initially either bullish (delta positive) or bearish (delta negative), but they always remain bullish or bearish no matter how market conditions change. Two options which expire at the same time and which have different exercise prices cannot have identical deltas. In the first example where the trader is long a May 100 call and short a May 105 call, the 100 call will always have a delta greater than the 105 call. If both options are either very deeply in-the-money, or very far out-of-the-money, the deltas may be almost identical. Even then, the 100 call will have a fractionally greater delta than the 105 call, resulting in a spread delta which is fractionally positive.

In the second example, the July 105 put will always have a negative delta greater than the July 95 put. Therefore, no matter how market conditions change, the spread will always be delta negative.

At expiration a vertical spread will always have a minimum value of zero if both options finish out-of-the-money, and a maximum value of the amount between exercise prices if both options finish in-the-money. If the market finishes anywhere below 100, a 100/105 call spread will be worthless because both options will be worthless. If the market finishes anywhere above 105, the same spread will be worth 5 points because the 100 call will be worth 5 points more than the 105 call. Similarly, a 95/105 put spread will be worthless if the market finishes above 105, and it will be worth 10 points if the market finishes anywhere below 95. The expiration value of of a bull and bear vertical spread is shown in Figure 10-1.

Since a vertical spread will be worth between zero and the amount between exercise prices at expiration, a trader should initially be willing to buy or sell a vertical spread for some amount within this range. A 100/105 call vertical spread should trade for an amount between zero and 5 points; a 95/105 put vertical spread should trade for an amount between zero and 10 points. The exact value of the spread, as generated by a theoretical pricing model, will depend on the expected return from the spread given a lognormal distribution of underlying futures prices.

A trader who does a vertical spread can be certain that his position will always reflect either a bullish or bearish market sentiment. If the trader is bullish, he can purchase the 100/105 call spread for some amount between zero and 5 points, say 2 points. If the market finishes above 105, the spread will widen to 5 points, and the trader will realize a 3 point profit. If the market finishes below 100, the spread will be worthless and the trader will lose his entire 2 point investment. The trader who is bearish on the market can sell the same spread, hoping to keep the total sale amount if the market falls below 100 by expiration.

It might seem that at some point the 100/105 call vertical spread is no longer delta positive, and therefore no longer bullish. For example, if the market rises to 150 both options will probably be so deeply in-the-money that they will be trading at parity (50 for the 100 call, 45 for the 105 call), and they will each have a delta of 100. The spread will have appreciated to its 5-point maximum, so there will be no purpose in the trader holding the position. He will want to sell the spread and take his 3-point profit now instead of waiting until expiration.

In theory this is true, but there is a practical problem here. We noted in the last chapter that deeply in-the-money options are relatively illiquid, which means that the bid/ask spread for such options will be wide. If the bid/ask for the individual options is wide, the bid/ask for the entire vertical spread will be even wider. The spread may in theory be worth 5 points, but the bid/ask may be 4.90/5.10. If the trader wants the full 3 point profit he will have to hold the position until expiration. At that time he will exercise his 100 call and be assigned on his 105 call, and he will be credited with the full 5-point value of the spread. However, if the trader must hold the position until expiration there is a chance, admittedly a remote one, that the underlying futures contract will fall below 105. If that happens the spread will lose some, if not all, of its 5-point value. The trader's presumed profit of 3 points might even turn into a loss of 2 points.

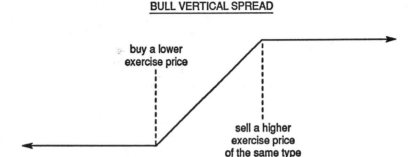

BULL VERTICAL SPREAD

buy a lower
exercise price

sell a higher
exercise price
of the same type

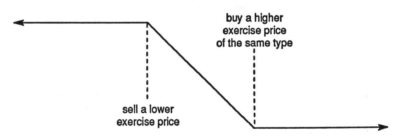

BEAR VERTICAL SPREAD

buy a higher
exercise price
of the same type

sell a lower
exercise price

Figure 10-1

If the trader is forced to hold the position until expiration, he would like to be as confident as possible that the spread will indeed be worth its maximum value of 5 points. His confidence level will be a function of how far above 105 the market is at any time prior to expiration. If the market is at 150, he will be more confident than if the market is at 125; if the market is at 175, he will be more confident than if the market is at 150. No matter where the market is, the trader will always want the market to go higher. The trader has, in theory, realized his 3 point profit. However, the higher the market goes, the more secure his profit becomes. This will be reflected in the delta of the spread being very slightly positive. The delta of the 100 call might be 99.999, and the delta of the 105 call might be 99.998. The .001 delta which the spread is long is indicative of the very slight possibility that the market could fall below 105.

A trader has basically four choices of vertical spreads. If he is bullish, he can choose either a bull call or a bull put vertical; if he is bearish, he can choose either a bear call or a bear put vertical. For example:

---

1. Bull Call Spread:	long a 100 call
	short a 105 call
2. Bull Put Spread:	long a 100 put
	short a 105 put
3. Bear Call Spread:	long a 105 call
	short a 100 call
4. Bear Put Spread:	long a 105 put
	short a 100 put

Notice that a trader who is bullish can buy a 100 call and sell a 105 call, or *buy a 100 put* and *sell a 105 put*. Call and put vertical spreads which expire at the same time, and which consist of long and short options at the same exercise prices, have identical delta values and are therefore identically bullish. The only real consideration when choosing between a call and a put vertical spread is market activity. If calls are being actively traded, a trader will, for reasons of liquidity, prefer the call spread. If puts are being actively traded, a trader will, for the same reasons, prefer the put spread.

Given the many different exercise prices and expiration months available, how can a trader choose the vertical spread which best reflects his expectations and which gives him the best chance to profit from those expectations?

A trader who thinks the market will rise must first determine his time horizon. If he sees upward movement, but perhaps not immediately, he will avoid near-term vertical spreads. If his expectations are very long-term, he may even have to go out several expirations to be certain that the upward movement will occur prior to expiration. Of course, as he moves further and further out, market liquidity will become more and more of a problem. He will have to counterbalance these two considerations.

Next, a trader will have to decide just how bullish or bearish he is, taking either a large or small delta position. Two factors will determine his total delta postion:

1. The delta of the specific vertical spread he has chosen.

2. The size in which he does the spread.

For example, a trader who wants to take a position which is 500 deltas long (equivalent to buying 5 futures contracts) can either choose to do a vertical spread which is 50 deltas long 10 times, or a different vertical spread which is 25 deltas long 20 times. Both positions will leave him with identical delta positions of +500.

The delta value of a vertical spread will be determined by the distance between exercise prices. The greater the distance, the greater the delta value. If all options expire at the same time, a 95/110 bull spread will be a more bullish than a 100/110 bull spread, which will, in turn, be more bullish than a 105/110 bull spread.

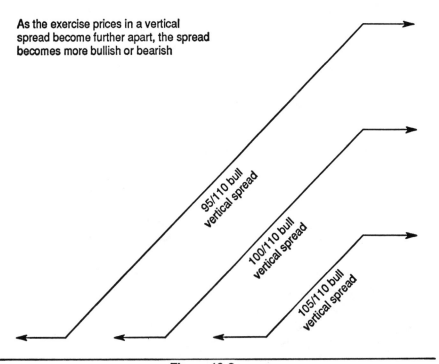

As the exercise prices in a vertical spread become further apart, the spread becomes more bullish or bearish

95/110 bull vertical spread

100/110 bull vertical spread

105/110 bull vertical spread

Figure 10-2

Once a trader decides on the expiration month in which to take a bull or bear position, and the size of the delta position he wishes to take, he must still choose specific exercise prices for his vertical spread. If he works around the at-the-money option, he will have the following choices:

Vertical Spreads
(working around the at-the-money option)

1. *Bull Call Spread*:	Buy an in-the-money call	*or*	Buy an at the-money call
	Sell an at-the-money call		Sell an out-of-the-money call
2. *Bear Call Spread:*	Buy an at-the-money call	*or*	Buy an out-of-the-money call
	Sell an in-the-money call		Sell an at-the money call
3. *Bull Put Spread:*	Buy an at-the-money put	*or*	Buy an out-of-the-money put
	Sell an in-the-money put		Sell an at-the-money put
4. *Bear Put Spread:*	Buy an in-the-money put	*or*	Buy an at-the-money put
	Sell an at-the-money put		Sell an out-of-the-money put

Figure 10-3

Since there are four different bull spreads and four different bear spreads, how can he choose the one which represents the best value? In Figure 10-4 a theoretical pricing model has been used to evaluate six different options—in-the-money, at-the-money, and out-of-the-money calls and puts. Any model requires us to make a judgement about volatility, and here we will assume that 20% represents our best estimate of volatility between now and expiration. From this table we can calculate the theoretical values and delta positions of four different vertical spreads:

Spread	Theoretical Value	Delta
95/100 call	2.87	20
100/105 call	1.88	20
95/100 put	2.04	20
100/105 put	3.03	20

Futures at 100.00;   Volatility = 20%;   Time = 12 weeks;   Interest = 8.00%

CALLS

Exercise Price	Theoretical Value	Delta	Gamma	Theta	Vega
95	6.63	71	3.4	-.017	.159
100	3.76	51	4.1	-.022	.188
105	1.88	31	3.7	-.020	.169

PUTS

Theoretical Value	Delta	Gamma	Theta	Vega
1.72	-27	3.4	-.019	.159
3.76	-47	4.1	-.022	.188
6.79	-67	3.7	-.019	.169

Volatility	95 call	95/100 spread	100 call	100/105 spread	105 call
16%	6.02	3.01	3.01	1.78	1.23
20%	6.63 (71)	2.87 (20)	3.76 (51)	1.88 (20)	1.88 (31)
24%	7.28	2.77	4.51	1.94	2.57

Volatility	95 put	95/100 spread	100 put	100/105 spread	105 put
16%	1.11	1.90	3.01	3.13	6.14
20%	1.72 (−27)	2.04 (20)	3.76 (−47)	3.03 (20)	6.79 (−67)
24%	2.37	2.14	4.51	2.97	7.48

Figure 10-5

Each of these spreads can be bought or sold, creating either a bull or bear position. Moreover, each spread has an identical delta value so that, in theory, each spread will have identical bull or bear characteristics. If a trader wants to take such a position, which spread represents the best means of doing so? The answer depends not only on the values of the spreads, but also on their prices in the marketplace.

The option trader's goal, whether he is a delta neutral volatility spreader, or a bull-bear spreader, is always to buy high value at a low price, or sell low value at a high price. Using our volatility estimate of 20%, we already know the values of these spreads. Now we need to know their prices. For an option trader, the relative prices of options in the marketplace is reflected in the implied volatility of the options. It is therefore logical to ask how the prices of these spreads would look at different implied volatilities. We can find out by using the theoretical pricing model to simulate the prices of the spreads at implied volatilities both lower and higher than our volatilty estimate of 20%. This is done in Figure 10-5, using volatilities of 16% and 24%.

Suppose we want to do a bull call spread. We have a choice of buying either the 95/100 or 100/105 call spread (buy the lower exercise price, sell the higher). If we assume a volatility of 20%, both spreads are identically long 20 deltas, with values of 2.87 and 1.88, respectively. However, if implied volatility is generally high, say

24%, the spreads may have prices of 2.77 and 1.94. In this case, the 95/100 call vertical represents a better value since we will be able to purchase a spread which is worth 2.87 for 2.77. If we purchase the 100/105 call vertical spread, we will have to pay 1.94 for a spread which is only worth 1.88.

On the other hand, if implied volatility is generally low, say 16%, the same spreads may have prices of 3.01 and 1.78. Now the 100/105 spread represents a better value since we will be able to purchase a spread which is worth 1.88 for 1.78. If we purchase the 95/100 call vertical spread, we will have to pay 3.01 for a spread which is only worth 2.87.

Since each spread is identically bullish with a delta of 20, whichever spread we buy, either the 95/100 or the 100/105, will leave us identically long. The question then is one of value, and the answer to the question rests on an important principle of option pricing discussed briefly in Chapter 6:

> When all options expire at the same time, an at-the-money option is always more sensitive, in total dollars, to a change in volatility than either an in-the-money or out-of-the-money option.

This simply means that when implied volatility is high, the at-the-money option will, in total dollars, be the most inflated.When implied volatility is low, the at-the-money option will, in total dollars, be the most depressed. The above principle leads to a simple rule for bull and bear vertical spreading:

> If implied volatility is high, bull and bear vertical spreads should focus on selling the at-the-money option. If implied volatility is low, bull and bear vertical spreads should focus on buying the at-the-money option.

Now we can see why the 95/100 call spread is a better value when implied volatility is 24%, and the 100/105 spread is a better value when implied volatility is 16%. If implied volatility is too high (24%) we want to sell the at-the-money option (the 100 call). Having done this, we only have one choice to complete the bull call spread: buy the 95 call. If implied volatility is too low (16%), we want to buy the at-the-money call (again, the 100 call). Having done this, we again only have one choice to complete the bull call spread: sell the 105 call.

The same principle of selling the at-the-money option when implied volatility is too high, and buying the at-the-money option when implied volatility is too low, is the determining factor in all vertical spreads, regardless of whether the spread is a bull or bear vertical, or whether it is a call or put vertical.

For example, suppose a trader wants to do a bull put spread when implied volatility is too high (24%). He must sell the at-the-money option (the 100 put). Now there is only one way to complete the bull put spread: purchase the out-of-the-money put (the 95 put). We can confirm this by looking at Figure 10-5. The spread is only worth 2.04, but if implied volatility is 24%, we will be able to sell it for 2.14.

Taking another example, suppose a trader wants to do a bear call spread when implied volatility is too low (16%). He must purchase the at-the-money option (the 100 call). Now there is only one way to complete the bear call spread: sell the in-the-money call (the 95 call). The trader is taking a position which is 20 deltas short by selling a spread which is only worth 2.87 for 3.01.

Of course, a trader is not required to execute any vertical spread by first buying or selling the at-the-money option. Such spreads always involve two options, and a trader can choose to either execute the whole spread in one transaction, or leg into the spread by trading one option at a time. In the latter case, he may decide to first trade an in-the-money or an out-of-the-money option. Regardless of how the spread is executed, the trader should always focus his attention on the at-the-money option; either buying it when implied volatility is low, or selling it when implied volatility is high.

A new trader who does not use a theoretical pricing model might take the view that it is always better to take a bull or bear position by either buying the least expensive spread or selling the most expensive. He can do a bull spread which is 20 deltas long by purchasing either the 95/100 call spread, or the 100/105 call spread. No matter what the implied volatility, the 100/105 spread will always be cheaper than the 95/100 spread, and a new trader might assume that this is the better spread. This overlooks the goal of option evaluation: to consider not only the initial cost of a strategy, but also the expected return from that strategy. A trader may have to lay out more for the 95/100 call spread, but if implied volatility is too high, that spread will also have a greater expected return. An option trader cannot look just at the price. He must always look at price versus value.

If both spreads are 20 deltas long, why *is* the 95/100 call spread always more expensive than the 100/105 call spread? Suppose we want to do a bull spread, and can buy either of these spreads for theoretical value, the 95/100 spread for 2.87 or the 100/105 spread for 1.88. Let's analyze both spreads on a simple win/lose basis.

If we are right and the market is above 105 at expiration, both spreads will be winners, since they will both widen to 5 points. If on the other hand we are wrong and the market is below 95 at expiration, both spreads will be losers, since they will both collapse to zero. Finally, suppose the market doesn't go up, but at least it also doesn't go down; it sits right at 100. The 100/105 spread will collapse to zero, resulting in a 1.88 point loss, while the 95/100 spread will widen to 5 points, resulting in a profit of 2.13 points. The trader who buys the 95/100 spread is paying for the luxury of having time on his side. If the market sits still, the 95/100 spread will be a winner, while the 100/105 spread will be a loser. This will be reflected in the 95/100 spread having a negative gamma and a positive theta, and the 100/105 spread having a positive gamma and a negative theta. (The reader may wish to confirm this by adding up the gammas and thetas of the various vertical spreads in Figure 10-5.)

Of course, if the market goes down, the 95/100 spread will also be the big loser, demonstrating that the direction of the market is still the most important factor in vertical spreads. If a trader finds that he is consistently wrong about the market direction, perhaps he should avoid bull and bear positions, and concentrate on delta neutral strategies.

Why might a bull or bear trader prefer a vertical spread to an outright long or short position in the underlying futures market? For one thing, vertical spreads are much less risky than outright futures positions. A trader who wants to take a position which is 500 deltas long, might either buy 5 futures contracts or buy 25 call vertical spreads with a delta of 20 each. The 25 vertical spreads may sound riskier than 5 futures contracts, until we remember that a vertical spread has limited risk, while the futures position has open-ended risk. Of course, greater risk also means greater reward, and there is no denying that the trader with an outright futures position can "hit a home run" if the market goes straight up. By contrast, the vertical spreader's profit is limited. But he will also be much less bloodied when the market makes an unexpected move in the opposite direction.

Experienced traders accept the fact that they are human, and that their directional forecasts are occasionally wrong. When that happens, the vertical spreader has a distinct advantage over the futures trader. By intelligently estimating volatility, an option trader can decide whether he wants time working for or against him. When he chooses to have time on his side, he can occasionally profit when the outright futures trader either breaks even or shows a small loss. And when he chooses to have time working against him, the option trader's losses, when he is wrong about market direction, will often be less than the losses from an outright futures position.

Buy and Sell Writes

There is one last position which has many of the characteristics of a bull vertical call spread, but isn't a true vertical spread. A *buy/write* involves buying a futures contract, and simultaneously selling a call (buy the futures contract, write the call). Like a vertical spread, this strategy is always done one-to-one (never ratioed). It tends to act like a bull vertical call spread, since it always has a positive delta. But unlike a vertical spread, a buy/write has unlimited downside risk; the call only offers partial protection against a drop in the underlying market.

Fund managers often hold portfolios which consist of long positions in securities, commodities, bonds, or similar optionable instruments. A common strategy in portfolio management is to sell calls against these instruments to protect the value of the holdings. The fact that a portfolio consists of long positions in these instruments means that the manager is bullish on the underlying markets. If, however, the market declines, the sale of the calls will at least partially offset the portfolio's loss in value. This strategy is essentially the same as a buy/write, but when the calls are sold against an existing long underlying position, the strategy is known as a *covered write*, or *overwrite*.

The amount of protection the portfolio manager is seeking, as well as the potential upside appreciation, will determine which calls are sold, whether in-the-money, at-the-money, or out-of-the-money. Selling in-the-money calls offers a high degree of protection, but will limit the potential upside profit. Selling out-of-the-money calls offers less protection, but will leave room for large upside profit potential. In fact most covered writes involve at-the-money calls, because these are the options with the greatest amount of extrinsic value (time premium). Such calls offer less downside protection than in-the-money calls, and less upside profit potential than out-of-the-money calls. But if the market sits still, the portfolio which consists of at-the-money covered/writes will show the greatest return. (See Figure 10-6.)

The covered write can be used by any market participant to hedge an essentially long position in the underlying market. Commodity producers, such as farmers or metal mining companies, can gain some protection agaist a drop in commodity prices by writing calls against their future production. In a similar manner, a party to a trade

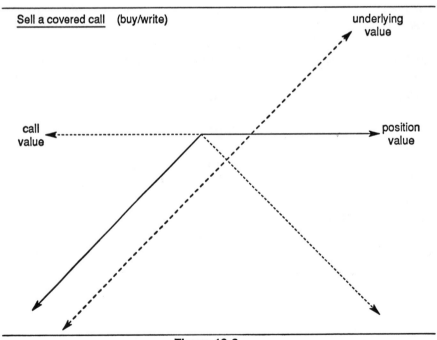

Figure 10-6

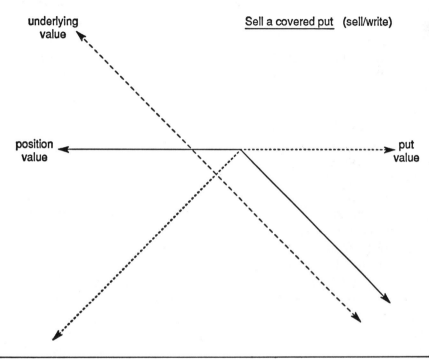

Figure 10-7

agreement who must make a future payment in a foreign currency begins with a long position in his domestic currency. He hopes the value of the domestic currency will rise so that, at the time of payment, he can purchase the needed foreign currency at a lower domestic currency cost. To partially offset the risk that the domestic currency will fall, he can sell calls against the domestic currency. Of course any covered write also limits the upside profit potential, and the covered writer will have to decide whether giving up this potential profit is worth the partial protection offered by the covered write.

While it is less common for a portfolio manager to have a short position in optionable instruments, such a position can be protected in exactly the same way as a long position. Instead of writing calls against a long position, the portfolio manager can write puts against his short position. This is similar to a covered write, but here the position to be protected is a short one. This is also a practical strategy for an end user of a commodity, such as a baking company needing grain, or a jewelry manufacturer needing gold and silver. These users want commodity prices to fall, so they begin with an essentially short position in the underlying commodity. If prices do rise, the sale of puts will partially offset the losses due to an increase in the cost of the needed commodities. For want of a better term, we will refer to the sale of puts against a short underlying position as a *sell/write*. (Figure 10-7.)

We noted above that a party to a trade agreement who must make payment in a foreign currency essentially has a long position in his domestic currency.This is identical to having a short position in the foreign currency: if the domestic currency is rising, the foreign currency is falling. If puts are available which are denominated in foreign currency units, a sell/write involving the sale of foreign currency puts will offer some protection against a possible rise in the value of the foreign currency.

For example, suppose an American firm expects to take delivery of DM 1,000,000 worth of German goods in six months. If the contract calls for payment in Deutschemarks at the time of delivery, the American firm has a short position in Deutschemarks. If the Deutschemark is currently trading at .6000 (60¢ per DM) and remains there for the next six months, the cost to the American firm will be $600,000. If, however, the value of the Deutschemark at delivery has risen to .7000 (70¢ per DM), and the firm has not hedged its position, the total cost will be $700,000. This risk of a rise in the value of the Deutschemark can be partially offset through the sale of Deutschemark puts. If the American firm wants a high degree of protection, with limited opportunity to profit from a fall in the Deutschemark, it can sell in-the-money puts with an exercise price higher than .60. If it wants only a low degree of protection, but with a correspondingly high profit potential, it can sell out-of-the-money puts with an exercise price lower than .60. If it wants an equal balance between protection and profit potential, it can sell at-the-money puts.

The sale of calls or puts is not the only way to hedge a position in a commodity. One can also buy puts to protect a long position, or buy calls to protect a short position. In theory, the choice of whether to buy or sell options will depend on the relative prices in the marketplace. If options are cheap, it makes sense to protect a long position by purchasing puts, or to protect a short position by pur-

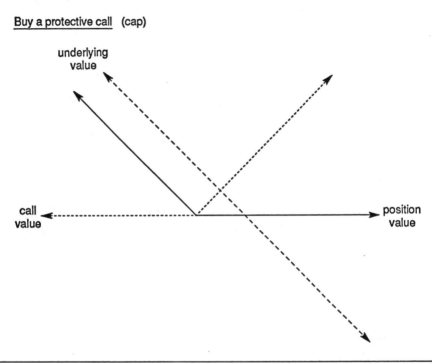

Buy a protective call (cap)

Figure 10-8

chasing calls. If options are expensive, it makes sense to sell calls against a long position, or sell puts against a short position. This may require a detailed volatility analysis which is, understandably, beyond the capabilities of most firms. In practice, the choice may come down to a question of risk versus reward. If a company needs to limit its risk to some known number, or wants unlimited profit potential, it can buy options to protect its position. If it is willing to accept limited protection, as well as limited profit potential, in order to profit from an option's time decay, it can sell options against its position.

The purchase of calls or puts to protect either a short or long market position is especially common in the interest rate market. A firm which borrows money based on a variable interest rate has a short interest rate position; a fall in interest rates will reduce its cost of borrowing. To *cap* the upside risk, the firm can purchase an interest rate call, thereby establishing a maximum amount it will have to

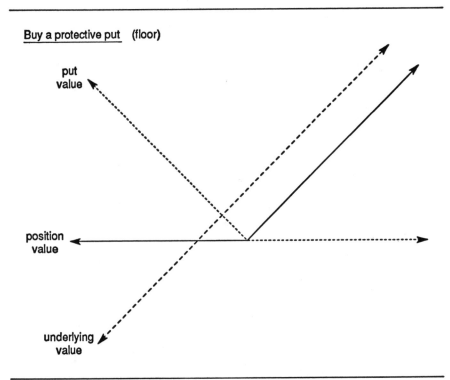

Figure 10-9

pay for borrowed funds, no matter how much interest rates rise (Figure 10-8). A lender at a variable interest rate has a long interest rate position; a rise in interest rates will increase the return on the loaned funds. To set a *floor* on its downside risk it can buy a put, thereby establishing a minimum amount it will receive on the loaned funds, no matter how much interest rates decline (Figure 10-9).

The purchase of options to hedge a position in the underlying commodity will result in a position with positive gamma (curvature). This means that as the market moves adversely, the purchased options are offering a better and better hedge; as the market moves favorably, the purchased options are eating up less and less of the profits. The opposite is true when options are sold to protect a position. A negative gamma position offers less and less protection when the market moves adversely, and eats up more of the profits when the market makes a favorable move.

It is also possible to combine these two strategies, by simultaneously selling a call and buying a put to protect an existing long position, or by selling a put and buying a call to protect an existing short postition. This strategy limits both the amount of appreciation from a favorable market move, and the amount of risk from an unfavorable move. Such a position is known by many names, most commonly as a *fence*, a *cylinder*, or a *range forward* postion. When used specifically to hedge an interest rate position, it is usually referred to as a *collar*.

The value of a bull fence and bear fence at expiration is shown in Figures 10-10 and 10-11. The resulting position appears to be identical to a bull and bear vertical spread. The positions are indeed equivalent; we shall see why in the next chapter when we look at synthetic positions.

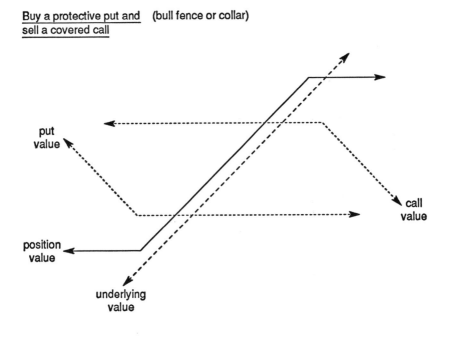

Figure 10-10

Hedging and portfolio management is a complex subject, and we have touched on only the most elementary strategies. Options offer an almost infinite variety of ways to structure the risk/reward characteristics of any postion. In this respect, a good advisior who is fully familiar with options and futures markets can be invaluable in helping a hedger understand his risk, and in explaining how to best control it.

Buy a protective call and   (bear fence or collar)
sell a covered put

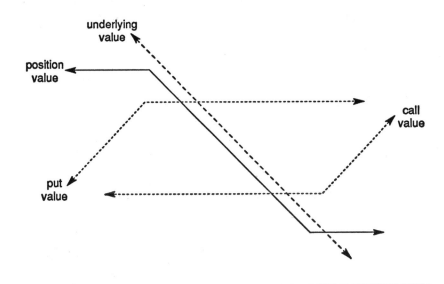

Figure 10-11

11

Arbitrage Strategies

Synthetic Positions

Suppose we have the following position where all options are European (no early exercise permitted):

long a July 100 call
short a July 100 put

What will happen to this position at expiration? If July futures are above 100, whoever owns the July 100 put will let it expire worthless, while we will exercise our July 100 call. This enables us to buy a July futures contract at 100. Conversely, if July futures are below 100, we will let our July 100 call expire worthless, but we will be assigned on the July 100 put. This will force us to buy a July futures contract at 100.

Ignoring for the moment the unique situation when July futures are right at 100, at expiration the above position will always result in our buying a July futures contract at 100. We will do it either by choice (July futures are above 100 and we exercise our call) or by force (July futures are below 100 and we are assigned on the put). The position is a *synthetic long future*. The primary difference between a synthetic and an actual long futures position is that the synthetic position will not become a long futures position until expiration.

259

If we take the opposite position, by selling the July 100 call and buying the July 100 put, we will have a *synthetic short future*. This position will always result in our selling a July futures contract at expiration, either by choice (the market is below 100 and we exercise our put) or by force (the market is above 100 and we are assigned on the call).

We can express these synthetic futures with the following simple equations:

synthetic long futures contract = long call + short put
synthetic short futures contract = short call + long put

where all options expire at the same time and have the same exercise price.

Synthetic positions act very much like their real equivalents. For each point the underlying futures contract rises, a synthetic long futures position will gain approximately one point in theoretical value, and a synthetic short futures position will lose approximately one point. This leads us to conclude, correctly, that the delta of a synthetic long futures contract is approximately 100, and the delta of a synthetic short futures contract is approximately -100. If the delta of the July 100 call is 75, the delta of the July 100 put will be approximately -25. If the delta of the July 100 put is -60, the delta of the July 100 call will be approximately 40. Ignoring positive or negative signs, the deltas of puts and calls with the same expiration date and exercise price add up to approximately 100. As we will see, interest considerations may cause the delta of a synthetic futures position to be slightly less than 100. Even then, the total delta is unlikely to be less than 98 or 99.

Rearranging the equations for synthetic futures, we can derive four other synthetic equivalents:

synthetic long call = long futures contract + long put
synthetic short call = short futures contract + short put
synthetic long put = short futures contract + long call
synthetic short put = long futures contract + short call

Again, all options must expire at the same time and have the same exercise price. Each of these synthetic positions has a delta approximately equal to its real equivalent, and will gain or lose value at approximately the same rate as the real equivalent.

Using a July futures contract and a July 100 call and put, we can write six synthetic positions:

---

synthetic long July future = long July 100 call + short July 100 put
synthetic short July future = short July 100 call + long July 100 put
synthetic long July 100 call = long July future + long July 100 put
synthetic short July 100 call = short July future + short July 100 put
synthetic long July 100 put = short July future + long July 100 call
synthetic short July 100 put = long July future + short July 100 call

---

We do not have to express the synthetic positions in terms of the 100 exercise price. We can choose any available exercise price. For example, long a July 110 call and short a July 110 put is still a synthetic long July futures contract. Here, however, at July expiration the July futures contract will be bought at 110. Short a July 95 call and long a July 95 put is still a synthetic short July futures contract, but at expiration the July futures contract will be sold at 95.

Suppose July futures are trading at 102.00 and we want to take a long position in this contract. We can simply go into the futures market and buy a July contract at 102.00. But we now have another choice. We can buy a synthetic futures contract by purchasing a July call and selling a July put at the same exercise price. Which of these strategies is best? As with any option strategy, the decision depends on the prices of the options in the marketplace. Suppose, for example, the July 100 call is trading at 5.00 and the July 100 put is trading at 3.00. If we take a synthetic long position by purchasing the call and selling the put, we will show an immediate debit of 2 points. Suppose July futures finish at 110. We will show a credit of 10 points at expiration by exercising our July 100 call, for a total gain of 8 points. If we ignore for the moment interest considerations, this is identical to the 8-point profit we would have realized had we bought a July futures contract at 102. (See Figure 11-1.)

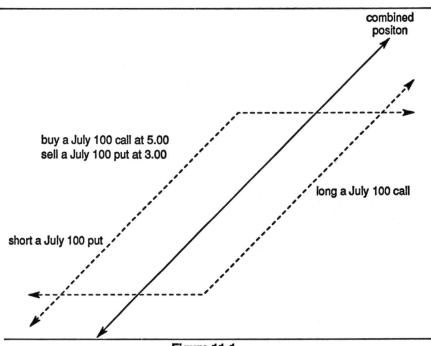

buy a July 100 call at 5.00
sell a July 100 put at 3.00

combined
positon

long a July 100 call

short a July 100 put

Figure 11-1

Suppose that July futures are still trading at 102.00, but now the July 100 call is trading at 4.98 and the July 100 put is trading at 3.02. If we take a synthetic long futures position by purchasing the 100 call at 4.98 and selling the 100 put at 3.02, we will show a debit of 1.96. Now if the futures contract finishes at 110 at expiration, we will show a total profit of 8.04 (1.96 debit from the option trade, plus a 10-point credit when we exercise our 100 call). This is .04 better than we would do by taking a long position in the actual July futures contract at 102.00.

If the price of the July 100 call is exactly 2 points more than the price of the July 100 put, the profit or loss from the synthetic long futures position will be identical to the profit or loss from the purchase of the July futures contract at 102.00. We refer to the difference between the call and put price as the *synthetic market*. In the absence of any interest considerations, the value of the synthetic market with respect to its real equivalent can be expressed as:

call price - put price = futures price - exercise price

If this equality holds, there is no difference between taking a long or short position in the actual futures contract, or taking the same position synthetically in the option market. With the July 100 call at 5.00 and the July 100 put at 3.00, we can write:

$$5.00 - 3.00 = 102.00 - 100.00$$
$$2.00 = 2.00$$

There is no difference between the synthetic and its real equivalent. However, with the 100 call at 4.98 and the 100 put at 3.02 we have:

$$4.98 - 3.02 \neq 102.00 - 100.00$$
$$1.96 \neq 2.00$$

Here the synthetic side is cheaper and is therefore a better method of taking a long position in the July futures contract.

If we raise the price of the 100 call to 5.02, drop the price of the 100 put to 2.98, and the July futures contract is still at 102.00, we have:

$$5.02 - 2.98 \neq 102.00 - 100.00$$
$$2.04 \neq 2.00$$

Now the real side is cheaper, so we will prefer to take our long position by purchasing the July futures contract. If we are bearish, we will prefer to sell the futures contract synthetically. By doing so, we will be able to sell a synthetic futures contract, which is only worth 2.00 points, for 2.04.

The reader may have noted that the synthetic and real markets will be the same price when the extrinsic value of the call and the extrinsic value of the put are identical. In our example, the synthetic and real futures markets are identical when the call and put both have 3 points of extrinsic value. If both options do not have identical extrinsic value, there is always a synthetic position which is either too expensive or too cheap.

Conversions and Reversals

If we take a synthetic long or short position, our primary concern, as with an actual long or short position, is market direction. If the market moves favorably, we expect to profit; if the market moves adversely, we expect to lose. If we do the synthetic at favorable prices, we may gain more or lose less, but it is still market direction in which we are interested.

Suppose, as before, with the July futures contract trading at 102.00, the July 100 call is trading at 5.02 and the July 100 put is trading at 1.98. The synthetic market should be 2.00 (futures price minus exercise price), but is actually 2.04. Without taking a directional position, is there any way we can profit from the fact that the synthetic futures contract and the real futures contract are trading at different prices?

Suppose we sell the synthetic (sell a 100 call at 5.02, buy a 100 put at 1.98) and buy the real futures contract at 102.00. We will immediately take in 2.04 on the option trades, and at expiration we will take in another 100.00 when we sell a futures contract at 100, either by exercising our put or being assigned on the call. The total credit resulting from the synthetic portion of the trade will be 102.04. From this we will have to subtract the debit of 102.00 when we purchase the July futures contract. But this will still leave us with a profit of .04, exactly the amount by which the synthetic futures contract was mispriced. Moreover, in the absence of any interest considerations, the position will always do .04 better than its real equivalent, no matter what the price of the futures contract at expiration. The profit of .04 is certain. (See Figure 11-2.)

This type of trade, where a synthetic short position is offset by an actual long position in the underlying market, is known as a *conversion*. The opposite position, where the synthetic is purchased and the actual futures contract is sold, is a *reverse conversion* or, more commonly, a *reversal*. The latter situation would be profitable if the futures contract were trading at 102.00, the 100 call at 4.98, and the 100 put at 3.02. Here, the synthetic is .04 underpriced. By purchasing the synthetic at 1.96 (buy a call at 4.98, sell a put at 3.02) and selling the futures contract at 2.00 (sell the future at 102.00 less the exercise price of 100.00), the reverse conversion would lock in a .04 profit in the same way that the conversion locked in a .04 profit when the synthetic was .04 too expensive.

Conversion =

synthetic short future + long future =
short call + long put + long future

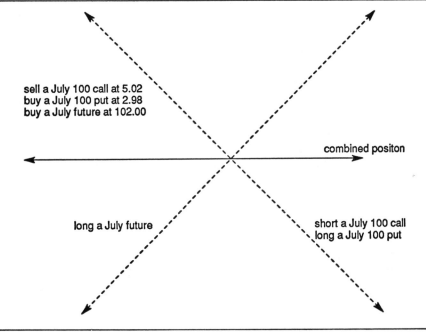

sell a July 100 call at 5.02
buy a July 100 put at 2.98
buy a July future at 102.00

combined positon

long a July future

short a July 100 call
long a July 100 put

Figure 11-2

Reversal =

synthetic long future + short future =

long call + short put + short future

As before both the call and put must have the same exercise price and expiration date.

Conversions and reversals are classified as arbitrage strategies because of their similarity to classical arbitrage. Typically, an arbitrageur will attempt to simultaneously buy and sell the same commodity in different markets for a very small profit. He might, for example, buy gold in New York for $450 per ounce and sell it in London for $453. The profit margin of $3, while small, is also very secure since the risk in one market is almost immediately offset in another market. Unlike the speculator, who tries to make a large profit on a small number of trades, an arbitrageur tries to make a small profit on many trades. He is willing to do much greater size than the speculator because his risk is much smaller.

Like classical arbitrages, conversions and reversals involve buying and selling the same thing in different markets. A conversion involves buying a futures contract in the futures market, and selling the same futures contract, synthetically, in the option market. A reversal involves selling a futures contract in the futures market, and buying the same futures contract, synthetically, in the option market. Whether these strategies are profitable depends on the difference between the synthetic futures price and the actual futures price.

Since the value of a conversion or a reversal is determined by the value of a synthetic position with respect to its real underlying, the synthetic market is sometimes refered to as the *conversion/reversal market*.

All experienced option traders are familiar with synthetic relationships, so that any temporary imbalance in the conversion/reversal market will be short-lived. If the synthetic is overpriced, all traders will try to sell a call, buy a put, and buy a futures contract (conversion). If the synthetic is underpriced, all traders will try to buy a call, sell a put, and sell a futures contract (reversal). This activity, where everyone is attempting to do the same thing, will quickly force the conversion/reversal market back to equilibrium. Indeed, imbalances in the conversion/reversal market are usually very small, and rarely exist for more than a few seconds. But when they do exist, an option arbitrageur will try to do them in very large size because of the low risk associated with such strategies.

Interest Considerations

In markets where there are no interest considerations, the synthetic relationship is defined simply as:

call price - put price = futures price - exercise price

This simple equation is valid if interest rates are zero, or in futures markets where the options are settled like futures contracts rather than like stock contracts. In the latter case, there is no interest component to a theoretical pricing model since no cash changes hands when options are traded.

In markets where options on futures are settled in cash, money will change hands when an option trade is made, and the carrying cost on this debit or credit must be taken into consideration.

Using the earlier example, with the July futures contract at 102, the July 100 call at 5.00, and the July 100 put at 3.00, we have:

call price - put price = futures price - exercise price
5.00 - 3.00 = 102.00 - 100.00
2 = 2

At these prices there does not appear to be any profit opportunity from either a conversion or a reversal. If we do a reversal by purchasing the synthetic for 2 points and selling the actual futures contract for 2 points more than the exercise price, the credit and debit will exactly offset each other at expiration.

Suppose, however, that the options are settled in cash, as is generally true on futures markets in the United States. We will have to lay out 2.00 points on the option trade, and we will not get this 2 points back until expiration. If interest rates are 8% per annum and expiration is 3 months away, there will be a 2% carrying cost on the debit. We expected to break even on the reversal, but in fact we will end up losing $2\% \times 2.00$, or .04, because of the cost of carrying our 2-point debit to expiration. If we really want to break even, we will have to find some way to offset this .04 interest loss. We can do this by purchasing the call for .04 less (4.96), by selling the put for .04 more (3.04), or by selling the future for .04 more (102.04). We can also use a combination of these three methods, for example by purchasing the call at 4.98, selling the put at 3.01, and selling the future at 102.01.

In futures markets where options are settled in cash, we can express the synthetic market as:

call price - put price = futures price - exercise price - carrying costs

where the carrying cost is calculated on the difference between the futures price and the exercise price.

Using this synthetic relationship, we can always express the value of one contract in terms of the other two:

---

call price = futures price - exercise price + put price - carrying costs
put price = exercise price - futures price + call price + carrying costs
futures price = call price - put price + exercise price + carrying costs

---

For example, with the July futures contract at 102.00 and the July 100 put at 2.75, we have:

call price = 102.00 - 100.00 + 2.75 - .04 = 4.71

With the July 100 call at 5.35 and the July futures contract at 101.90, we have:

put price = 100.00 - 101.90 + 5.35 + .04 = 3.49

With the July 100 call at 3.25 and the July 100 put at 1.25, we have:

futures price = 3.25 - 1.25 + 100.00 + .04 = 102.04

While synthetic relationships are most likely to be of interest to option traders, these relationships can also be be useful to futures traders. For example, suppose a futures market is locked limit up at 102.00, but the options are still trading. Ignoring carrying costs, the call price less the put price must be equal to the futures price less the exercise price. If the 102 call is trading at 4.00 and a 102 put is trading at 1.00, the trader knows that the futures contract, if it were still trading, would be approximately 103.00 (exercise price of 100, plus the three point difference between the call and put). This can be useful to a trader because it enables him to determine the price at which the large arbitrage houses are still trading the underlying commodity in the cash market.

A trader who does not wish to participate in option markets would still be well advised to learn the synthetic relationships. It will occassionally enable him to take a long or short futures position, synthetically, at a better price than would otherwise be possible in the futures market. In those futures markets which have limits, he may find that when the market is locked, options may be the only route by which he can protect himself against further losses, or maximize the profits he does have.

Conversion/Reversal Risk

New option traders are often told to go into the market and do only conversions and reversals because these strategies are riskless. Beware: *There are no riskless strategies*. There are only strategies with higher risk and strategies with lower risk. The risks in the conversion/reversal market may not be immediately apparent, but they exist nonetheless.

Interest Rate Risk

Where options are settled in cash, part of the value of the conversion or reversal depends on the carrying costs to expiration on the credit or debit balance. This is a function of interest rates, and since interest rates are not necessarily constant, this carrying cost can change. If part of the profit we expect from a trade depends on our getting 7% on credit balances, a reduction in interest rates to 6% will certainly reduce our profit, and might even result in a loss. If part of the profit depends on paying 8% on a debit balance, a rise in interest rates to 9% will likewise cut into our profit. In practice, large changes in interest rates over the limited lifetime of an option are the exception rather than the rule. For this reason, the interest rate risk associated with conversions and reversals is relatively small.

Execution Risk

Since no market participant wants to give away money, a trader is unlikely to be offered a profitable conversion or reversal all at one time. Consequently, he will have to execute one or two legs of the strategy, and hope to complete the final leg(s) at a later time. He may, for example, simultaneously buy futures and buy puts, and hope to later complete the conversion by selling calls. However, if call prices begin to fall, he may never be able to profitably complete the conversion. Even a floor trader, who would seem to be in a good position to know the prices of all three contracts, can be fooled. He may buy a call and sell a put (synthetic long future) at what he thinks are good prices. However, when he turns around to sell the futures contract, he may find that the price of the future is much lower than what he thought it was. Anytime a spread has to be executed a leg at a time, there is always an execution risk.

Pin Risk

In our earlier discussion of synthetic positions we made the assumption that at expiration the futures market would either be above the exercise price and all calls would be exercised, or below the exercise price and all puts would be exercised. We must also deal with the rare, but not impossible, situation where the futures contract is right at, or *pinned* to, the exercise price at expiration.

Suppose a trader has done a July 100 conversion: he is short a July 100 call, long a July 100 put, and long a July futures contract. If the market is above or below 100 at July expiration there is no problem. He will either be assigned on his short call, or exercise his put. Either procedure will offset his long futures position so that he will have no position on the day following expiration.

Now suppose the market finishes right at 100. The trader would like to be rid of his futures position, but he doesn't know whether to exercise his put, because he doesn't know whether he will be assigned on the call. If he is assigned, he will want to let the put expire; if he isn't assigned, he will want to exercise the put. What should he do?

He might try to guess whether he will be assigned. If the market seems to be strong on the last trading day, he might assume that he will be assigned on the call, in which case he will choose not to exercise his put. Unfortunately, if he is wrong and does not get an assignment notice, he will find himself with a long futures position which he would rather not have. Conversely, if the market seems weak on the last trading day, the trader might assume that he will not be assigned on the call, in which case he will choose to exercise his put. But, again, if he is wrong and does get an assignment notice, he will find himself with a short futures position on the day following expiration.

The risk of a wrong guess can be further compounded by the fact that conversions and reversals, because of their low risk, are usually done in large size. If the trader guesses wrong, he may find himself naked long or short not one but several hundred futures contracts.

There can be no sure solution to the problem of pin risk. With thousands of open contracts outstanding, some calls will be exercised and some won't. The trader is at the mercy of the fates, and that is a position which option traders prefer to avoid. The practical solution to the problem is to avoid carrying conversions or reversals to expiration when there is a clear danger of expiration right at the exercise price. If a trader has a large number of July 100 conversions or reversals, and expiration is approaching with the futures market close to

100, the sensible course is to reduce the pin risk by reducing the size of the position. If he doesn't reduce his size, he may find that he is under considerable pressure to get out of a large number of risky positions at the last moment.

Sometimes even a careful trader will find that he still has some at-the-money conversions or reversals as expiration approaches. One solution is to simply trade out of the positions at whatever price the market dictates. Unfortunately, this is likely to be a losing proposition because the trader will be forced to buy at the offer and sell at the bid. Fortunately, it is often possible to trade out of such positions all at once at a fair price.

Since conversions and reversals are common strategies in any option market, a trader who has at-the-money conversions and is worried about pin risk can be fairly certain that there are also traders in the market with at-the-money reversals who are also worried about pin risk. If the trader can find one of these other traders, and cross positions with him, everyone will avoid the risk of expiration right at the exercise price. This is why, as expiration approaches, one often hears traders asking if anyone wants to trade conversions or reversals at even money. This simply means that a trader wants to trade out of his position at a fair value so that he can avoid any pin risk. Whatever profit a trader expects from the conversion or reversal resulted from the initial trade, not from the closing trade.

Some futures contracts, such as Eurodollars and stock indices, are settled at expiration in cash rather than with the delivery of the physical commodity. When options on such contracts expire on the same day as the futures contract, the options, at expiration, are also settled in cash. The amount of cash which flows into a trader's account, if he is long an in-the-money option, or out of his account, if he is short an in-the-money option, is simply the difference between the exercise price and the settlement price of the futures contract on the last trading day. When options and futures settle in this manner, there is no pin risk because no futures position results from exercise or assignment.

Futures Risk

Returning now to our earlier example where there are 3 months to July expiration with interest rates at 8% per annum, if the underlying futures contract is at 102.00, the value of the July 100 synthetic market is as follows:

July 100 call - July 100 put =
102 - 100 - (carry on 2 points for 3 months) = 1.96

Suppose a trader is able to sell a July 100 call for 5.00, buy a July 100 put for 3.00, and buy a July futures contract for 102.00. He has done the July 100 conversion by selling a synthetic futures contract at 2.00. Since the synthetic is only worth 1.96, he has, in theory, made a profit of .04. Apparently, if interest rates do not fall, and assuming there will be no problem with pin risk, the trader can simply sit on the position until expiration, at which time he will realize his .04 profit.

Suppose that a day after the trader initiates the conversion, the market drops 2 points to 98.00. The synthetic (short) side of the position will now be profitable: the 100 call, which he is short, will drop in value, and the the 100 put, which he is long, will rise in value. But because the options are settled like stock, these profits are only on paper and will not be realized until expiration, when either the call or put is exercised. On the other hand, the trader is also long a futures contract, and this part of the conversion will require an immediate 2-point outlay of cash when the market drops. This 2-point outlay must either be borrowed, or taken out of an existing interest bearing account. In either case, there will be a loss in interest, and this interest loss will *not* be offset by the paper profit on the options.

Most traders think of conversions and reversals as being delta neutral strategies, but in fact they are not quite delta neutral. For example, the deltas in the previous example might be approximately:

Option Position	Delta Position
short 100 call	-75
long 100 put	-24
long future	+100
total delta	+1

This one long delta reflects the fact that the trader would prefer the market to move up rather than down so that cash will flow into his account. The interest on this cash credit can represent an unexpected profit or, in the case of a downward move in the underlying market, an unexpected loss.

One delta may not seem like a very great risk, except when we remember that conversions and reversals, because of their low risk, are often done in very large size. A trader who has 1000 conversions in his account, has a risk equal to 1000×1 delta = 1000 deltas. This is the same as being naked long 10 futures contracts. No trader can afford to ignore the risk associated with a naked futures position.

While it is unusual for a trader to be forced out of business from conversions and reversals, it can happen. During the last half of 1983 and the first half of 1984, the market in U.S. Treasury Bonds declined steadily from 72-00 to 59-00. During this period many traders initially sold futures contracts, and later, as the market continued to decline, locked in their profits by purchasing calls and selling puts (synthetic long futures). The result was that many traders had large numbers of reversals in their accounts. However, when the Treasury Bond market reached 59, it turned around and began an extended rise. Now, each up move required a large cash outlay to feed the short futures portion of the reversal. If a trader had 1000 reversals (short 1000 actual futures contracts) and the market moved up 1 full point ($1,000), the trader received a call for $1,000,000. Traders who did not have access to such large amounts of cash were forced to liquidate, and went out of business. Even those traders who had sufficient funds in their accounts, or who were able to borrow the necessary funds, lost more in interest than they originally expected to make on the reversal.

The amount by which the total delta will be less than 100 in a conversion or reversal depends on the interest risk. This in turn depends on interest rates and the amount of time to expiration. A 10% interest rate with 9 months to expiration represents a greater risk than a 6% interest rate with 2 months to expiration. In the former case, the deltas of opposing calls and puts may add up to only 96; in the latter case they may add up to 99.

What can a trader do to reduce the futures risk associated with conversions and reversals? One possibility is to ratio the strategy so that it is delta neutral. For example, if a trader has 1000 conversions (short 1000 calls, long 1000 puts, long 1000 futures), so that he is 1000 deltas long, he can sell off 10 of his futures contracts. Now he is long 990 futures versus short 1000 synthetic futures. If the market rises, the loss from the extra 10 short synthetic futures should be offset by the interest gain from the cash inflow associated with the actual long futures contracts. If the market falls, the loss in interest should be offset by the 10 extra short synthetic futures.

Another approach is to replace the futures contract with something that isn't a futures contract but which acts just like one. An option which is so deeply in-the-money that its delta is 100, or in the case of puts -100, often serves this purpose. If a trader can replace a long futures contract in a conversion with either a long call or short put, with deltas of 100 and -100 respectively, he will no longer have to worry about the interest rate risk from his futures position. Such positions, where a deeply in-the-money option replaces the futures portion of a conversion or reversal, is known as a *3-way*.

While 3-ways have characteristics which are very similar to conversions and reversals, it is important to remember that they are not exactly alike. If the options are American (early exercise permitted), the trader who is short a deep in-the-money option is still subject to the risk of early exercise. Moreover, even though a deep in-the-money option may currently have a delta of 100, there is still the slight possibility of the futures contract going through the exercise price. If the futures market moves towards the option's exercise price, the delta of the option will begin to move away from 100 (-100 in the case of puts), and the option will act less and less like a futures contract.

Boxes

Is there any other way to eliminate the futures portion of the conversion or reversal so that we can eliminate any futures risk? Again we can ask, what acts like a futures contract but isn't a futures contract? The answer is a synthetic futures contract. By replacing the futures contract with a synthetic futures contract at a different exercise price, we will eliminate the risk of an adverse move in the futures price.

For example, suppose a trader has a July 100 conversion:

> short a July 100 call
> long a July 100 put
> long a July futures contract

He can consider replacing the long futures contract with a synthetic long futures contract at a different exercise price. (If he were to use the same exercise price, he would simply be liquidating his position.) He might, for example, sell the futures contract and replace it with a synthetic long futures contract at a 105 exercise price:

Initial Position	Replacement Trade
short a July 100 call	long a July 105 call
long a July 100 put	short a July 105 put
long a July future	short a July future

The long and short July futures contracts cancel each other out, leaving:

short a July 100 call	long a July 105 call
long a July 100 put	short a July 105 put

The trader has a synthetic short at a 100 exercise price, and a synthetic long at a 105 exercise price. The position is simply a conversion at one exercise price, and a reversal at a different exercise price, where the long and short futures contracts offset each other.

This position, where a conversion and reversal are done in the same expiration month but at different exercise prices, is known as a *box*. A trader is long (short) a box when he is long (short) the lower exercise price call and the higher exercise price put. Our example position is short the July 100/105 box.

Regardless of the price of the underlying futures contract, at expiration a box will always be worth exactly the difference between exercise prices—in our example 5 points. If the options are settled like stock rather than like futures, the value of the box today will be the value at expiration less carrying costs. If our 5-point box expires in 3 months with short-term interest rates at 8%, we must deduct the 2% carrying cost, or .10, from its expiration value. Thus, its value today is 4.90.

Since we have eliminated the futures risk, boxes are even less risky than conversions and reversals, which were already relatively low-risk strategies. Indeed, when there is no possibility of early exercise because the options are European, and there is no pin risk because the options and underlying futures are settled in cash, the purchase or sale of a box is identical to lending or borrowing short-term funds. In our example, a trader who buys the 5-point box at 4.90 has essentially lent funds for 3 months at a rate of 8%. A trader who sells the box has essentially borrowed funds for 3 months at the same rate. When no other method is available, a trading firm can often raise needed short term capital by selling boxes in the option market. Of course, no trader wants to just break even on a trade, so the firm will probably be forced to sell the boxes at less than theoretical value. This will increase borrowing costs. Moreover, if the options can be exercised early, or if at expiration the options are settled with a futures contract instead of cash, this method of borrowing may not be without risk.

We originally defined a box as a conversion and reversal at different exercise prices. We wrote our short July 100/105 box as:

| short a July 100 call | long a July 105 call |
| long a July 100 put | short a July 105 put |

Notice that instead of interpreting this box as a 100 conversion and a 105 reversal, we can also interpret it as a 100/105 bear vertical call spread together with a 100/105 bull vertical put spread. In fact a long (short) box is simply a bull (bear) vertical call spread combined with a bear (bull) vertical put spread with the same exercise prices. This knowledge can help a trader evaluate a spread without knowing the theoretical value of the individual options.

For example, with 3 months to expiration and 8% interest rates, the value of the 100/105 box is 4.90 (5 point expiration value less .10 carrying costs). Suppose a trader knows that the July 100/105 call vertical spread is trading actively at 3.00 points. Without any additional information, the trader can estimate a fair market price for the July 100/105 put vertical spread. He knows that the 100/105 box is worth 4.90, and that the value of a call and put vertical spread with the same exercise prices and expiration date must add up to the value of the corresponding box. If the market value of the 100/105 call vertical is 3.00, the market value of the 100/105 put vertical must be 1.90. If a floor trader believes he can either buy or sell the call vertical at 3.00, and is asked to give a market for the put vertical, he will very likely base his market on an assumed spread value of 1.90. He might, for example, give a market of 1.85 bid/1.95 ask. If he is able to buy the 100/105 put vertical at 1.85, he will attempt to buy the 100/105 call vertical at 3.00, thereby paying a total of 4.85 for a box which is worth 4.90. Conversely, if he is able to sell the put vertical at 1.95, he will attempt to sell the call vertical at 3.00, thereby selling a box which is only worth 4.90 for 4.95.

This type of spread evaluation based on arbitrage relationships is extremely useful to market makers. A floor trader, for example, may not have access to up-to-the-minute theoretical values. If he is forced to make a market, his only tools may be his knowledge of option values based on arbitrage relationships. These arbitrage relationships are summarized in Appendix F.

Jelly Rolls
Another type of arbitrage strategy consists of a long synthetic position in one delivery month and a short synthetic position in a different month, where both synthetic positions are done at the same exercise price. For example:

---

buy a July 100 call	sell an October 100 call
sell a July 100 put	buy an October 100 put
(synthetic long)	(synthetic short)

The combined long and short synthetic positions is known as a *jelly roll*.[1] Like boxes, jelly rolls consist of offsetting conversions and reversals, but instead of using different exercise prices we use dif-

---

[1]This very unscientific-sounding term seems to have originated among traders on the Chicago Board Options Exchange.

ferent expiration months. What should the value of a jelly roll be? Suppose that the futures market for a certain commodity is based solely on the cost of carrying the physical commodity from one delivery month to another. If interest rates are 8% and the current spot price of a commodity is 100.00, with 3 months to July expiration the price of the July futures contract should be:

$$100.00 + (3/12 \times .08 \times 100.00) = 102.00$$

From this we can calculate the value of the July 100 synthetic market (July 100 call minus the July 100 put):

futures price - exercise price - carry on 2 points for 3 months =
$$102.00 - 100.00 - .04 = 1.96$$

In the same way, with 6 months remaining to October expiration the price of the October futures contract should be:

$$100.00 + (6/12 \times .08 \times 100.00) = 104.00 \ [2]$$

The value of the October 100 synthetic market is then:

futures price - exercise price - carry on 4.00 points for 6 months =
$$104.00 - 100.00 - .16 = 3.84$$

The value of the jelly roll market is the difference between the October and July synthetic markets:

$$3.84 - 1.96 = 1.88$$

Putting all our calculations together, we can write the jelly roll market as:

long-term synthetic market - short-term synthetic market =
carry between futures months - carry on the long-term synthetic +
carry on the short-term synthetic

In our example, this works out to:

October/July 100 jelly roll =
2.00 - carry on 4.00 points to October + carry on 2.00 points to July =
$$2.00 - .16 + .04 = 1.88$$

---

[2]For simplicity, we will ignore any compound interest considerations.

A trader's knowledge of the jelly roll market can also help him evaluate call and put time spreads. We can rewrite the jelly roll market:

long-term synthetic market - short-term synthetic market =
(long-term call - short-term call) - (long-term put - short-term put)

From this we have:

long-term call - short-term call =
long-term put - short-term put + jelly roll

and

long-term put - short-term put =
long-term call - short-term call - jelly roll

This simply means that the value of call and put time spreads with the same exercise prices must differ by exactly the value of the jelly roll. In our example, the October/July 100 jelly roll is worth 1.88, so the value of the October/July 100 call time spread must be exactly 1.88 more than the value of the October/July 100 put time spread. If the October 100 put is trading at 3.00 and the July 100 put is trading at 2.00 (put time spread at 1.00), the 100 call time spread must be trading at 2.88 (put time spread plus the jelly roll). Taking this a step further, if the July 100 call is trading at 2.50, the October 100 call must be trading at 5.38.

Like other option arbitrage strategies, jelly rolls and time spreads are sensitive to changes in interest rates. If interest rates rise, the value of the jelly roll will rise, since carrying the synthetic position to October expiration will cost less than carrying the actual physical commodity. In our example, if interest rates double from 8% to 16%, the value of July and October futures contracts will rise to 104.00 and 108.00 respectively. The value of the October/July 100 jelly roll will then be:

cost of carry between futures months - carry on 8.00 to October
expriation + carry on 4.00 to July =
4.00 - .64 + .16 = 3.52

The rise in interest rates has caused the jelly roll market to widen by 1.64 from 1.88 to 3.52. At the same time, the difference between the October/July 100 call and put time spreads will also widen from 1.88 to 3.52.

When the difference in futures prices is affected by factors other than the cost of carry, a jelly roll may begin to act less and less like an arbitrage. In agricultural markets, especially, the prices of different delivery months may be very sensitive to short-term supply and demand. It is even possible for a near-term delivery month to trade at a premium to a long-term delivery month. When this happens, the jelly roll market will carry risks not normally associated with arbitrage strategies.[3]

Synthetic Volatility Spreads

A trader need not restrict himself to using synthetics as part of an arbitrage strategy. He can also replace any part of a volatility spread with its synthetic equivalent.

For example, suppose a trader wants to purchase 10 July 100 straddles (buy 10 July 100 calls, buy 10 July 100 puts). He can achieve the same result, synthetically, by purchasing 20 July 100 calls and selling 10 July futures contracts. This *synthetic straddle* has characteristics almost identical to its real equivalent.

Using synthetic relationships, we can also see why call and put butterflies, with the same expiration date and exercise prices, are equivalent:

Long Call Butterfly	Synthetic Equivalent
long a July 95 call	long a July 95 put/long a July future
short 2 July 100 calls	short 2 July 100 puts/short 2 July futures
long a July 105 call	long a July 105 put/long a July future

---

[3]Jelly rolls are most common among stock option traders, where the cost of carrying stock is relatively stable. The value of a stock option jelly roll is:

long-term synthetic market - short-term synthetic market =
cost of carry on the exercise price between expiration months
- dividend payout between expiration months

The two long and short futures contracts in the synthetic equivalent cancel each other out, leaving:

long a July 95 put
short 2 July 100 puts
long a July 105 put

When a trader is considering the purchase or sale of an option, he should always look at the price of the synthetic equivalent. Occassionally, he will find that he can trade the synthetic at a better price. Even if the price of the synthetic is only fractionally better, such small savings can add up over many years of trading.

For example, suppose with the underlying July futures contract at 102.00, a trader wants to execute the following volatility spread:

buy 10 July 100 calls at 5.00
sell 20 July 105 calls at 2.00

The current bid/ask spreads in these options are:

July 100 call: 5.00 bid/5.10 offer
July 105 call: 2.00 bid/2.05 offer

If the trader can buy July 100 calls at 5.00, he intends to sell July 105 calls at 2.00. If he can sell July 105 calls at 2.05, he intends to buy July 100 calls at 5.10. In either case he will achieve his goal of executing the spread for a 1.00 point debit:

$$-5.00 + (2 \times 2.00) = -5.10 + (2 \times 2.05) = -1.00$$

Suppose that eventually a bid of 2.05 for July 105 calls appears. The trader immediately sells July 105 calls and is about to pay 5.10 for July 100 calls when, almost simultaneously, someone offers July 100 puts at 3.10. The trader now has a choice. He can buy July 100 calls for 5.10. Or he can buy July 100 calls synthetically by purchasing July 100 puts for 3.10 and July futures for 102.00. Which strategy is best?

If there are 3 months to expiration with interest rates at 8%, and the trader has done his homework, he will know that:

$$\text{synthetic July 100 call} =$$
$$\text{put price + futures price - exercise price - carry on 2 points} =$$
$$3.10 + 102.00 - 100.00 - (2.00 \times .08 \times 3/12) = 5.06$$

The trader is being offered a chance to buy a July 100 call synthetically, for 5.06 when he would have to pay 5.10 if he purchased the actual option. By purchasing the synthetic, he will save .04.

Of course, synthetic volatility spreads which include long or short futures contracts, have the same futures risk and pin risk as conversions and reversals. An adverse move in the futures contract will result in a loss in interest because of the cash drain from the futures settlement procedure. There will be pin risk if the short synthetic option expires with the futures contract right at the exercise price. However, these risks are small, and if given the choice it is almost always preferable to do the synthetic at a better price.

12

Early Exercise of American Options

Thus far we have assumed that all option strategies involve holding a position to expiration. Since the great majority of listed options traded throughout the world permit early exercise, it will be worthwhile to consider some of the characteristics of American options. Specifically, we will want to answer two questions:

1. Under what circumstances should a trader consider exercising an American option prior to expiration?
2. How much more should a trader be willing to pay for the right to exercise an option early?

If we break down a futures option's theoretical value into its individual components we might write:

theoretical value = intrinsic value + time value
= intrinsic value + volatility - carrying costs

Each of these components—intrinsic value, volatility, and carrying costs—either adds to or subtracts from the option's value. Since no option can have a negative theoretical value, no matter how far out-of-the-money it might be, intrinsic value must always be a nonnegative component. Likewise, volatility can only enhance the value of an option, so its effect must also be positive. Carrying costs, on the other hand, have a negative effect on futures options. An increase in interest rates will make options a less desirable alternative to a position in the underlying futures contract.

As an example, suppose we have the following inputs into the Black-Scholes model:

time to expiration	= 60 days
futures price	= 110.00
volatility	= 20%
interest rate	= 8.00%

Using these inputs we find that the theoretical value of the 100 call is 10.36. Since we know that the intrinsic value is 10.00, the time value (volatility and carrying cost components together) must be .36. In order to calculate the approximate volatility and carrying cost components, we can set the interest rate to zero, keep all other inputs the same, and recalculate the theoretical value. If we do this, the new value for the option is 10.50. With the interest rate at zero, the .50 time value must be all volatility value. The carrying cost component when we originally used an interest rate of 8.00% must therefore have been .14. Summarizing, we have:

theoretical value   = +10.00 + .50 - .14 = 10.36

Suppose 30 days pass and the underlying futures contract has risen to 113.00. Using the same volatility of 20% and interest rate of 8.00%, we find that the new theoretical value of the 100 call is 12.95. Notice that the value of the option is now less than its intrinsic value. We can see why if we use the same method as before to break down the option's value into its individual components. We now find that the volatility component is .04 and the carrying cost component is .09, so that:

theoretical value   = +13.00 + .04 - .09 = 12.95

The carrying cost of .09 is now greater than the volatility component of .04. If this option is a European option, no trader will want to pay even as much as the option's intrinsic value, since the insurance value of the option is less than the cost of holding the option to expiration.[1]

Given the fact that the carrying cost component of an option can, under some circumstances, be greater than the volatility component, there will be times when early exercise will be desirable in order to avoid these carrying costs.

Suppose the option in our example, with its European theoretical value of 12.95, is an American option. Is there any advantage to exercising this option now? In considering the desirability of early exercise, we must really compare three alternatives:

1. Do nothing.

2. Exercise the option.

3. Sell the option and buy a futures contract.

How will each of these alternatives affect our account? If we choose the first alternative and do nothing, there is obviously no change to our account. The position we take home is identical to the one with which we begin the next trading day.

If we choose the second alternative and exercise the 100 call, it is just as if we had gone into the futures market and purchased a futures contract for 100. Since we are now subject to futures style settlement, if the futures contract settles at 113.00, 13.00 points will be credited to our account. With 30 days to expiration, and an interest rate of 8.00%, the total interest earned to expiration on this 13 points is:

$$13.00 \times .08 \times 30/365 = .09$$

Sometimes, of course, this .09 earnings in interest will be reduced, because the underlying futures contract will crash through the call's exercise price. In that case we would have preferred not exercising early because the loss to the option position is limited to its intrinsic value, while the loss to the futures position is potentially unlimited.

---

[1]Note that a European option with a theoretical value which is less than its intrinsic value will have a *positive* theta. The value of the option will gradually *rise* to its intrinsic value as expiration approaches.

Still, the fact that the option's theoretical value is less than its intrinsic value tells us that in the long run we will do better exercising the option now in order to earn interest on the settlement proceeds.

What about the third choice, selling the call and buying a futures contract? If the 100 call is trading at exactly its intrinsic value of 13.00 and we can buy the futures contract at 113.00, there is no difference between exercising the option, or selling the option and buying a futures contract. Both strategies will result in the same 13.00 points being credited to our account, and we will earn the same interest to expiration of .09.

Suppose, however, that the 100 call is not trading at parity. Could it be trading for less than its intrinsic value? This is clearly impossible in a market where early exercise is permissible. If the 100 call were really trading at 12.95 with the underlying futures contract at 113.00, all traders would buy calls, sell an equal number of futures contracts at 113.00, exercise their calls, and realize an immediate and riskless profit of .05.

What if the option is trading for more than parity, say 13.10? If we sell the call and buy a futures contract for 113.00, we will end up with the same position we would have had through early exercise. But now, instead of 13.00 points, 13.10 points will be credited to our account. We will realize an additional profit of .10 through the sale of the option, as well as the slight additional interest earnings which go with it.

From the foregoing discussion, we can infer two conditions necessary for early exercise:

1. The option must have a theoretical value, using a European pricing model, no greater than parity.
2. The option must be trading at parity.

The first condition ensures that the interest earned on the proceeds from early exercise will be more valuable than the insurance value, or volatility component, of the option. If the option has a theoretical value greater than parity, early exercise will result in the loss of this insurance value. Rather than exercise early, a trader will do better in the long run by hedging the option against the underlying futures contract and continuing to make delta neutral adjustments.

The second condition ensures that a trader does not miss an additional profit opportunity when the option is trading at more than parity. In that case, selling the option in the marketplace and replacing it with a futures contract will be a more sensible strategy.

If a trader is trying to decide whether an option should be exercised early, but must make his decision based on a European pricing model, he probably will not go too far wrong simply by adhering to our two rules. If the option has a theoretical value of less than parity, and if it is trading at parity in the marketplace, then it should probably be exercised in order to earn interest on the cash which will be credited to the trader's account.

There is however a practical problem associated with early exercise, and that is the accuracy of the trader's theoretical value. The desirability of early exercise depends on the interest rate component in an option's value being greater than the volatility component. If a trader incorrectly estimates either of these components, he will find that he is often exercising when he shouldn't, or not exercising when he should. Since futures options are very sensitive to changes in volatility, and only slightly sensitive to changes in interest rates, a trader who is considering early exercise must be very concerned with the accuracy of his volatility estimate. Returning to our example where the 100 call is worth 12.95 with 30 days to expiration and a volatility of 20%, if we raise our volatility estimate to 25%, the option will now have a theoretical value of 13.05. Since this value is greater than parity, the option is no longer a candidate for early exercise.

An experienced trader who is considering early exercise knows how difficult it is to guess the future volatility of any commodity, and he will allow for the widest possible margin for error in his volatility estimate. If his best volatility guess is 20%, he may use a volatility as high as 25%, or even 30%, to confirm that the option is indeed an early exercise candidate.

Because a swift rise in volatility can alter the desirability of early exercise, options are more likely to be early exercise candidates in markets where the volatility of the underlying commodity is relatively stable. Options are less likely to be early exercise candidates in markets where there are wide swings in volatility. The volatilities of metals and agricultural products, in particular, can fluctuate wildly. (Note the greater volatility swings of metals versus currencies in Appendix C.) Indeed, a trader will lose very little in the long run if he *never* exercises a futures option on a metal or agricultural product early. There is simply too great a chance that his volatility estimate will be low. The loss in interest from not exercising early is a small price to pay for protection on those occasions when the option unexpectedly goes out-of-the-money.[2]

Thus far we have only addressed the question of when it will be desirable to exercise an American option early. There should also be an additional value associated with an American option over a European option because the former carries with it additional rights. Even an out-of-the-money option might eventually go deeply enough into-the-money to be an early exercise candidate. This possibility should make an American option more valuable than an identical European option.

How much more should a trader be willing to pay for the right of early exercise? The Black-Scholes model does not address this problem because it was developed to evaluate European options only. There are however two models which are commonly used to evaluate the early exercise value of an American option. These are the Cox-Ross-Rubenstein model, sometimes referred to as the binomial model, and the Whaley, or quadratic model.

The Cox-Ross-Rubenstein Model

The model developed by John Cox, Stephen Ross, and Mark Rubenstein takes much the same approach as we took in Chapter 4 with our pinball maze. Recall that when a ball dropped down and encountered a nail, it had only two routes it could follow, either to the left or to the right. We can apply the same approach to option evaluation by dividing the time to expiration into smaller time periods of equal length. Over each time period we will allow the price of the underlying contract to move either up or down a specified amount. This price movement will determine a *binomial* distribution of possible underlying prices at expiration (Figure 12-1).

---

[2]Option traders in stocks and physical commodities are less reluctant to exercise early because of the greater interest to be earned.

Example of a 6-period Binomial Distribution Tree

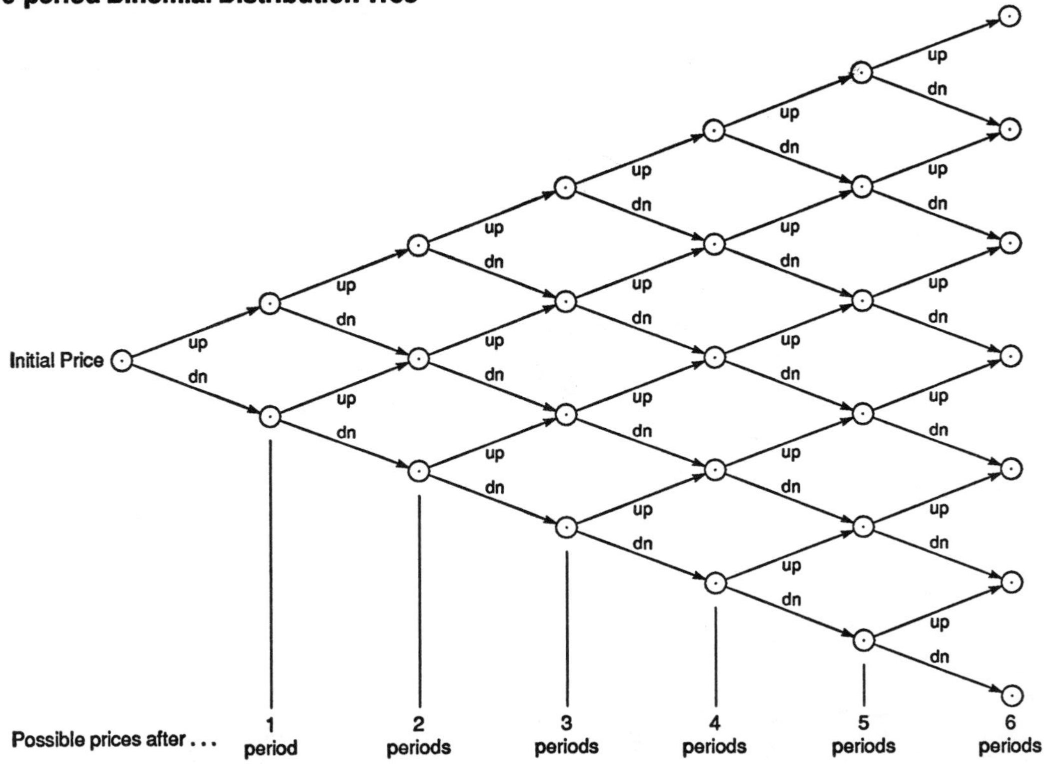

Figure 12-1

Since an option's value at expiration is either zero or its intrinsic value, the option's initial value can be determined by adding up all the possible option values at expiration times the probability of each value. (This is analogous to looking at every possible path for each ball dropped into the pinball maze as illustrated in Figure 4-1.)

This binomial approach to option pricing not only enables us to calculate the total value of an option if it is held for the full time to expiration, but it also allows us to calculate the value of the option at the beginning of each intermediate time period. In particular, if we want to evaluate an American option we can assume that if at any intermediate time period the option's value is less than its intrinsic value, the option will be exercised early, and therefore valued at parity. By taking into consideration the possibility of early exercise at each intermediate time period and adding up the values at each time period, we can approximate the true value of an American option.

To effectively use the Cox-Ross-Rubenstein model, the price distribution of the underlying contract at expiration must closely approximate a normal distribution. To achieve this it is necessary to divide the total time to expiration into smaller and smaller time periods of equal length. As this is done, the resulting binomial price distribution will more and more closely resemble the normal distribution assumed in the Black-Scholes model. At the same time, the computed value of the option will come closer and closer to the true value of an American option. If no early exercise is permitted, the Cox-Ross-Rubenstein model will simply converge to the Black-Scholes model.

Ideally, we would like to divide the time to expiration into an infinite number of smaller time segments since the binomial distribution, when carried out an infinite number of times, will yield a true normal distribution. In practice, however, the values for American options derived from the Cox-Ross-Rubenstein model become quite accurate using as few as 50 time periods. Unfortunately, even 50 time periods will require numerous repetitive computations. While the Cox-Ross-Rubenstein model yields more accurate values for American options, many traders still prefer the Black-Scholes model because of its computational simplicity.

The Whaley Model

In order to avoid the cumbersome calculations required in the Cox-Ross-Rubenstein model, Robert Whaley and Giovanni Barone-Adesi have taken a different approach to American option evaluation. In their model, an attempt is made to find a critical underlying price above which a European call (or below which a European put) will be worth less than parity. Above this critical price, an American option will always be exercised in order to avoid carrying costs. The value of an American call option is then the value of the European call below the critical price, plus the intrinsic value of the call above the critical price. (See Figure 12-2.)

The Whaley model is mathematically more complex than the Cox-Ross-Rubenstein model since it requires the solution of a quadratic equation, as well as an iterative procedure to locate the critical price of the underlying contract. In spite of this, the model yields accurate American option values with less computation than the Cox-Ross-Rubenstein model.

No matter what model a trader uses, the accuracy of model generated values will depend at least as much on the inputs to the model as the technical precision of the model itself. If a trader evaluates an American call option using an incorrect volatility, an incorrect interest rate, or an incorrect underlying contract price, the fact that he is deriving his values from an American pricing model rather than from a European pricing model will make very little difference. Both models will generate incorrect values because the inputs are incorrect. The American pricing model may produce less error, but that will be small consolation if the incorrect inputs lead to a large trading loss.

American option values become most important where there is a significant carrying cost associated with the underlying contract. Put options on stock or physical commodities are very often exercised early to earn interest on the cash proceeds of the sale. Additionally, a call option on a stock may be exercised early in order to capture a sufficiently large dividend.

Since futures contracts pay no dividends, early exercise of futures options is totally dependent on interest considerations. If there is no cost of carry on either the underlying contract or on an option on that contract, there can be no interest rate considerations and therefore no

Arbitrage Boundary for Early Exercise

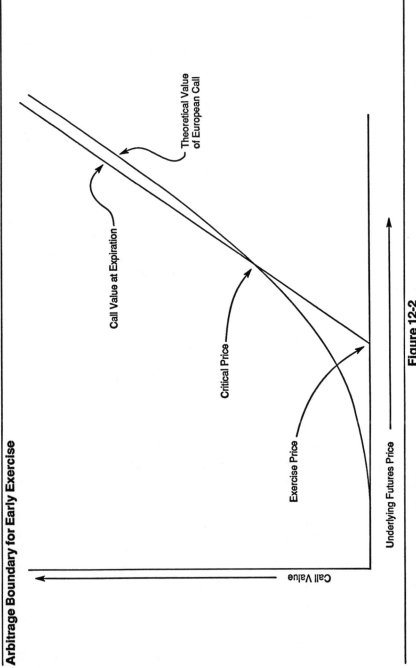

Call Value at Expiration

Theoretical Value
of European Call

Critical Price

Exercise Price

Call Value

Underlying Futures Price

Figure 12-2

value to early exercise. This will be true if both the underlying contract and options on that contract are settled futures style.[3] Under these conditions the interest rate component to any theoretical pricing model effectively becomes zero. By setting the interest rate to zero, all option models, whether European of American, will yield identical values.

In the United States, even though exchange traded futures contracts are settled futures-style, the options on those contracts are presently settled like stock, requiring full and immediate payment of the option premium. As we have seen, the interest component in the evaluation of such options is small, so the early exercise value will also be small. Indeed, the difference in values for such options derived from the Black-Scholes model, the Cox-Ross-Rubenstein model, or the Whaley model will be very slight. Any differences which do occur are almost certain to be less than the bid-ask spread for the option in the marketplace. A trader is unlikely to profit significantly because he is using an American pricing model while other traders in the marketplace are using a European pricing model. Practical considerations, such as the accuracy of a trader's volatility estimate, his ability to anticipate directional trends, and his ability to control risk through effective spreading strategies, will far outweigh any small advantage gained from an American versus a European model.

The Effect of Early Exercise on Vertical Spreads

The early exercise value of an American option on a futures contract, where the option is settled like stock, is most evident in the pricing of vertical spreads. If all options are European, with no possibility of early exercise, the maximum value of a vertical spread will always be the amount between exercise prices. If both options are so deeply in-the-money that they are valued at parity, the value of the spread ought to be the amount between exercise prices less carrying costs. For example, with interest rates at 8% and three months remaining to expiration, the maximum value of a 90/95 call vertical spread, where all options are European, will be:

---

[3]Such settlement procedures currently exist on several European and Australian futures exchanges.

$$5.00 - (5.00 \times .08 \times 3/12) = 5.00 - .10 = 4.90$$

If, however, these options are American, and the 90 and 95 calls are so deeply in-the-money that they become early exercise candidates, both calls will be exercised to avoid carrying costs. Under these conditions, the spread will have a value of exactly 5.00 points.

A trader will always be willing to pay the full intrinsic value for a deeply in-the-money vertical spread so that he can exercise his long option and earn interest on the proceeds. In our example, if the underlying futures contract is at 150 and the 90 call is an early exercise candidate, a trader will gladly pay 5.00 points for the 90/95 call vertical spread. He will immediately offset the 5-point debit from the purchase of the spread by exercising his 90 call and collecting 60 points (the difference between the exercise price and settlement price of the futures contract). He can now earn interest to expiration on the 55-point credit in his account. This will amount to:

$$55.00 \times .08 \times 3/12 = 1.10$$

If the trader is fortunate enough not to be assigned on the 95 call, he will profit by the full interest earnings of 1.10.

What will happen if the trader is assigned on the 95 call? He will have to pay out 55 points, and this will eliminate the interest profit he expected. But he still has not lost anything. At worst he will break even.

The same reasoning that leads a trader to pay full value for a deeply in-the-money vertical spread also dictates that he pay full value for a deeply in-the-money box. If all options are European, the value of a 90/95 box will be 5.00 points less the .10 carrying costs to expiration. The 4.90 value of the box is identical to the value of the deeply in-the-money call vertical spread. However, if the box is deeply in-the-money and the options are American rather than European, a trader will always be willing to pay the full 5-point value for the box because he will immediately exercise either the deeply in-the-money call or put. If, as before, the underlying futures contract is at 150 and a trader has purchased the 90/95 box for 5.00, he will immediately exercise the 90 call and collect interest on the 55-point credit now in his account. If he is assigned on the 95 call he will, like the trader with the vertical spread, do no worse than break even. In the case of the box, however, he will be left with an additional asset in the form of a bear vertical put spread:

long a 95 put/short a 90 put

This spread can never be worth less than zero, and might have some positive value should the market make a swift downward move.

The same conditions which lead a trader to exercise an option early are also likely to lead to early assignment, and every trader should be prepared for this possibility. Margin requirements established by the clearing houses usually require a trader to keep sufficient funds in his account to cover the possibility of early assignment. But this is not always true. If he is short deeply in-the-money options on which he might be assigned, and these are offset with other options rather than with futures contracts, an early assignment notice may cause a cash squeeze. If this happens, he will need access to sufficient capital to cover the situation. Otherwise, he may be forced to liquidate other option positions. Forced liquidations are invariably losing propositions.

The sensible trader tries to be prepared for as many contingencies as possible. The risk of early assignment should simply be one more item on his checklist.

A Comparison of European and American Option Values

The theoretical values and deltas in Figure 12-3 are for options on futures contracts where the options are settled like stock. The European values (upper value) were calculated using the Black-Scholes Model. The American values (lower value) were calculated using the Whaley Model.

Note that the value of an American option over a European option increases as the option goes more deeply into-the-money, as interest rates increase (Part A), or as the time to expiration increases (Part B). Note also how the delta of a American option approaches 100 (-100 for puts) more quickly than its European counterpart.

European vs. American Option Values

Futures Price = 100.00; Time = 60 days; Volatility = 20%

Interest = 4.00%	*80*	*90*	*100*	*110*	*120*
calls	19.88 (99)	10.28 (90)	3.21 (51)	.50 (13)	.04 (1)
	20.00 (100)	10.30 (91)	3.23 (51)	.50 (12)	.04 (1)
puts	.01 (0)	.35 (−9)	3.21 (−48)	10.43 (−87)	19.91 (−98)
	0 (0)	.34 (−9)	3.23 (−48)	10.46 (−87)	20.01 (−99)

Interest = 8.00%	*80*	*90*	*100*	*110*	*120*
calls	19.75 (98)	10.22 (90)	3.19 (51)	.50 (13)	.04 (1)
	20.00 (100)	10.27 (91)	3.22 (51)	.50 (12)	.04 (1)
puts	.01 (0)	.35 (−9)	3.19 (−48)	10.36 (−86)	19.78 (−97)
	0 (0)	.34 (−9)	3.22 (−48)	10.42 (−87)	20.00 (−100)

Interest = 12.00%	*80*	*90*	*100*	*110*	*120*
calls	19.62 (98)	10.15 (89)	3.18 (51)	.40 (13)	.04 (1)
	20.00 (100)	10.24 (91)	3.20 (51)	.50 (13)	.04 (1)
puts	.01 (0)	.34 (−9)	3.17 (−47)	10.30 (−86)	19.65 (−97)
	0 (0)	.34 (−9)	3.20 (−48)	10.39 (−87)	20.00 (−100)

Figure 12-3A

Futures Price = 100.00;   Volatility = 20%;   Interest = 8.00%

	80	90	100	110	120
Time = 30 days					
calls	19.87 (99)	10.00 (96)	2.27 (51)	.12 (5)	0 (0)
	20.00 (100)	10.04 (97)	2.29 (51)	.12 (5)	0 (0)
puts	0 (0)	.07 (−3)	2.27 (−49)	10.05 (−94)	19.87 (−99)
	0 (0)	.07 (−3)	2.29 (−49)	10.09 (−95)	20.00 (−100)
Time = 60 days					
calls	19.75 (98)	10.22 (90)	3.19 (51)	.50 (13)	.04 (1)
	20.00 (100)	10.27 (91)	3.22 (51)	.50 (12)	.04 (1)
puts	.01 (0)	.35 (−9)	3.19 (−48)	10.36 (−86)	19.78 (−97)
	0 (0)	.34 (−9)	3.22 (−48)	10.42 (−87)	20.00 (−100)
Time = 120 days					
calls	19.58 (95)	10.77 (81)	4.46 (51)	1.33 (21)	.29 (6)
	20.00 (99)	10.88 (82)	4.50 (51)	1.34 (22)	.28 (6)
puts	.10 (−2)	1.03 (−16)	4.46 (−47)	11.07 (−76)	19.77 (−91)
	.09 (−2)	1.04 (−16)	4.50 (−47)	11.19 (−77)	20.10 (−95)
Time = 240 days					
calls	19.51 (88)	11.73 (73)	6.13 (51)	2.77 (29)	1.10 (14)
	20.16 (94)	11.99 (75)	6.24 (51)	2.82 (29)	1.12 (14)
puts	.53 (−7)	2.27 (−22)	6.13 (−44)	12.26 (−66)	20.08 (−81)
	.53 (−7)	2.29 (−22)	6.24 (−45)	12.51 (−68)	20.65 (−86)

Figure 12-3B

13

Let the User Beware

Thus far the reader has been asked to accept, mostly on good faith and with some carefully prepared examples, that theoretical pricing models can in fact accurately evaluate options. Can we indeed trust these models? Or are there potential weaknesses in models of which a trader should be aware?

Let's look at some of the basic assumptions made in theoretical pricing models and consider whether these assumptions are truly valid. If they are not, then perhaps they represent a danger to a trader who is pursuing strategies based on model-generated values.

Assumption 1: *Interest rates are constant over the life of an option, and all traders can either borrow or lend at the same rate.*

Clearly, this assumption—that interest rates are constant and uniform for everyone—is not true. We know that interest rates, like commodity prices, tend to fluctuate over time. Moreover, anyone who has compared the interest a bank pays on a savings account, and the interest it charges for a loan, knows that borrowing and lending rates are not identical. This principle applies especially to an individual trader, who will always pay more for borrowed funds and receive less for lent funds, than a large brokerage house or banking firm.

If interest rates are not constant and uniform, as assumed in the model, how is this likely to affect the accuracy of model-generated values? The answer depends on the type of underlying instrument. Futures options which are settled like futures contracts are essentially insensitive to changes in interest rates because no capital is required to trade either the underlying contract or options on that contract.[1] This is reflected in the fact that we can effectively evaluate such options using an interest rate of zero.

Futures options which are settled like stock are somewhat more sensitive to changes in interest rates because some capital is required to trade the options. We noted in Chapter 11 (Arbitrage Strategies) that a trader should be aware of his own personal borrowing and lending rates, and that there is some danger that these rates may change. But even here the effect is slight because the value of the underlying futures contract, which requires no capital outlay, is so much greater than the value of the option.

As we move away from options on futures and towards options on physicals, the risk of a change in interest rates becomes increasingly important. The purchase or sale of stocks, bonds, or foreign currencies will result in a large debit or credit, and such a position can be highly sensitive to changes in interest rates. Since an option position can be thought of as a substitute for a position in the underlying, the value of options on these underlying instruments will also be sensitive to changes in interest rates. Foreign currency option traders, in particular, are at risk because they must worry about two different interest rates, the rate in the foreign (deliverable) currency as well as the rate in the domestic currency. If these rates should move in opposite directions, the value of a foreign currency option can change dramatically.

There is no practical way to deal with the risk of a change in interest rates other than to be aware that such changes are possible. For large positions, the rho will be useful in helping a trader analyze the

---

[1] Of course, a futures contract itself may be sensitive to changes in interest rates. But that is a risk associated with trying to evaluate the futures contract, rather than trying to evaluate an option on that contract.

interest rate risk. As with any position, if the risk becomes too great, some offsetting trade may be worthwhile, even if it reduces the total theoretical edge of the position.

Assumption 2: *The possible prices of an underlying contract are lognormally distributed over the life of an option.*

Suppose every trader in the world believed that the Black-Scholes model was a highly effective method of evaluating options. Suppose moreover that each trader based his trading strategies in a specific commodity on values generated by the model. Each trader would enter his volatility estimate into the model and, based on the resulting theoretical values, go into a market and buy underpriced options and sell overpriced options. Buying pressure would force up the price of undervalued options, and selling pressure would force down the price of overvalued options.

Eventually each option price would reach an equilibrium which would translate into an implied volatility. The result would be a single uniform implied volatility for every option because every trader would be working with exactly the same model.

If this scenario were real, a trader would have no trouble determining the marketplace's consensus implied volatility, since the implied volatility of every option would be identical. Unfortunately, as most traders are aware, no matter what model is used, the implied volatilities of all options on the same underlying never seem to line up. Some implied volatilities are too high, and some are too low. And whether we use the Black-Scholes model, or the Cox-Ross-Rubenstein model, or some other model, the discrepancies in implied volatilities never seem to disappear.

A good example of this problem is shown in Figure 13-1, a listing of prices and implied volatilities for options on June 1988 crude oil futures on the NYMEX as of the close on March 31,1988. The numbers were generated using the Black-Scholes model. The implied volatilities range from a low of 25.1 for the 17 call, to a high of 43.1 for the 13 put, with implied volatilities increasing as we move away from the at-the-money options. How can we account for this?

A new trader might make the assumption that everyone trading at-the-money options thinks the volatility of June crude oil futures

Distribution of Implied Volatilities
31 March 1988

June Crude Oil at 16.98; Time to Expiration = 43 days; Interest rate at 7.00%

Exercise Price	Calls		Puts	
	Price	Implied Volatility	Price	Implied Volatility
13	-----	-----	.02	43.1
14	-----	-----	.04	37.3
15	2.06	32.1	.08	31.1
16	1.19	27.6	.21	27.3
17	.53	25.1	.56	25.6
18	.19	25.2	1.21	25.4
19	.06	26.1	-----	-----
20	.03	29.8	-----	-----
21	.02	34.3	-----	-----

Figure 13-1

will be approximately 25.5, while everyone trading away-from-the-money options thinks the volatility will be some higher number. The problem with this assumption is that an active option trader is probably trading options at every different exercise price. If a trader were trading the at-the-money options and really believed that the volatility of the June contract would be 25.5, he would certainly want to sell the 20 and 21 calls, with their implied volatilities of 29.8 and 34.3, or the 14 and 15 puts, with their implied volatilities of 37.3 and 31.1. This selling pressure would eventually force the prices of these options towards an implied volatility of 25.5.

Is there another possible explanation? Suppose we were to take a poll of all the June crude oil option traders and ask each one whether he thought the possible prices of June crude oil futures at expiration were lognormally distributed. If every trader voted yes, then, as before, we would expect a uniform volatility across every exercise price. But if enough traders said no, then we would expect to see prices with different implied volatilities depending on how the majority of traders viewed the likely distribution of crude oil prices at expiration.

If we look at the distribution of implied volatilities for a particular underlying, we are actually looking at an *implied distribution* of underlying prices at expiration. Through the pricing of each option, the marketplace is telling us how accurate it believes the lognormal assumption in a theoretical pricing model to be. If implied volatilities are generally uniform across all exercise prices, the marketplace believes that the lognormal assumption is a reasonable one. If implied volatilities vary greatly from one exercise price to another, the marketplace believes the the lognormal assumption is unrealistic.

In order to more easily grasp what the marketplace is telling us, it might be helpful to draw a graph of implied volatilities. Figure 13-2 is such a graph for June crude oil options. From this graph it appears that, in relative terms, the marketplace values the away-from-the-money exercise prices (13, 14, 20, 21) more highly than the at-the-money exercise prices (16, 17, 18). The marketplace apparent-

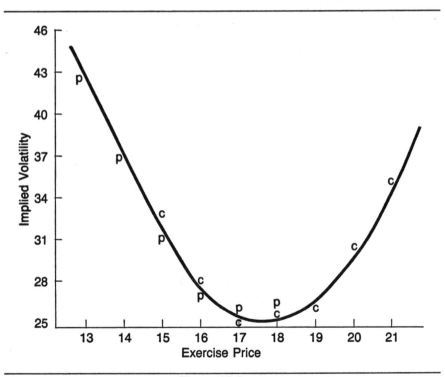

Figure 13-2

ly believes the theoretical pricing model undervalues away-from-the-money options in relation to at-the-money options. Option prices seem to reflect a belief that there is a greater chance for June crude oil futures to go through these extreme exercise prices than is predicted by the theoretical pricing model.

If we draw an approximate graph of the implied price distribution of June crude oil futures, it might look something like Figure 13-3. Note how the implied distribution curve differs from the lognormal distribution curve. The tails of the implied curve are "fatter" than the tails of the lognormal curve. This fat tail characteristic reflects a belief that there is a greater chance of a large move in the underlying than is predicted by the lognormal distribution assumed in most theoretical pricing models. Additionally, the implied distribution curve has a higher peak in the middle, reflecting a belief that the likelihood of very small changes in price are also greater than predicted by a lognormal distribution.

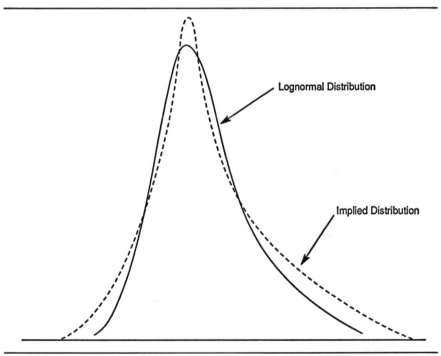

Figure 13-3

Who should we believe, the theoretical pricing model or the marketplace? There is no conclusive evidence, but practical experience seems to indicate that the marketplace does have a good feel for how prices act in the real world, and that there is indeed a better chance for both large and small price changes than is assumed in most theoretical pricing models.

As an example of an unusually large price change, we can look to the events of October 19, 1987. The volatility based on daily settlement to settlement price changes of the S&P 500 index for all of 1987 was approximately 32%. From this we can calculate an approximate one standard deviation daily price change:

$$32\% / 16 = 2.00\%$$

On October 19, the S&P 500 dropped about 25%, or more than 12 standard deviations. If we look at a table of probabilities to find the likelihood of such an occurance, we will find that it is so unlikely it doesn't even appear in the table. (The author's calculator can handle numbers up to 10 to the power of 500, but even 12 standard deviations results in an overflow.) In other words, one would not expect to see a move of 12 standard deviations during the lifetime of our universe, or any other universe for that matter. Nevertheless, in spite of what probability theory predicts, we did see such a move on October 19th.

While this particular example is unique, it does appear that these larger than expected moves happen more often than a lognormal distribution predicts. The marketplace senses this, and raises the value of the away-from-the-money exercise prices to correct for the inaccuracy of the model.

What does this mean to a trader? It means that whatever the model says an option with an extreme exercise price is worth, it is probably worth more. How much more, nobody really knows. But because of the apparent inaccuracy in the model, no experienced trader is likely to sell such an option for its theoretical value. If the model says a far out-of-the-money option is worth .05, no experienced trader will sell such an option for .05 because he knows the model has probably undervalued it in the real world. Even a bid of .10 or .15 may be insufficient. Of course, every trader has his price, and if someone bids .50 the trader may finally be willing to sell. The model may be wrong, but at a price of .50, the trader may decide that he can live with that risk.

Because of the danger that the model has undervalued far out-of-the money options, experienced traders will also avoid ratio vertical spreads with a high ratio of short to long options. Such spreads almost always include a large number of far out-of-the-money options. For example, if an at-the-money call with a delta of 50 seems underpriced, and an out-of-the-money call with a delta of 5 seems overpriced, our impulse is to buy the at-the-money call and sell 10 of the out-of-the-money calls. But are we really certain that the out-of-the-money call is overpriced? We know the model tends to underprice such options. Furthermore, we can't be certain that the delta of the option is 5, since the delta is also dependent on the lognormal distribution assumption built into the model. If the delta is really 10, the correct ratio is 1 to 5, rather than 1 to 10.

The practical solution to this problem is to avoid ratio vertical spreads with exercise prices which are very far apart. If we restrict ourselves to ratio vertical spreads where the long and short options have adjacent exercise prices, or which are separated by no more than one exercise price, we can greatly reduce the risk that the model has incorrectly evaluated an option. The model may indeed have mispriced the options. But because the options have exercise prices which are close to each other, both options are likely to be mispriced to the same degree.

As a trader becomes more sophisticated, particularly an active local trader or market maker, he is likely to give increasingly greater thought to the problem of price distributions in the real world. How can a trader use a theoretical pricing model if he knows the model makes an assumption which is not correct? One solution is to correct the model by making a more accurate assumption about how prices move in the real world. Then we can replace the lognormal distribution assumption with our new price distribution assumption, and thereby generate more accurate theoretical values.

There are two problems with this approach. First, in the absence of any extensive studies of commodity price distribution, no one can say with any certainty what the future price distribution for a given commodity is likely to be. Secondly, even if we were able to come up with a new and more accurate distribution, describing this distribution mathematically—which would be necessary in order to integrate it into our model—could prove so complex as to be impractical.

Given the fact that most traders are not theoreticians, is there any way we can make use of the existing theoretical pricing models to more accurately evaluate options? There is no perfect solution to this problem, but there is an approach which many traders use based on two not unreasonable assumptions. The first assumption is that, given a correct volatility forecast, the model will accurately evaluate an at-the-money option. The second assumption is that the distribution of implied volatilties in the marketplace is a reasonable approximation of the relative value of options.

Using this approach, a trader will first make a volatility forecast and use that volatility to evaluate at-the-money options. Next, the trader will look at a distribution of implied volatilities, such as in Figure 13-2. From this he will evaluate every other option using an incrementally higher or lower volatility consistent with the distribution of volatilities in the marketplace.

For example, suppose we are trying to evaluate the crude oil options in Figure 13-1. First we must make a volatility forecast for the at-the-money (17) exercise price. Let us assume our best guess about volatility to June expiration is 30%. Looking at the distribution of implied volatilties, we note that the implied volatility of the 18 call and put is approximately the same as the 17 call and put, so we will also use a volatility of 30% to evaluate the 18 exercise price. Moving up another exercise price, the 19 call has an implied volatility which is approximately 1 percentage point higher than the at-the-money option. Thus, we can add one percentage point to our base volatility of 30%, and use 31% to evaluate the 19 call and put. In the same manner, we will use a volatility 4 percentage points higher (34%) to evaluate the 20 exercise price, and a volatility 8 percentage points higher (38%) to evaluate the 21 exercise price.

Note that we must always assign the same volatility to calls and puts with the same exercise price. If we did not do this, we would be violating the put/call/underlying arbitrage relationship.

The resulting theoretical values for June crude oil options, using our base volatility of 30% and the volatility distribution implied by the marketplace, appear in Figure 13-4.

Theoretical Evaluation Based on Implied Distribution of Volatilities
June Crude Oil at 16.98; Time to Expiration 43 days; Interest Rate 7.00%

Exercise Price	Calculating Volatility	Call Value	Put Value
13	48	4.00	.05
14	42	3.05	.09
15	36	2.13	.16
16	32	1.30	.33
17	30	.68	.70
18	30	.32	1.33
19	31	.14	2.15
20	35	.09	3.08
21	40	.07	4.05

Figure 13-4

Theoretical Evaluation Based on Implied Per Cent Distribution of Volatilities
June Crude Oil at 16.98; Time to Expiration 43 days; Interest Rate 7.00%

Exercise Price	Calculating Volatility	Call Value	Put Value
13	51	4.02	.07
14	44	3.07	.11
15	38	2.15	.19
16	33	1.32	.35
17	30	.68	.70
18	30	.32	1.33
19	31	.14	2.15
20	35	.09	3.08
21	41	.08	4.06

Figure 13-5

An additional modification to this method is to increase or decrease the volatility as a percent of the at-the-money volatility. For example, we see in Figure 13-1 that the implied volatility of the 21 call is approximately 9 percentage points higher than the volatility of the 17 call. In percent terms, this is about 36% higher than the 17 call (9/25 = 36%). If we use a base volatility of 30% for the at-the-money option, the correct volatility for the 21 call will be 36% more than 30%, or about 41%. This type of ratio volatility estimation is useful in evaluating options on very high volatility underlying commodities. An example of the resulting values for crude oil is given in Figure 13-5.

This modification of model-generated theoretical values, whereby a trader assigns different volatilities to different exercise prices, has become increasingly popular. As a result, some option evaluation software already has this modification built into the system. The user need only select a base volatility and an incremental change from one exercise price to another. The software will then calculate theoretical values for every exercise price.

A trader who uses this approach will find that the implied distribution may vary from commodity to commodity. Some examples of volatility distributions are shown in Figures 13-6A through 13-6D. For example, while gold and Deutschemarks are symmetrically distributed around the at-the-money option, Treasury bonds show a strong downward bias (downside implied volatilities are high), and soybeans show a strong upward bias (upside implied volatilities are high). In each case, the distribution of implied volatilites reflects the consensus of the marketplace as to the likely distribution of underlying prices at expiration.

Assumption 3: *The volatility of an underlying contract is constant over the life of an option.*

When we forecast a future volatility for an underlying contract, we are forecasting the magnitude of the price changes over the life of the option. If we assume that the percent price changes are normally distributed, we expect 68% of the price changes to be between zero and one standard deviation, 27% of the price changes to be between one and two standard deviations, and about 5% of the price changes to be between two and three standard deviations. Moreover, we as-

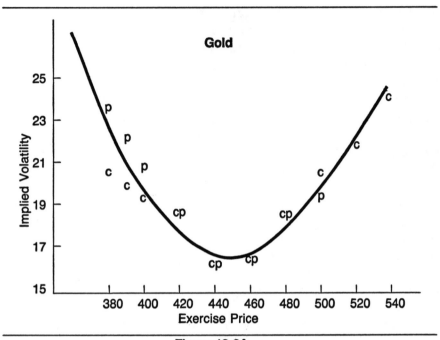

Figure 13-6A

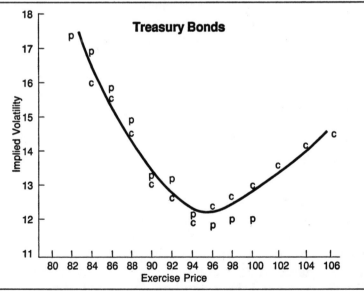

Figure 13-6B

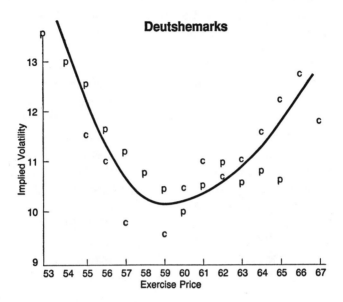

Figure 13-6C

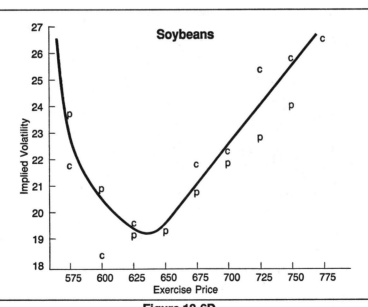

Figure 13-6D

sume that these one, two, and three standard deviation price changes will be evenly distributed over the life of the option. That is, we assume that the volatility of the underlying contract will be constant over the life of the option.

In real life, however, volatility is unlikely to be evenly distributed. Over the life of any option the underlying market may experience extended periods of both very low volatility and very high volatility. Sometimes prices sit still for weeks on end; at other times, the market jumps all over the place. If we were to look a a bar chart of price movement, we would have little difficulty identifying periods of high and low volatility. Such a chart might look like Figure 13-7.

A theoretical pricing model really doesn't care how volatility is distributed over the life of an option. A period of high volatility followed by a period of low volatility is theoretically identical to a period of low volatility followed by a period of high volatility. The model is only interested in the total volatility, not the order in which it occurs. In practice, however, the sequence of volatility can affect the value of an option.

As an option's gamma increases, it becomes more and more sensitive to changes in the volatility of the underlying contract.

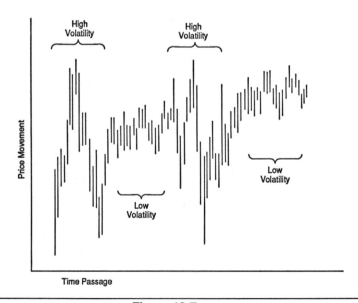

Figure 13-7

However, the gamma, like the delta, is constantly changing as market conditions change. Therefore, even though an option's life includes periods of both high and low volatility, if the period of high volatility occurs when the option's gamma is high, the model will tend to undervalue the option. If the period of high volatility occurs when the option's gamma is low, the model will tend to overvalue the option.

For example, suppose we have the two different volatility scenarios represented by Figures 13-8A and 13-8B. If we were to calculate the volatility for both scenarios we would find that they are identical. Even though the order of volatility is different, the total volatility is the same.

Now suppose we use a theoretical pricing model to evaluate an at-the-money option under these two scenarios. Since we are using the same volatility number in both cases, the theoretical value of the option in both cases will be identical. Yet in a real life trading situation we would find that the option is more valuable in scenario 13-8B than in scenario 13-8A. The reason is that with a great deal of time remaining to expiration, all options have relatively low gammas. But as expiration approaches, the gamma of an at-the-money option can increase dramatically (see Figure 6-7), thereby magnifying the effect of any increased volatility.

Another way of looking at the situation is to recall, from Chapter 5, that the value of an option, if it is hedged against the underlying futures contract, is dependent on the size of the adjustments needed to remain delta neutral. The more adjustments the holder of an option is able to make, the more valuable the option. The size of the adjustments depends on the rate at which the delta of the option changes, and this in turn is determined by the size of the option's gamma. In practice, this means that in a rising volatility market the model will tend to undervalue at-the-money options, while in a falling volatility market it will tend to overvalue at-the-money options, even though theoretically both scenarios yield identical option values.

If the fact that volatility is either rising or falling is simply random and the degree of error is identical in both cases, the principle may seem moot. But based on practical experience, most traders agree that the model tends to undervalue at-the-money options more in a rising volatility market rather than overvalue them in a falling volatility market.

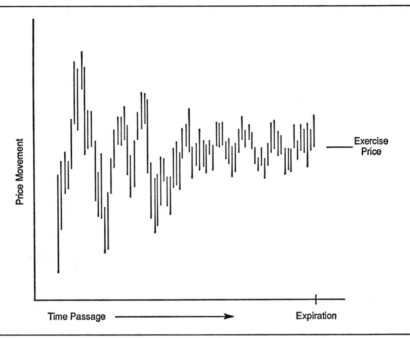

Exercise
Price

Price Movement

Time Passage ⟶   Expiration

Figure 13-8A

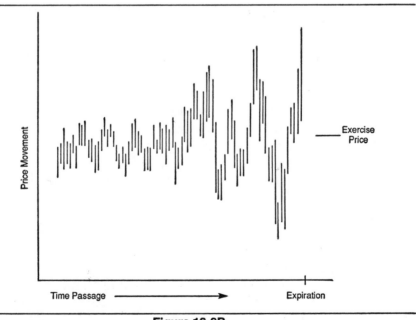

Exercise
Price

Price Movement

Time Passage ⟶   Expiration

Figure 13-8B

As traders we would like to know which options will be deeply in-the-money or far out-of-the-money at expiration (low gamma), and which will be at-the-money (high gamma). We know that the former are likely to be overvalued by the model and that the latter are likely to be undervalued. Unfortunately, underlying markets constantly move around, and today's at-the-money option may be tomorrow's in- or out-of-the-money option. There is simply no way of knowing which exercise price will be at-the-money at expiration.

If we don't know which option will be at-the-money at expiration, the point may seem nothing more than an interesting aberration in the model. However, if we make the assumption that as expiration approaches there is an increasingly greater likelihood that the current at-the-money option will also be the expiration at-the-money option, it follows that as we get closer and closer to expiration, the model is more and more likely to undervalue the current at-the-money option. This does indeed seem to be born out by experience.

Assumption 4: *Trading in an underlying contract is continuous, with no gaps in the price of the underlying.*

An additional and important assumption in most theoretical pricing models is that trading in an underlying contract is continuous. That is, trading proceeds 24-hours per day, seven days per week, without interruption. Moreover, the model assumes that there are no gaps in trading. If a commodity price moves from 101.05 to 101.08, it must have also traded at some time in between at 101.06 and 101.07.

In the real world, however, trading is not continuous, and price gaps can occur at any time. A commodity might close one day at 101.00, and open the next day at 103.00. Under these circumstances a trader who plans to adjust at 102.00 will have no chance to do so. In effect, the market has moved too fast to allow him to adjust. Even though world markets in many commodities seem to be moving toward 24-hour trading, there are still periods when no exchange trading takes place. Moreover, even during regular trading hours there are times when commodities may gap from one price to another.

If the model assumes that trading is continuous when in fact it isn't, and that there are no price gaps when in fact there are, will this result in inaccurate theoretical values? And if so, how can a trader make allowances for these inaccuracies?

It may help to think of a price gap as a swift increase in volatility. In the last section we noted that any increase in volatility will have its greatest effect on the value of an at-the-money option close to expiration. In exactly the same way, gaps in trading will have the greatest effect on at-the-money options close to expiration. This characteristic is again a result of such options having the highest gamma, and therefore changing their delta characteristics most quickly when there is significant movement in the price of the underlying contract.

For example, suppose that the following conditions exist:

Futures price	= 100.00
Volatility	= 20%
Interest rate	= 7.00%
Time to expiration	= 9 months

A trader decides to do a synthetic short straddle by purchasing one futures contract at 100.00, and selling two 100 calls at their theoretical value of 6.56. What will happen if the market gaps up 3 points at the next day's opening? Holding all other inputs constant, except for the underlying futures price which is now 103.00, we find that the 100 call is now worth 8.18. The trader's loss on the position is:

$$+3.00 - 2 \times (8.18 - 6.56) = -.24$$

Now suppose all conditions are as before, with the futures contract at 100.00, volatility at 20%, and interest rates at 7.00%. But instead of 9 months to expiration, there is only one day to expiration. If we establish the same position by purchasing one futures contract at 100.00 and selling two 100 calls at their theoretical value of .42, what will happen now if the market gaps up 3 points at the next day's (expiration day) opening? With less than a day remaining to expiration, and the underlying futures contract at 103.00, we find that the 100 call has a theoretical value of exactly parity, or 3.00. The loss to the position is therefore:

$$+3.00 - 2 \times (3.00 - .42) = -2.16$$

Notice that with 1 day to expiration a 3-point gap caused a loss 9 times greater than the loss to the same position with 9 months to expiration. We can see why the risk is so much greater with 1 day to expiration by comparing gammas. With 9 months to expiration the 100 call has a gamma of 6.6. The same call, with 1 day to expiration, has a gamma of 38.1. The higher the gamma, the greater the sensitivity to a large market move.

Intuitively, we can also see that with 9 months to expiration, even if the market gaps up to 103.00, there is still plenty of time for it to fall back to 100.00. But with one day to expiration there is not enough time for the market to drop back. The 100 call will quickly take on the characteristics of a futures contract, leaving the trader naked short one futures contract in a market which has made a violent upward move. The trader would, in theory, have adjusted between 100.00 and 103.00. But because the market gapped, the trader was unable to make the required adjustment.

Expiration Backspreads

Because theoretical pricing models assume that volatility is constant though it is not, and because trading is not continuous but from time to time exhibits price gaps, a theoretical model may incorrectly evaluate an option. While the model may inaccurately evaluate options at any time during an option's life, the effects are likely to be greatest for at-the-money options close to expiration. Under these circumstances, when the option's gamma is high and the option is very sensitive to any changes in volatility, the model will often generate values lower than the true value of the option in the real world. How much lower, no one knows; but just like the trader who is short a large number of far out-of-the-money options, the trader who is short a large number of at-the-money options going into expiration has a hidden risk that may one day put him out of business.

Indeed, even if a trader is delta neutral, one of the riskiest positions he can assume is to be short at-the-money options as expiration approaches. The large negative gamma position resulting from such a spread means that either a swift increase in volatility or a gap in the underlying market will certainly leave the trader poorer, if not totally devastated. For this reason new traders in particular are advised to avoid such positions. No clearing firm will appreciate even experienced and well-capitalized traders being short large numbers of at-the-money options as expiration approaches.

If a trader should avoid selling at-the-money options as expiration approaches, perhaps there is some sense in taking the other side by purchasing at-the-money options as expiration approaches. This may seem to contradict conventional option wisdom, which says that a trader should sell at-the-money options as expiration approaches to take advantage of increased time decay. What traders tend to forget is that there is always a tradeoff between reward and risk. The reward may be an accelerated profit if the market doesn't move, but the risk is an increased loss if the market does move. Because of the inaccuracies in the model, the hidden risk in this case is often greater than the reward. The losses from an occasional increase in volatility will more than offset any profits resulting from increased time decay. An experienced trader will therefore tend to do just the opposite of the conventional wisdom. He will tend to buy at-the-money options close to expiration if he can do so at a theoretically favorable price. Because so many traders are intent on selling time premium as expiration approaches, it is often possible to find cheap at-the-money options.

As with any strategy based purely on volatility, the trader must still establish a delta neutral hedge. We can hedge the position by either establishing a ratio vertical spread or a backspread. If we do a ratio vertical spread we will be forced to sell out-of-the-money options. But with so little time remaining to expiration such options will have a very low delta, and our spread will consequently require a high ratio of short to long options. Based on our previous discussion about the possibility of a larger than expected price change, this is the type of spread we specifically want to avoid. We are therefore restricted to backspreading our long at-the-money options against in-the-money options or against the underlying contract. Expiration backspreads which include long at-the-money options are very popular among experienced traders because of the likelihood that the theoretical pricing model has undervalued such options. With one or two weeks remaining to expiration many traders spend extra time looking for relatively cheap at-the-money options with which to establish a backspread.

An expiration backspread, like any backspread, ought to be periodically adjusted so that the spread remains delta neutral. However, with very little time remaining to expiration, it may be impractical to adjust very often. If there is only one day remaining to expiration, a trader will find it difficult to make many adjustments at equal intervals. For this reason, a trader who initiates an expiration backspread will often sit on the position to expiration without adjusting.

Even if a trader carefully chooses his expiration backspreads, the most likely outcome in any single case will be a loss. This seems to contradict the reason for doing any spread—to make money. What the trader must remember is that the primary concern is not the gain or loss from any single trade, but rather the long-term gain or loss reflected by a positive theoretical edge. Going back to our roulette bet, a player who buys a number at a roulette table can expect to win only once in every 38 plays. Still, if he can buy a bet for less than its theoretical value of 92¢, he expects to be a winner *in the long run*. When his number does come up, the winnings will more than offset the losses. The same is true of expiration backspreads. A trader may end up losing several times in a row. But the one time he does win, he can expect a return great enough to more than offset all the previous losses. The long-term theoretical edge is still a positive one, and this is the trader's primary concern.

Because he knows that the probability of a loss in any one instance is high, no trader will invest more than he is willing to lose in any one expiration backspread. But a trader ought to be willing to invest in such spreads when conditions are right, knowing that even if he loses several times in succession, an overall profit will eventually result from such strategies.

By way of example of an expiration backspread, on Thursday, May 16, 1985, one day prior to expiration of June options, the June Treasury Bond futures contract on the Chicago Board of Trade closed at 74-04. At that time, June 74 calls were trading at 23/64. Suppose a trader had purchased two June 74 calls at 23/64 and sold one June futures contract at 74-04, a typical expiration backspread. What would have happened? At the 2:00 P.M. close on Friday, May 17, the June futures contract was at 73-28. The trader might assume that this was one instance when such a strategy was unsuccessful. He would buy in his June futures contract for 73-28, and let his June 74 calls expire worthless, for a total result of:

$$+8/32 - (2 \times 23/64) = -62/64 \ (-\$937.50)$$

But something unexpected happened at 2:15 P.M. on that Friday. The Federal Reserve Board announced a cut of 1/2% in the discount rate. The cash market in Treasury Bonds immediately reacted to this announcement by jumping 1 1/2 points. This meant that June Treasury Bond futures would probably open 1 1/2 points higher when trading resumed on the following Monday morning. Prior to this news everyone had assumed that all June 74 calls were worthless, and would expire unexercised. But even though trading in options and futures ended at 2:00 P.M. on Friday, the options did not actually expire until the following Saturday. Holders of June 74 calls quickly filled out exercise notices to purchase June futures at 74-00. When the market did in fact open at 75-08 on the following Monday, they were able to close out each contract for a profit of 1-8/32. Since the spread originally included two 74 calls for each short futures contract, the actual result became:

$$-62/64 + (2 \times 1-8/32) = + 1-17/32 \ (+\$1,531.25)$$

The situation is perhaps not a perfect example of an expiration backspread since the long calls were actually unhedged at the time of exercise. However, the example does emphasize the possibility of a gap in trading, and such gaps can dramatically magnify the value of an at-the-money option if there is very little time remaining to expiration.

How likely is it that such a gap will occur as expiration approaches? Not very. And yet gaps and unexpected increases in volatility do seem to occur often enough to result in model-generated values which are too low. When this happens, an expiration backspread can be a very profitable strategy.

Because the use of a theoretical model requires us to make certain assumptions about market conditions which are obviously untrue, the reader may conclude at this point that model-generated values are likely to be too inaccurate to be of use to anyone but a theoretician. In fact, just the opposite is true. Experienced traders know that with intelligent inputs theoretical pricing models can be quite accurate.

Losses resulting from model-generated values are due most often to inaccurate inputs, rather than to weaknesses in the model itself. Only in a limited number of situations must the user of a theoretical pricing model be sceptical of model-generated values.

In fact, the greatest benefit from a theoretical pricing model may not even derive from its ability to identify profit opportunities. Once a trader has found what he thinks is a theoretically profitable trade, the model becomes especially valuable because it allows the trader to analyze not just what will happen when things go right, but also what will happen when things go wrong. A model's real value derives from its ability to analyze risk, and to help a trader prepare for protective action if conditions move against him. It is in this area of risk analysis that traders often fail to make the best use of a model.

This brings us to one final and perhaps most important principle of option trading: *There is no substitute for common sense.* A trader who slavishly uses the model to make his every trading decision is heading for certain disaster. Only the trader who has a full understanding of what a model can and cannot do for him will be able to make the model his servant rather than his master.

Appendix A

A Glossary of Option Terminology

All Or None (AON)—An order which must be filled in its entirety or not at all.

American Option—An option which may be exercised at any time prior to expiration.

Arbitrage—The simultaneous purchase and sale of the same product in different markets for a small profit.

Assignment—The process by which the seller of an option is notified of the buyer's intention to exercise.

At-the-Money—An option whose exercise price is approximately equal to the current market price of the underlying.

Automatic Exercise—The exercise by the clearing house of an in-the-money option at expiration, unless the holder of the option submits specific instructions to the contrary.

Back Spread—A spread in which more options are purchased than sold, and where all options have the same underlying and expire at the same time. Back spreads are usually delta neutral.

Backwardation—A futures market where the more distant delivery months for a commodity trade at a discount to the near term delivery months.

Bear Spread—Any spread in which a decline in the price of the underlying will theoretically increase the value of the spread.

Box—A long call and short put at one exercise price, and a short call and a long put at a different exercise price. All four options must have the same underlying and expire at the same time.

Bull Spread—Any spread in which a rise in the price of the underlying will theoretically increase the value of the spread.

Butterfly—The sale (purchase) of two identical options, together with the purchase (sale) of one option with an immediately higher exercise price, and one option with an immediately lower exercise price. All options must be of the same type, have the same underlying, and expire at the same time.

Buy/Write—The purchase of an underlying contract and the simultaneous sale of a call.

Calendar Spread—Another name for a time spread.

Call Option—A contract between a buyer and a seller whereby the buyer acquires the right, but not the obligation, to purchase a specified stock, commodity, futures contract, or cash index, at a fixed price on or before a specified date. The seller of the call option assumes the obligation of delivering the stock, commodity, futures contract, or cash index should the buyer wish to exercise his option.

Cap—A contract between a borrower and lender whereby the borrower is assured that he will not have to pay more than some maximum interest rate on borrowed funds. This type of contract is analogous to a call option where the underlying is an interest rate on borrowed funds.

Christmas Tree—A type of ratio vertical spread where options are sold at two or more different exercise prices.

Class—All options with the same underlying. The term is more generally used in futures options to refer to all options with the same underlying commodity.

Clearing Member—A member firm of an exchange which is authorized by the clearing house to process trades for its customers, and which guarantees, through the collection of margin and variation monies, the integrity of its customer's trades.

Collar—A contract between a borrower and a lender whereby the borrower is assured that he will not have to pay more than some maximum interest rate on the borrowed funds, and whereby the lender is assured of receiving some minimum interest rate on the loaned funds. This is analogous to an option fence, with an interest rate as the underlying.

Combination—A two-sided option spread which does not fall into any well defined category of spreads. More specifically, it is often used to refer to a long call and short put, or short call and long put, which together make up a synthetic position in the underlying.

Condor—The sale (purchase) of two options with consecutive exercise prices, together with the purchase (sale) of one option with an immediately lower exercise price and one option with an immediately higher exercise price. All options must be of the same type, have the same underlying, and expire at the same time.

Contango—A futures market where the more distant delivery months for a commodity trade at a premium to the near term delivery months.

Contingency Order—An order which becomes effective only upon the fulfillment of some condition in the marketplace.

Conversion—A long underlying position together with a short call and long put, where both options have the same exercise price and expiration date. A conversion is a long underlying position offset by a synthetic short underlying position.

Covered Write—The sale of a call option against an existing long underlying position.

Cylinder—Another name for either a fence or collar.

Delta—The sensitivity of an option's theoretical value to a change in the price of the underlying.

Delta Neutral Spread—A spread where the total delta position on the long side and the total delta position on the short side add up to approximately zero.

Diagonal Spread—A 2-sided spread consisting of options at different exercise prices and with different expiration dates. All options must be of the same type and have the same underlying.

Exercise—The process by which the holder of an option notifies the seller of his intention to take delivery of the underlying, in the case of a call, or make delivery, in the case of a put, at the specified exercise price.

Exercise Price—The price at which the underlying will be delivered in the event an option is exercised.

Expiration—The date and time after which an option may no longer be exercised.

European Option—An option which may only be exercised on the expiration date.

Extrinsic Value—The price of an option less its intrinsic value. The entire premium of an out-of-the-money option consists of extrinsic value.

Fair Value—Another name for theoretical value.

Fence—A long (short) underlying position, together with a long (short) out-of-the-money put and a short (long) out-of-the-money call. All options must expire at the same time. When the fence includes a long (short) underlying position, it is sometimes known as a risk conversion (reversal).

Fill Or Kill (FOK)—An order which must be filled immediately, and in its entirety. Failing this, the order will be cancelled.

Floor—A contract between a borrower and lender whereby the lender is assured that he will receive at least some minimum interest rate on the loaned funds. This type of contract is analogous to a put option where the underlying is an interest rate on loaned funds.

Forward Contract—A contract between a buyer and a seller whereby the buyer is obligated to take delivery and the seller is obligated to make delivery of a fixed amount of a commodity at a predetermined price on a specified future date. Payment in full is due at the time of delivery. (This differs from a futures contract where settlement is made daily, resulting in partial payment over the life of the contract.)

Front Spread—Another name for a ratio vertical spread.

Futures Contract—A contract between a buyer and a seller whereby the buyer is obligated to take delivery and the seller is obligated to make delivery of a fixed amount of a commodity at a predetermined price on a specified future date. Futures contracts are usually traded on an exchange and are settled daily based on their current value in the marketplace. (This differs from a forward contract where no payment is made until the actual delivery date.)

Futures Type Settlement—A settlement procedure used by commodity exchanges in which the purchase of a contract requires no immediate cash outlay. Cash settlement is made daily based on the difference between the current day's closing price, and either the previous day's closing price or the original trade price.

Gamma—The sensitivity of an option's delta to a change in the price of the underlying.

Good Til Cancelled (GTC)—An order to be held by a broker until it can be filled, or until cancelled.

Guts—A strangle where both the call and the put are in-the-money.

Haircut—On equity option exchanges, money deposited by a trader with the clearing house to ensure the integrity of his trades. This is similar to a margin requirement on an commodity exchange.

Hedger—A trader who enters the market with the specific intent of protecting an existing position in an underlying.

Horizontal Spread—Another name for a time spread.

Immediate Or Cancel (IOC)—An order which must be filled immediately or which will be cancelled. IOC orders need not be filled in their entirety.

In-the-Money—An option which could be exercised and immediately closed out against the underlying contract for a cash credit. A call is in-the-money if its exercise price is lower than the current market price of the underlying. A put is in-the-money if its exercise price is higher than the current market price of the underlying.

Intermarket Spread—A spread consisting of opposing positions in instruments with two different underlyings.

Intrinsic Value—The amount by which an option is in-the-money. Out-of-the-money options have no intrinsic value.

Iron Butterfly—The combination of a long (short) straddle and a short (long) strangle. All options must have the same underlying and expire at the same time.

Jelly Roll—A long call and short put in one expiration month, and a short call and long put in a different expiration month. All four options must have the same underlying commodity, stock, or index, and typically also have the same exercise price. Note that this is simply a long synthetic position in one month offset by a short synthetic position in a different month.

Kappa—Another name for vega.

Leg—One side of a spread position.

Limit (Move)—The maximum daily allowable price movement for an exchange traded contract.

Limit Order—An order to be filled at a specified price or better.

Local—An independent trader on a commodity exchange. Locals perform functions similar to market makers on stock and stock option exchanges.

Locked Market—A market where trading has been halted because prices have reached their limit. Trading can resume the same day if prices come off limit.

Long—A position resulting from the purchase of a contract. The term is also used to describe a position which will theoretically increase (decrease) in value should the underlying market rise (fall). Note that a long put position is a short market position.

Long Premium—A position in which a large price move in the underlying in either direction will theoretically increase the value of the position.

Margin—A deposit made by a trader with a clearing house to ensure that he will fulfill any future financial obligations resulting from his trades.

Market Maker—An independent trader or trading firm which is prepared to both buy and sell contracts in a designated market. Market makers on stock or stock option exchanges perform functions similar to locals on commodity exchanges, the primary difference being that market makers must make a two-sided (bid and ask) market.

Market If Touched (MIT)—A contingency order which becomes a market order if a contract trades at a specified price.

Market On Close (MOC)—An order to be filled at the current market price as close as possible to the close of that day's trading.

Market Order—An order to be filled immediately at the current market price.

Naked—A long (short) market position with no offsetting short (long) market position. A trader who executes one side of a two-sided spread is said to be naked until he executes the other side.

Neutral Spread—Another name for a delta neutral spread. Spreads may also be lot neutral, where the total number of long contracts and the total number of short contracts of the same type are approximately equal

Not Held—An order submitted to a broker, and over which the broker has descretion as to the prices and time at which the order will be executed.

Omega—Another name for vega.

One Cancels the Other (OCO)—Two orders submitted simultaneously, either of which may be filled. If one order is filled, the other is considered to be cancelled.

Order Book Official (OBO)—An exchange official responsible for executing limit orders in a trading pit.

Out-of-the-Money—An option which currently has no intrinsic value. A call is out-of-the-money if its exercise price is higher than the current market price of the underlying. A put is out-of-the-money if its exercise price is lower than the current price of the underlying.

Out Trade—A trade made on an exchange which cannot be processed due to conflicting terms reported by the two parties involved in the trade.

Overwrite—The sale of an option against an existing position in the underlying.

Parity—Another name for intrinsic value.

Pin Risk—The risk to a trader who has sold an option that at expiration the price of the underlying will be identical to the exercise price of the option. The trader will not know whether the option is likely to be exercised.

Position—The sum total of a trader's open contracts in a particular underlying.

Position Limit—For a single trader the maximum number of allowable open contracts with the same underlying.

Premium—The price of an option.

Put Option—A contract between a buyer and a seller whereby the buyer acquires the right, but not the obligation, to sell a specified stock, commodity, futures contract, or cash index, at a fixed price on or before a specified date. The seller of the put option assumes the obligation of taking delivery of the stock, commodity, futures contract, or cash index should the buyer wish to exercise his option.

Range Forward—Another name for a fence.

Ratio Spread—Any spread where the number of long market contracts and the number of short market contracts are unequal.

Ratio Vertical Spread—A spread where more contracts are sold than are purchased, with all contracts having the same underlying and expiration date. Ratio vertical spreads are usually delta neutral.

Reverse Conversion (Reversal)—A short underlying position, together with a long call and short put, where both options have the same exercise price and expiration date. A reverse conversion is a short underlying position offset by a long synthetic underlying position.

Rho—The sensitivity of an option's theoretical value to a change in interest rates.

Risk Conversion/Reversal—Another name for a fence.

Scalper—An exchange trader who hopes to make a profit by buying at the bid and selling at the offer. Scalpers try to close out all positions at the end of each trading day.

Serial Expiration—Options on the same futures contract which expire in more than one month.

Series—All options of the same class with the same exercise price and expiration date.

Short—A position resulting from the sale of a contract. The term is also used to describe a position which will theoretically increase (decrease) in value should the underlying market fall (rise). Note that a short put position is a long market position.

Short Premium—A position in which a large price move in the underlying in either direction will theoretically decrease the value of the position.

Specialist—A market maker given exclusive rights by an exchange to make a market in a specified underlying. A specialist may buy and sell for his own account, or act as a broker for other exchange members. In return, a specialist is required to maintain a fair and orderly market in his underlying.

Speculator—A trader who hopes to profit from a specific directional move in an underlying.

Spread—A long market position and an offsetting short market position usually, but not always, in contracts with the same underlying.

Stock Type Settlement—A settlement procedure in which the purchase of a contract requires immediate and full payment by the buyer to the seller. In stock type settlement the actual cash profit or loss from a trade is not realized until the position is liquidated.

Stop Limit Order—A contingency order to buy or sell a contract at a limited price or better if the contract trades at a specified price.

Stop (Loss) Order—A contingency order to buy or sell a contract at the current market price if the contract trades at a specified price.

Straddle—A position consisting of a long (short) call and a long (short) put, where both options have the same underlying, the same expiration date, and the same exercise price.

Strangle—A position consisting of a long (short) call and a long (short) put, where both options have the same underlying, the same expiration date, but different exercise prices. Typically, both options are out-of-the-money. *See also* **Guts.**

Strap—A position consisting of two long (short) calls and one long (short) put, where all options have the same underlying, the same expiration date, and the same exercise price.

Strike Price—Another name for exercise price.

Strip—A position consisting of one long (short) call and two long (short) puts, where all options have the same underlying, the same expiration date, and the same exercise price.

Synthetic Call—A long (short) underlying position together with a long (short) put.

Synthetic Put—A short (long) underlying position together with a long (short) call.

Synthetic Underlying—A long (short) call together with a short (long) put where both options have the same underlying, exercise price, and expiration date.

Theoretical Value—An option value generated by a mathematical model given certain prior assumptions about the terms of the option, the characteristics of the underlying, and prevailing interest rates.

Theta—The sensitivity of an option's theoretical value to a change in the amount of time to expiration.

Time Spread—A spread consisting of one long and one short option of the same type and with the same exercise price, but which expire in different months. All options must have the same underlying stock or commodity.

Time Premium—Another name for extrinsic value.

Time Value—Another name for extrinsic value.

Type—The designation of an option as either a call or a put.

Underlying—The stock, commodity, futures contract, or cash index to be delivered in the event an option is exercised.

Vega—The sensitivity of an option's theoretical value to a change in volatility.

Vertical Spread—A spread in which one option is bought and one option is sold, where both options are of the same type, have the same underlying, and expire at the same time. The options differ only by their exercise prices.

Volatility—The degree to which the price of an underlying tends to fluctuate over time.

Appendix B
The Mathematics of
Option Pricing

1. The Black-Scholes Model and its variations

Abbreviations used in the following mathematical formulae:

C = the theoretical value of a call
P = the theoretical value of a put
U = the price of the underlying
E = the exercise price
t = the time to expiration in years
v = the annual volatility in per cent
r = the risk free interest rate
e = the base of the natural logarithm
$\ln$ = the natural logarithm
$N'(x)$ = the normal distribution curve

$$= \frac{1}{\sqrt{2\pi}} e^{-x^2/2}$$

$N(x)$ = the cumulative normal density function

A. *The Black-Scholes Model* for evaluating European options on non-dividend paying stocks (U = price of the underlying stock):

$$C = Ue^{-rt}N(h) - Ee^{-rt}N(h - v\sqrt{t})$$

$$P = -Ue^{-rt}N(-h) + Ee^{-rt}N(v\sqrt{t} - h)$$

where

$$h = \frac{\ln\left[U/(Ee^{-rt})\right]}{v\sqrt{t}} + \frac{v\sqrt{t}}{2}$$

For stocks which pay dividends, the current stock price (U) can be replaced by the current price less the present value of the expected dividends:

$$U - \sum_{i=1}^{n} d_i e^{-rt_i}$$

where d_i = each expected dividend payout
t_i = the time to payout

The sensitivities of the Black-Scholes formula are:

$$\text{call delta} = N(h)$$

$$\text{put delta} = -N(-h)$$

$$\text{call gamma} = \text{put gamma} = \frac{N'(h)}{Uv\sqrt{t}}$$

$$\text{call theta} = \frac{UvN'(h)}{2\sqrt{t}} + rEe^{-rt}N(h - v\sqrt{t})$$

$$\text{put theta} = \frac{UvN'(h)}{2\sqrt{t}} - rEe^{-rt}N(v\sqrt{t} - h)$$

$$\text{call vega} = \text{put vega} = U\sqrt{t}N'(h)$$

$$\text{call rho} = tEe^{-rt}N(h - v\sqrt{t})$$

$$\text{put rho} = -tEe^{-rt}N(v\sqrt{t} - h)$$

B. *The Black Model* for evaluating European options on futures contracts, where the option is subject to stock type settlement (U = the price of the underlying futures contract):

$$C = Ue^{-rt}N(h) - Ee^{-rt}N(h - v\sqrt{t})$$
$$P = -Ue^{-rt}N(-h) + Ee^{-rt}N(v\sqrt{t} - h)$$

where

$$h = \frac{\ln (U/E)}{v\sqrt{t}} + \frac{v\sqrt{t}}{2}$$

The sensitivities of the Black formula are:

$$\text{call delta} = e^{-rt}N(h)$$

$$\text{put delta} = -e^{-rt}N(-h)$$

$$\text{call gamma} = \text{put gamma} = \frac{e^{-rt}N'(h)}{Uv\sqrt{t}}$$

$$\text{call theta} = -rUe^{-rt}N(h) + rEe^{-rt}N(h - v\sqrt{t})$$
$$+ Ue^{-rt}N'(h)v/(2\sqrt{t})$$

$$\text{put theta} = rUe^{-rt}N(-h) - rEe^{-rt}N(v\sqrt{t} - h)$$
$$+ Ue^{-rt}N'(h)v/(2\sqrt{t})$$

$$\text{call vega} = \text{put vega} = e^{-rt}U\sqrt{t}N'(h)$$

$$\text{call rho} = -tC$$

$$\text{put rho} = -tP$$

If options on futures are subject to futures type settlement, simply set $r = 0$ in each of the above formulae.

C. *The Garman Kohlhagen Model* for evaluating European options on foreign currencies ($U =$ the price of the foreign currency in domestic currency units):

$$C = e^{-r_f t}UN(h) - e^{-r_d t}EN(h - v\sqrt{t})$$
$$P = e^{-r_f t}U(N(h) - 1) - e^{-r_d t}E(N(h - v\sqrt{t}) - 1)$$

where

$$h = \frac{\ln (U/E) + [r_d - r_f - (v^2/2)]t}{v\sqrt{t}}$$

$r_d =$ the risk-free interest rate in the domestic currency
$r_f =$ the risk free rate in the foreign currency

The sensitivities of the Garman-Kohlhagen formula are:

$$\text{call delta} = e^{-r_f t} N(h)$$

$$\text{put delta} = -e^{-r_f t} N(-h)$$

$$\text{call gamma} = \text{put gamma} = \frac{e^{-r_f t} N'(h)}{U v \sqrt{t}}$$

$$\text{call theta} = r_f e^{-r_f t} U N(h) - r_d e^{-r_d t} E N(h - v\sqrt{t})$$
$$- e^{-r_f t} U v N'(h)/(2\sqrt{t})$$

$$\text{put theta} = -r_f e^{-r_f t} U N(-h) + r_d e^{-r_d t} E N(v\sqrt{t} - h)$$
$$- e^{-r_f t} U v N'(h)/(2\sqrt{t})$$

$$\text{call vega} = \text{put vega} = e^{-r_f t} U \sqrt{t} N'(h)$$

$$\text{call domestic rho} = t e^{-r_d t} E N(h - v\sqrt{t})$$

$$\text{put domestic rho} = -t e^{-r_d t} E N(v\sqrt{t} - h)$$

$$\text{call foreign rho} = -t e^{-r_f t} E N(h)$$

$$\text{put foreign rho} = t e^{-r_f t} E N(-h)$$

The only difficulty in using the Black-Scholes Model or its variations may be the computation of $N(x)$, the cumulative normal density function. The following approximation is suitable for most practical uses:

If $x \geqslant 0$, then

$$N(x) = 1 - N'(x)(.4361836 k - .1201676 k^2 + .9372980 k^3)$$

where $k = 1/(1 + .33267 \, |x|)$ and $N'(x)$ is the normal distribution curve previously described.

If $x < 0$, then $N(x) = 1 - N(x)$.

2. The Cox-Ross-Rubenstein (Binomial) Model.

We first define:

n = the number of intervals to expiration
t = the time to expiration in years
r = the risk free interest rate

The basic form of the model for evaluating European options is then:

$$C = \frac{1}{(rr)^n} \left[\sum_{k=0}^{n} \frac{n!}{k!(n-k)!} q^k (1-q)^{n-k} \max(0, u^k d^{n-k} U - E) \right]$$

$$P = \frac{1}{(rr)^n} \left[\sum_{k=0}^{n} \frac{n!}{k!(n-k)!} q^k (1-q)^{n-k} \max(0, E - u^k d^{n-k} U) \right]$$

where

$$u = e^{v\sqrt{t}/n}$$

$$d = \frac{1}{u}$$

$$rr = 1 + \frac{rt}{n} \quad \text{(one plus the risk free interest rate over each period, } n)$$

and for an option on stock:

$$q = \frac{rr - d}{u - d}$$

and for an option on a futures contract:

$$q = \frac{1 - d}{u - d}$$

If n is chosen large enough in the above formula, the Cox-Ross-Rubenstein model will converge to the Black-Scholes model.

In order to use the model to evaluate an American option, we need to check whether, at each possible underlying price after each time interval, the current value of the option is such that early exercise is warranted. If we define $U(i,j)$ as the jth underlying price at the end of time period i (see Figure A-1), and $C(i,j)$ or $P(i,j)$ as the call or put value at each $U(i,j)$, then we must check to see if $C(i,j) < U(i,j) - E$ in the case of a call, or if $P(i,j) < E - U(i,j)$ in the case of a put.

We begin by computing each : $U(n,j)$ for $j = 0, \ldots, n$

$$U(i,j) = U \, u^j \, d^{(n-j)}$$

At the end of the nth period (expiration), the value of a call at each $U(n,j)$ is the maximum of either zero or $U(n,j) - E$, and the value of a put is the maximum of either zero or $E - U(n,j)$. From each of these possible values we work backward towards either $C(0,0)$ or $P(0,0)$ (the current value of the call or put), checking at each intermediate $U(i,j)$ whether it is better to exercise the option or hold it. Using this technique, for $i = n - 1$ to 0 and for $j = 0$ to i, we can express the value of an American call:

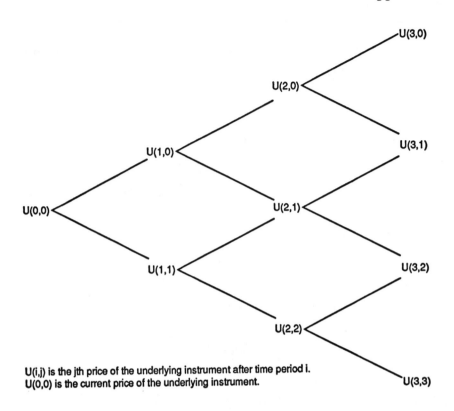

U(i,j) is the jth price of the underlying instrument after time period i.
U(0,0) is the current price of the underlying instrument.

Figure A-1

$C(i,j)$ = the greater of either

$$\frac{qC(i+1,j) + (1-q)C(i+1,j+1)}{rr} \text{ or } U(i,j) - E$$

and the value of an American put:
$P(i,j)$ = the greater of either

$$\frac{qP(i+1,j) + (1-q)P(i+1,j+1)}{rr} \text{ or } E - U(i,j)$$

Further, we can calculate:

$$\text{call delta} = \frac{C(1,1) - C(1,0)}{U(1,1) - U(1,0)}$$

$$\text{put delta} = \frac{P(1,1) - P(1,0)}{U(1,1) - P(1,0)}$$

The larger n is chosen, the more accurate the option value generated by the model will be. Unfortunately, as we increase n, the number of calculations required increases geometrically. At some point, the additional accuracy is not worth the extra computer time needed for a larger n. Many services which use the Cox-Ross-Rubenstein model have settled on $n = 50$ as a reasonable tradeoff between accuracy and computer time.

3. The Whaley Model

We first define:

C = the value of an American call
c = the value of a European call
r = the risk free interest rate
b = carrying costs on the underlying instrument
   ($b = r$ for stocks)
   ($b = 0$ for futures)

To find the value of an American call, we must solve the following equation for the critical underlying price, U^*:

$$U^* - E = c(U^*) + \frac{[1 - e^{(b-r)t}N(h^*)]U^*}{q_2}$$

where $c(U^*)$ = the value of the European call at U^*

$$h^* = \frac{\ln [U^*/(Ee^{(b-r)t}]}{v\sqrt{t}} + \frac{v\sqrt{t}}{2}$$

$$q_2 = \frac{-N + 1 + \sqrt{(N-1)^2 + 4M/K}}{2}$$

$$K = 1 - e^{-rt}$$

$$M = 2r/v^2$$

$$N = 2b/v^2$$

Then:

$$C(U) = c(U) + A_2(U/U^*) \qquad \text{when } U < U^*$$

and

$$C(U) = U - E \qquad \text{when } U \geqslant U^*$$

where

$$A_2 = \frac{U^*}{q_2}(1 - e^{(b-r)t})N(h^*)$$

The only real difficulty in using the Whaley model is in solving for the critical underlying price, U^*. Whaley and Barone-Adesi suggest an iterative approach:

Let $U_i = E$

Define $L(U_i) = U_i - E$ (the left side of the critical equation)

Define $R(U_i) = c(U_i) + \dfrac{[1 - e^{(b-r)t}N(h_i)]U_i}{q_2}$ (the right side of the critical equation)

Choose a margin for error, ε.

Then we continue iteration until

$$|L(U_i) - R(U_i)| \leqslant \varepsilon$$

at which point we can use U_i as our approximation of U^*.

In order to generate each subsequent U_i we take the derivative Δ_i of the right hand side:

$$\Delta_i = e^{(b-r)t}N(h_i)\left(1 - \frac{1}{q_2}\right) + \frac{[1 - e^{(b-r)t}N'(h_i)]/v\sqrt{t}}{q_2}$$

Then

$$U_{i+1} = \frac{E + R(U_i) - \Delta_i U_i}{1 - \Delta_i}$$

Finally, when we arrive at the critical underlying price, U^*, we also have as a byproduct the delta of the call which is the last Δ_i.

To solve for an American put, P, the method is analogous to that for a call, except that the critical underlying price, U^*, is found by solving:

$$E - U^* = p(U^*) - \frac{[1 - e^{(b-r)t}N(-h^*)]U^*}{q_1}$$

where $p(U^*)$ is the value of a European put at U^*, K, M, N, and h^* are as previously defined

and

$$q_1 = \frac{-N + 1 - \sqrt{(N-1)^2 + 4M/K}}{2}$$

Then:

$$P(U) = p(U) + A_1(U/U^*) \qquad \text{when } U > U^*$$

and

$$P(U) = E - U \qquad \text{when } U \leqslant U^*$$

where

$$A_1 = -\left(\frac{U^*}{q_1}\right)(1 - e^{(b-r)t})N(-h^*)$$

Using the same iterative approach to finding U^* we let:

$$L(U_i) = E - U_i$$

and

$$R(U_i) =$$

and continue until

$$|L(U_i) - R(U_i)| \leqslant$$

at which point we can use U_i as our approximation of U^*.

In order to generate each subsequent U_i we again take the derivative Δ_i of the right hand side, which for a put is:

$$\Delta_i = -e^{(b-r)t}N(-h_i)\left(1 + \frac{1}{q_1}\right) - \frac{[1 - e^{(b-r)t}N'(-h_i)]/v\sqrt{t}}{q_1}$$

Then

$$U_{i+1} = \frac{E + R(U_i) - \Delta_i U_i}{1 - \Delta_i}$$

Note that when working with the same underlying instrument it is only necessary to use this iterative method to find one critical underlying price, U^*, for one exercise price, E^*. Once U^* has been found, the critical underlying price, U^{**}, for another exercise price, E^{**}, is:

$$U^{**} = (U^*/E^*)E^{**}.$$

4. Volatility

A. *Mean and Standard Deviation:* Since a volatility figure is a standard deviation, it will be useful to know how a standard deviation is calculated. We must first define the mean (m) of n occurences (x_i):

$$m = \frac{1}{n}\sum_{i=1}^{n} x_i$$

The standard deviation (σ) is then defined as:

$$\sigma = \sqrt{\frac{1}{n-1} \sum_{i=1}^{n} (m - x_i)^2}$$

For example, we can calculate the mean and standard deviation of the pinball distribution in fig. 4-6. In order to arrive at the mean, we multiply the number of balls in each trough by the number of that trough, add up the total (565), and divide by the total number of balls (75):

$$m = 565/75 = 7.5333 \text{ (see Figure A-2)}$$

To arrive at the standard deviation, for each ball we square the difference between its trough and the mean, add up each of these 75 results, divide by the number of occurrences less one, and take the square root of this number:

$$\sqrt{\frac{1}{n-1} \sum_{i=1}^{n} (m - x)^2} = \sqrt{\frac{1}{74} \sum_{i=1}^{75} (7.5333 - x_i)^2}$$

$$= \sqrt{\frac{42.6667}{74}}$$

$$= \sqrt{8.6847}$$

$$= 2.9470$$

B. Historical volatility is the standard deviation of a series of price changes measured at regular intervals. Most commonly, the price changes are defined as either the per cent price changes or the logarithmic price changes.

Using per cent price changes, we define:

$$X_i = \frac{P_{i+1} - P_i}{P_i}$$

Using logarithmic price changes, we define:

$$X_i = \ln\left(\frac{P_{i+1}}{P_i}\right)$$

where in both cases p_i is the price at the end of each interval i.

In order to annualize the resulting standard deviation we must muliply by the square root of the number of intervals in year. A standard deviation based on weekly price changes must be multiplied by $\sqrt{52}$; a standard deviation based on monthly price changes must be multiplied by $\sqrt{12}$.

Value	Number of Occurences	Trough		Deviation from the Mean	Deviation Squared
0	0	0		7.533	56.746
1	1	1		6.533	42.680
4	2	2		5.533	30.614
9	3	3		4.533	20.548
24	6	4		3.533	12.482
40	8	5		2.533	6.416
42	7	6		1.533	2.350
70	10	7		.533	.284
88	11	8		.467	.218
81	9	9		1.467	2.152
50	5	10		2.467	6.086
66	6	11		3.467	12.020
48	4	12		4.467	19.954
13	1	13		5.467	29.888
14	1	14		6.467	41.822
15	1	15		7.467	55.756
565	75	totals			

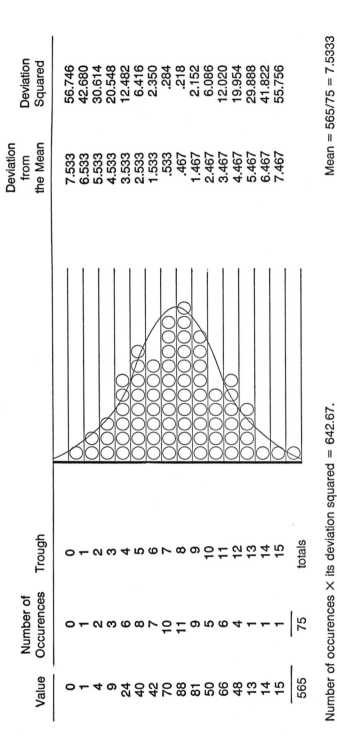

Number of occurences × its deviation squared = 642.67.

Mean = 565/75 = 7.5333

Figure A-2

These two approaches to computing volatility differ only in the manner in which price changes are assumed to occur. Per cent changes assume that prices change at fixed intervals. Logarithmic changes assume that prices are continuously changing. This is similar to a bank paying compounding interest on a savings account at regular intervals (per cent changes) versus compounding interest continuously (logarithmic changes).

The logarithmic approach may initially seem more appropriate because it more accurately reflects the continuous trading assumption in most theoretical pricing models. In the real world however trading is not continuous, so per cent changes seem to offer a realistic alternative. In fact, numbers generated by the two methods are unlikely to differ significantly. More importantly the trader should remember that volatility is at best only an approximation of how prices are distributed over time. How a volatility figure is used will be more important in the long run than small errors in its accuracy.

As an example of a volatility calculation, we can use the logarithmic method to calculate the volatility of the underlying commodity in Figure A-3. (See also Figure 5-1.)

C. *Implied volatility:* While it is not possible to invert the Black-Scholes model to arrive at an implied volatility for an option, a Newton search can be used to compute this number. We first make a guess as to the option's implied volatility, and then use the option's sensitivity to a change in volatility (vega) to converge on the true implied volatility. This method is illustrated in Figure A-4.

Because an option's vega is relatively linear, the method converges very quickly, usually with no more than three passes through the loop, even with a poor first guess. The iterative process is:

$$x_{i+1} = x_i - \frac{y_i - p}{v_i}$$

until $|y_i - p| \leqslant \varepsilon$, at which point:

$$x_i = \text{the implied volatility}$$

where p = the option's price
x_i = the volatility
y_i = the options theoretical value at volatility x_i
v_i = the option's vega at theoretical value y_i
ε = the desired degree of accuracy

Week	Underlying Price	$\ln \frac{p_n}{p_{n-1}}$	Mean	Deviation from Mean	Deviation Squared
0	101.35				
1	102.26	+.008939		.007772	.000060
2	99.07	−.031692		.032859	.001080
3	100.39	+.013236		.012069	.000146
4	100.74	+.003480		.002313	.000005
5	103.59	+.027898	Mean = .011674/10 = .001167	.026731	.000715
6	99.26	−.042698		.043865	.001924
7	98.28	−.009922		.011089	.000123
8	99.98	+.017150		.015983	.000255
9	103.78	+.037303		.036136	.001306
10	102.54	−.012020		.013187	.000174
		+.011674 (sum)			.005788 (sum)

0005788/9 = $\sqrt{.000643}$ = .025360 = .025360
Annualized Volatility = .25360 × $\sqrt{52}$ = .182871

Figure A-3

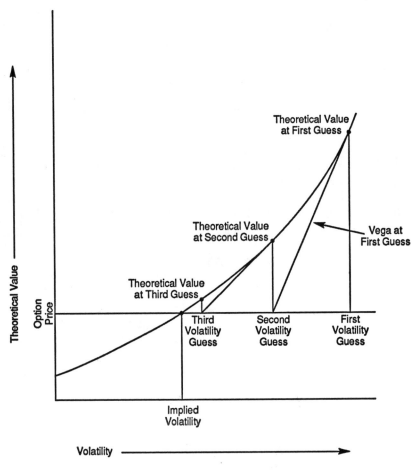

Figure A-4

Appendix C

Some Historical Volatilities

The following graphs represent the historical volatilities of commodities on which options are actively traded in the United States. Because the graphs have been smoothed out considerably, the reader should not draw any conclusions about the short-term volatility of a commodity. The graphs are intended only as a general guide to a commodity's characteristic range of volatilities. Where possible, commodities with similar characteristics have been grouped together.

The volatility at each data point represents a 10-week moving average of a 10-week annualized volatility. Calculations were made using the per cent change in the settlement price from one Friday to the next, using the near-term futures contract except in the delivery month.

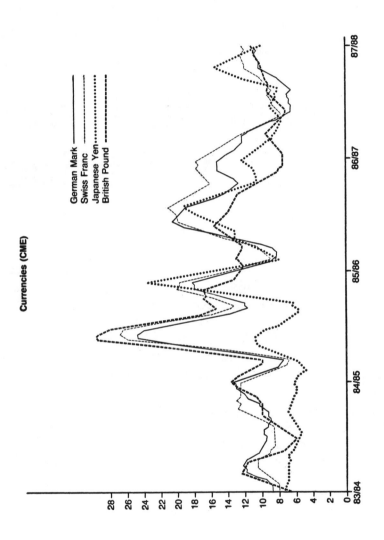

Currencies (CME)

German Mark
Swiss Franc
Japanese Yen
British Pound

28
26
24
22
20
18
16
14
12
10
8
6
4
2
0

83/84   84/85   85/86   86/87   87/88

Currencies

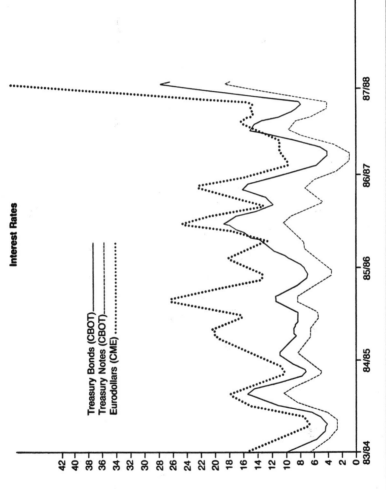

Interest Rates

Treasury Bonds (CBOT) ———
Treasury Notes (CBOT) ———
Eurodollars (CME) ·············

Interest Rates

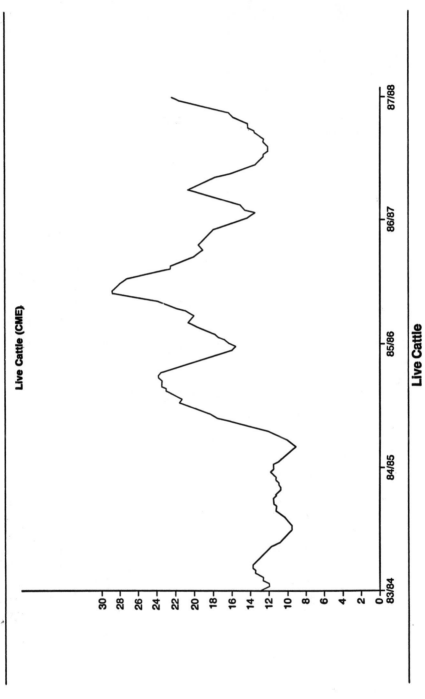

Live Cattle (CME)

Live Cattle

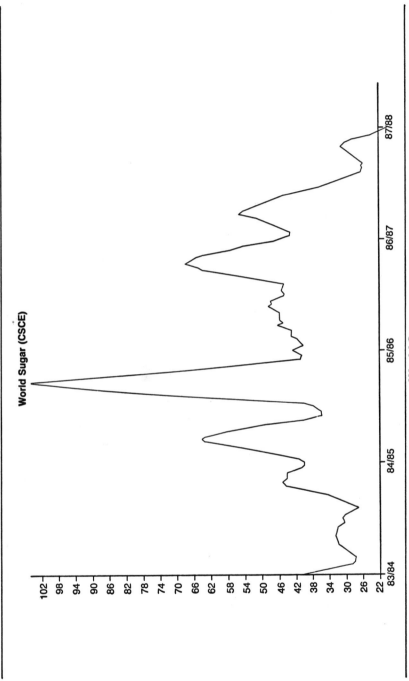

World Sugar (CSCE)

World Sugar

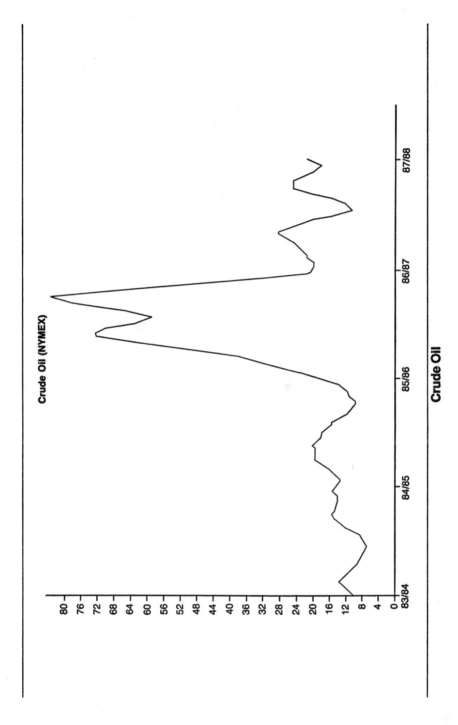

Crude Oil (NYMEX)

Crude Oil

Precious Metals

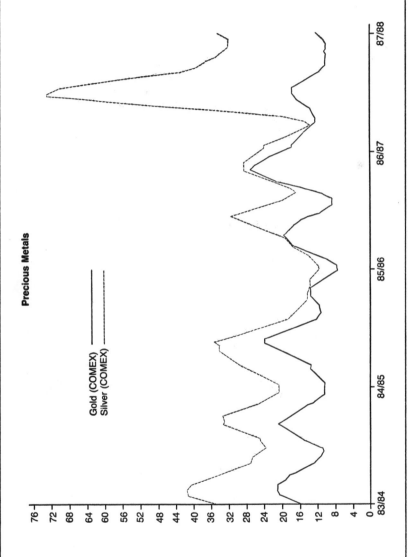

Gold (COMEX) ———
Silver (COMEX) -------

Precious Metals

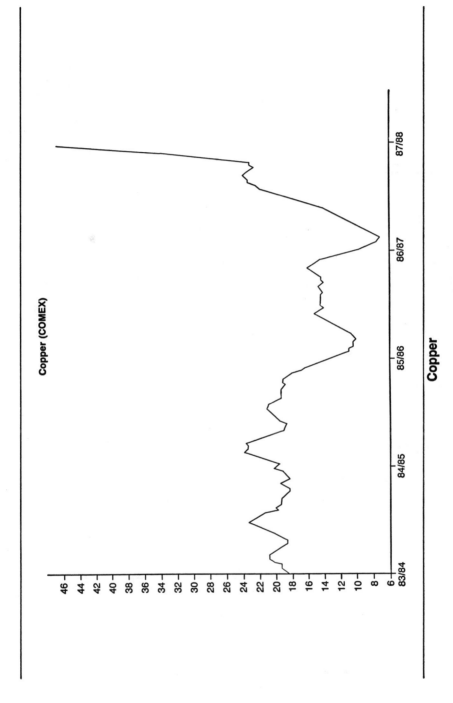

Copper (COMEX)

Copper

Grains

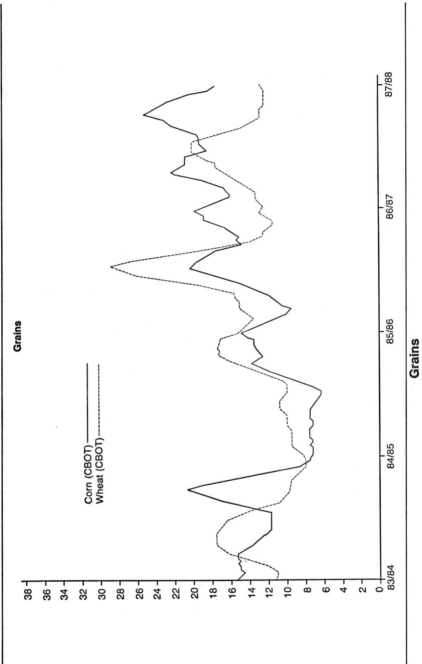

Grains

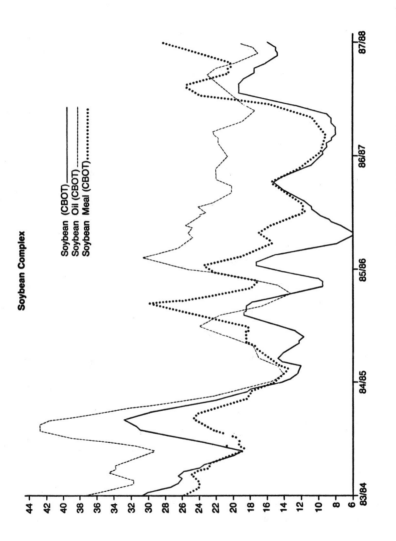

Soybean Complex

Soybean (CBOT) _____
Soybean Oil (CBOT) _ _ _ _ _
Soybean Meal (CBOT)••••••••

Soybean Complex

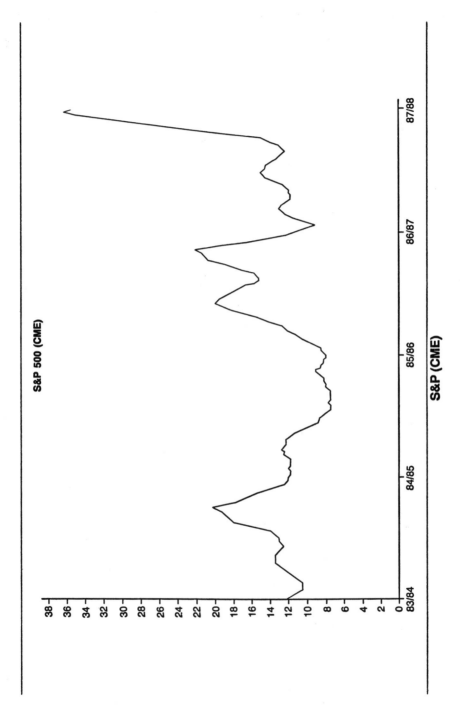

S&P 500 (CME)

S&P (CME)

Appendix D

Characteristics of Volatility Spreads

Spread Type	Initial Delta	Initial Gamma	Initial Theta	Initial Vega	A Large Move in the Underlying Generally	An Increase (Decrease) in Implied Volatility Generally	The Passage of Time Generally	Maximum Upside Risk/Reward	Maximum Downside Risk/Reward
Call Backspread	0	+	–	+	helps	helps (hurts)	hurts	unlim. reward	lim. reward
Put Backspread	0	+	–	+	helps	helps (hurts)	hurts	lim. reward	unlim. reward
Call Ratio Vertical Spread	0	–	+	–	hurts	hurts (helps)	helps	unlim. risk	lim. risk
Put Ratio Vertical Spread	0	–	+	–	hurts	hurts (helps)	helps	lim. risk	unlim. risk
Long Straddle	0	+	–	+	helps	helps (hurts)	hurts	unlim. reward	unlim. reward
Short Straddle	0	–	+	–	hurts	hurts (helps)	helps	unlim. risk	unlim. risk
Long Strangle	0	+	–	+	helps	helps (hurts)	hurts	unlim. reward	unlim. reward
Short Strangle	0	–	+	–	hurts	hurts (helps)	helps	unlim. risk	unlim. risk
Long Butterfly	0	–	+	–	hurts	hurts (helps)	helps	lim. risk	lim. risk
Short Butterfly	0	+	–	+	helps	helps (hurts)	hurts	lim. reward	lim. reward
Long Time Spread	0	–	+	+	hurts	helps (hurts)	helps	lim. risk*	lim. risk*
Short Time Spread	0	+	–	–	helps	hurts (helps)	hurts	lim. reward*	lim. reward*

All spreads are assumed to be approximately delta neutral.

"unlim." = unlimited.

"lim." = limited.

*Assuming the spread between underlying contracts remains unchanged.

Appendix E

What's the Best Strategy?

The following chart is designed to help the reader choose the types of strategies which are likely to be profitable given a trader's opinion on market direction and implied volatility. Even though several strategies may be appropriate under the same market conditions, each strategy will have different risk/reward characteristics. The reader should refer to the text for a detailed analysis of each strategy.

Any appropriate strategy may also be done synthetically. For example, instead of selling the underlying contract (moderate implied volatility, bearish market perspective), a trader can instead sell a call and buy a put with the same exercise price (synthetic short underlying). Instead of selling naked puts (high implied volatility, bullish market perspective), a trader can instead buy the underlying contract and sell a call (buy/write, equivalent to a synthetic short put).

The only scenario for which there is no appropriate strategy is the one in which a trader has no opinion on either implied volatility or market direction. When there is no apparent profit opportunity, a disciplined trader will choose to sit on the sidelines.

Chart Abbreviations: **ITM**=in-the-money
                                      ATM=at-the-money
                                      OTM=out-of-the-money

In-the-money call butterflies and time spreads, and out-of-the-money put buttterflies and time spreads, are those in which all exercise prices are lower than the current price of the underlying.

Out-of-the-money call butterflies and time spreads, and in-the-money put butterflies and time spreads, are those in which all exercise prices are higher than the current price of the underlying.

	Implied Volatility		
	Low	**Moderate**	**High**

Bearish	buy naked puts
	vertical spreads:
	  buy ATM calls/sell ITM calls
	  buy ATM puts/sell OTM puts
	sell OTM call butterflies
	sell ITM put butterflies
	buy ITM call time spreads
	buy OTM put time spreads
		sell the underlying	sell naked calls
			vertical spreads:
			  sell ATM calls/buy OTM calls
			  sell ATM puts/buy ITM puts
			buy ITM call butterflies
			buy OTM put butterflies
			sell OTM call time spreads
			sell ITM put time spreads

Neutral	call backspreads (slightly bullish) put backspreads (slightly bearish) buy straddles buy strangles sell ATM call or put butterflies buy ATM call or put time spreads	go on vacation	call ratio vertical spreads put ratio vertical spreads sell straddles sell strangles buy ATM call or put butterflies sell ATM call or put time spread

Bullish	buy naked calls
	vertical spreads:
	  buy ATM calls/sell OTM calls
	  buy ATM puts/sell ITM puts
	sell ITM call butterflies
	sell OTM put butterflies
	buy OTM call time spreads
	buy ITM put butterflies
		buy the underlying	sell naked puts
			vertical spreads:
			  sell ATM calls/buy OTM calls
			  sell ATM puts/buy ITM puts
			buy OTM call butterflies
			buy ITM put butterflies
			sell ITM call time spread
			sell OTM put time spreads

Market Direction

Appendix F

Synthetic and Arbitrage Relationships

1. *Synthetic equivalents:*   synthetic long underlying = long call + short put
synthetic short underlying = short call +long put

synthetic long call = long underlying + long put
synthetic short call = short underlying + short put

synthetic long put = short underlying + long call
synthetic short put = long underlying + short call

where all options have the same exercise price and expiration data

2. *Arbitrage strategies:*   conversion = long underlying + synthetic short underlying
= long underlying + short call + long put

reverse conversion = short underlying + synthetic long underlying
= short underlying + long call + short put

box = synthetic long underlying at one exercise price +
synthetic short underlying at a different exercise price

jelly roll = synthetic long underlying in one delivery month +
synthetic short underlying in a different delivery month

3. *Arbitrage Values for European Options (no early exercise permitted):*

In the following equations the "present value" is defined to be the value at expiration less carrying costs.

i. For futures markets where options are settled like futures:

synthetic underlying market = call price − put price = exercise price − underlying price

box market = the amount between exercise prices

jelly roll market = long-term synthetic market − short-term synthetic market
= (long-term call − long-term put) − (short-term call − short-term put)
= carrying costs on the underlying between short-term and long-term expiration

ii. For futures markets where options are settled like stock:

synthetic underlying market = call price − put price
= present value (exercise price − underlying price)

box market = present value (the amount between exercise prices)

jelly roll market = long-term synthetic market − short-term synthetic market
= carry on the underlying between expiration dates
− carry on the long-term synthetic market
+ carry on the short-term synthetic market

3. *Arbitrage Values for European options (no early exercise permitted)—continued:*
iii. *For stocks*
synthetic underlying market = call price − put price
= exercise price − underlying price
+ present value (exercise price) − expected dividends

box market = present value (the amount between exercise prices)

jelly roll market = long-term synthetic market − short-term synthetic market
= carry on the underlying between expiration dates − expected dividends

4. *Other Useful Relationships*

box = conversion at one exercise price + reverse conversion at a different exercise price
= bull (bear) vertical call spread + bear (bull) vertical put spread

call butterfly = put butterfly with the same exercise prices

long (short) call butterfly + short (long) put butterfly with the same exercise prices
= one long and one short box

long (short) butterfly = long (short) iron butterfly
= long (short) straddle + short (long) strangle

jelly roll = long (short) call time spread + short (long) put time spread

Appendix G

A Guide to Option Software and Computer Services

The following guide to computer and software vendors for option traders is designed to help the trader locate computer support appropriate to his area of interest. The material in the guide was compiled from a questionnaire sent to each of the vendors listed. Due to the large number of vendors, no attempt has been made to verify the information contained in this guide. A prospective user should contact each company individually and ask for a detailed description of the services or software. A physical demonstration, as well as serveral references, will also be helpful in making a final decision.

The letter codes used in the guide are as follows:

Types of Options Evaluated

A. Stock options

B. Futures options

C. Index options

D. Foreign currency options

E. Debt or interest rate option

F. Customized "over-the-counter" options

Models Used

A. Black-Scholes or a variation, including the Black model for futures and the Garman-Kohlhagen model for foreign currencies.

B. Cox-Ross-Rubenstein (binomial)

C. Whaley

D. Proprietary

Modification of Distribution or Volatilities

The user may use other than a lognormal distribution, or may assign different volatilities to each exercise price.

Analytical Capabilities

A. Theoretical values

B. Delta (hedge ratio)

C. Gamma (curvature)

D. Theta (time decay)

E. Vega (volatility sensitivity)

F. Implied volatility

Volatility Analysis

The user can calculate and display either the historical volatility of the underlying instrument, or the implied volatility of options on the instrument.

Plotting Capabilities

A. Simple spread postions

B. Complex positions consisting of options on more than one underlying instrument

C. Plot evaluation by change in:

    i. Underlying price

    ii. Volatility

    iii. Time to expiration

    iv. Interest rates

Online or Real-Time Analysis

A. U.S. stock exchanges

B. Foreign stock exchanges

C. U.S. commodity exchanges

D. Foreign commodity exchanges

Compatabilites

A. IBM and compatable

B. Apple and compatables

C. Proprietary hardware

D. Other

Company	Types of Options Evaluated	Models Used	Modification of Distribution or Volatilities	Analytical Capabilities	Volatility Analysis	Plotting Capabilities	On Line or Real-Time Analysis	Compatabilities
The Applied Research Co. 53 West Jackson, Suite 318 Chicago, IL 60604 (312) 922-7882	A, B, C, D, E	A, B	Yes	A, B, C, D, E, F	Yes	A, B, C i, ii, iii		A
Astrogamma, Inc. 3 Hanover Square New York, NY 10004 (212) 825-2341	D	A, B	Yes	A, B, C, D, E, F		A, B, C i, ii, iii, iv		A
Automated Trading Systems, Inc. 40 Exchange Place New York, NY 10005 (212) 968-0800	A, B, C, D, E	A, B		A, B, C, F	Yes	A, B, C i, ii, iii, iv	A, C	A
Bloomberg Financial Markets 499 Park Ave. New York, NY 10022 (800)448-5678	A, B, E	A	Yes	A, B, C, D, E, F	Yes	A, B, C i, ii, iii, iv	A, B, C, D	C
Bond-Tech, Inc. P.O. Box 192 Englewood, OH 45322 (513) 836-3991	A, B, C, D, E, F	A, B		A, B, C, D, E, F				A
CCF, Inc. 45 Broadway, 22nd Floor New York, NY 10006 (212) 943-0171	A, B, C, D, E, F	A, B, D		A, C, D, E, F		A C i, ii, iii, iv		D
Chicago Mercantile Exchange 30 South Wacker Drive Chicago, IL 60606 (312) 930-4596	A, B, C, D, E	A, C,		A, B, C, D, E, F		A, B, C i, ii, iii, iv		

Company								
Chronometrics, Inc. 250 South Wacker Drive, 4th Floor Chicago, IL 60606 (312) 993-4120	B, C, D, E, F	A, B		A, B, C, D, E, F	Yes	A, B, C i, ii, iii, iv	C	C
Citymax Integrated Information Systems Rush Lane, 80 Cannon Street London EC4N 6HH (01) 588-1156	A, B, C, D, E, F	A	Yes	A, B, C, D, E, F	Yes	A, C i	B	A, D
Colplan Systems Limited 20 Page Heath Lane Bromley, Kent BR1 2DS England (01) 464-7563	A, B, C,	A		A, B, C, D, E, F	Yes	A, B, C i, ii, iii, iv		A
Commodity Communications Corp. 420 Eisenhower Lane North Lombard, IL 60148 (800)621-2628	B, C, D E	A		A, B, F		A, B, C i, ii, iii, iv	C	A
Commodity Exchange, Inc. Four World Trade Center New York, NY 10048 (800) 333-2900	B	A		A, B, D, E, F		A, B, C i, ii, iii, iv		A, B
Comtech Software 141 West Jackson Blvd., Suite 1531-A Chicago, IL 60604 (312) 341-7547	A, B, C, D, E, F	A, C	Yes	A, B, C, D, F	Yes	A C i, iii,		A
David Bruce & Co. 211 West Wacker Dr., Suite 1230 Chicago, IL 60606 (312) 641-2207	A, B, C, D, E, F, G	A, B C, D	Yes	A, B, C, D, E, F,	Yes	A, B, C i, ii, iii, iv	A, C	A, D

Company	Types of Options Evaluated	Models Used	Modification of Distribution or Volatilities	Analytical Capabilities	Volatility Analysis	Plotting Capabilities	On Line or Real-Time Analysis	Compatabilities
Devon Systems International, Inc 430 Park Ave., 12th Floor New York, NY 10022 (212) 371-1116	A, B, C, D, E, F	A		A, B, C, D, E, F	Yes	A, B, C i, ii		A, D
Dollar Soft P.O. Box 822 Newark, CA 94560 (415) 487-7616	A, B, C, D, E	A	Yes	A, B, C, D, E, F	Yes	A, B, C i	A, C	A, D
FX Systems, Inc. 1760 Market Street Philadelphia, PA 19103 (215) 563-6037	A, B, C, D, E, F	D	Yes	A, B, C, D, E, F		A, B, C i, ii, iii, iv		A
H & H Scientific 13507 Pendleton St. Fort Washington, MD 20744 (301) 292-2958	A	A		A, B, F		A, B, C i		A, B
Intelligent Trading Systems, Inc. 327 South LaSalle, St., Suite 545 Chicago, IL 60604 (312) 341-9599	A, C, D,	A		A, B			A, C	A
International Advanced Models, Inc. P.O. Box 1019 Oak Brook, IL 60522 (312) 369-8461	A, C	A	Yes	A, B, F		B, C i, iii		A
Investment Support Systems, Inc. 1455 Broad St. Bloomfield, NJ 07003 (201) 338-0321	B, D, E, F	A, B, C		A, B, C, D, E, F	Yes	A, B, C i, ii, iii, iv	A, C, D,	A

Market Soft 431 South Dearborn St. Chicago, IL 60605 (312) 347-5775	A, B, C, D	A		A, B, C, D, E, F	Yes	A, B, C i, ii, iii, iv	C	A
Market Vision Corp. 40 Rector St. New York, NY 10006 (212) 227-1610	B	A		A, B, C, F	Yes		C	D
Marketview Software, Inc. 37 W 228 Route 64 St. Charles, IL 60174 (312) 377-5135	A, B, C, D, E	A, C	Yes	A, B, C, D, E, F	Yes	A, C i, ii, iii, iv	A, B, C, D	A
Monetary Investments International 30 South Wacker Drive, Suite 2200 Box 45, Chicago Mercantile Exchange Chicago, IL 60606 (312) 902-1997	A, B, C, D, E, F	A, B, C		A, B, C, D, E, F	Yes	A, B C i, ii, iii, iv	B, C, D	A
National Computer Network 175 West Jackson Blvd., Suite A 1038 Chicago, IL 60604 (312) 427-5125	A, B, C, D, E, F	A, B		A, B, C, D, E, F	Yes	A, B, C i, ii, iii, iv	A, C	A, B, C
OPA Software P.O. Box 90658 Los Angeles, CA 90009 (213) 545-3716	A, B, C, D, E, F	B, D		A, B, C, D, E, F		A, C i, ii, iii, iv	A, C	A
Optionomics Corp. P.O. Box 9340 Bend OR 97708 (503) 389-7719	B, C, D, E, F	A, E		A, B, D, F	Yes	A, B, C i, ii, iii, iv	C, D	A

Company	Types of Options Evaluated	Models Used	Modification of Distribution or Volatilities	Analytical Capabilities	Volatility Analysis	Plotting Capabilities	On Line or Real-Time Analysis	Compatabilities
Options-80 Box 471 Concord, MA 01742 (617) 369-1589	A	A, E		A, F		A, C i		A, B
The Options Group 50 Broadway, Stuie 2000 New York, NY 10004 (212) 785-5555	B, C, D E, F	A	Yes	A, B, C D, E, F		A, B, C i, ii, iii, iv	B, D	A, B, C
Options Research 256 Sutter St. San Francisco, CA 94108 (415) 981-0243	A, B, C	A, B D		A, B, C D, E, F	Yes	A, C i, ii, iii, iv	A	A, B
Option Systems International, Inc. 175 East Hawthorn Parkway, Suite 180 Vernon Hills, IL 60061 (312) 816-6610	A, C	A	Yes	A, B, C D, E		A, B, C i, ii, iii, iv	A	A
PC Quote, Inc. 401 South LaSalle St. Chicago, IL 60605 (312) 786-5400	A, C, D,	D	Yes	A, B, C D, F		A, B, C i, ii, iii	A	A
Programmed Press 599 Arnold Rd. West Hempstead, NY 11552 (516) 599-6527	A, B, C D, E, F	A, D	Yes	A, B, D, E	Yes			A, B, D
Reuters Information Services, Inc. 327 South LaSalle St. Chicago, IL 60604 (312) 294-2557	A, B, C D, E, F	A, B	Yes	A, B, C D, E, F	Yes	A, B, C i, ii, iii, iv	A, B	A

Company								
Roberts-Slade, Inc. 750 North 200 West, Suite 301B Provo, UT 84601 (801) 375-6847	A, B, C, D, E, F	A		A, B, F			A, C, D	A, B
Savant Corp. P.O. Box 440278 Houston, TX 77244-0278 (800) 231-9900	A	A		A, F				A
Software Options, Inc. 210 Sylvan Ave. Englewood Cliffs, NJ 07632 (201) 568-6664	A, B, C, D, E, F	A, B, D	Yes	A, B, C, D, E, F	Yes	A, B, C i, ii, iii, iv	A, B, C, D	A
Spectra Soft, Inc. 11 Harrison St. New York, NY 10013 (212) 219-0404	A, B, C, D, E	A, B, C		A, B, C, D, E, F	Yes	A, B, C i, ii, iii, iv		A, D
Standard & Poor's Trading Systems 11 Broadway New York, NY 10004 (212) 412-0100	A, B, C, D, E	A, B		A, B, C, D	Yes	A, B, C i	A, C	C
Systems Development Corp. 141 West Jackson Blvd., Suite 1636 Chicago, IL 60604 (312) 435-2800	A, B, C, D, E, F	A, B, C	Yes	A, B, C, D, E, F		A, B, C i, ii, iii, iv	A, B, C, D	A, C
Telerate Systems, Inc. One World Trade Center, 104th Floor New York, NY 10128 (212) 938-5788	B, E	A, B	Yes	A, B, C, D, E, F	Yes	A, B, C i, ii, iii, iv	A	C
Terco Computer Systems P.O. Box 388206 Chicago, IL 60638 (312) 495-7123	A, B, C, D, E, F	A, B		A, B, F				A

Company	Types of Options Evaluated	Models Used	Modification of Distribution or Volatilities	Analytical Capabilities	Volatility Analysis	Plotting Capabilities	On Line or Real-Time Analysis	Compatibilities
Townsend Analytics, Ltd. 30 South Wacker Dr., Suite 1117 Chicago, IL 60606 (312) 559-0642	A, B, C, D, E	A, D	Yes	A, B, C, D, E, F	Yes	A, B, C i, ii iii	A, C	A
Track Data Corp. 61 Broadway New York, NY 10006 (212) 943-4555	A, C	A, B		A, B, C, D, E, F	Yes	A C i, ii, iii, iv	A, C	D
Wang Financial Information Services, Corp. 120 Wall St. New York, NY 10005 (212) 208-7600	A, B, C, D, E	A, B	Yes	A, B, F		A, B, C i, ii, iii, iv	A, B, C	A, D
Xcaliber Trading Systems, Inc. 401 South LaSalle St., Suite 403 Chicago, IL 60605 (312) 786-5353	A, B, C D, E, F	A, B, D	Yes	A, B, C, D, E, F		A, B, C i, ii, iii, iv	A, B, C, D	A, D

Appendix H

Recommended Readings

The following reading list includes those books which are likely to contribute substantially to the serious option trader's understanding of the subject. An effort has been made to categorize the books according to the difficulty of the material: elementary (E), intermediate (I), and advanced (A). The categorization is based on both the complexity of the mathematics and sophistication of the strategies presented.

Clasing, Henry K., Jr.
*The Dow Jones-Irwin Guide
 to Put and Call Options* **(E)**
Dow Jones-Irwin; Homewood, IL
1978; 290 pp.

Brenner, Menachem
*Option Pricing: Theory and
 Applications* **(A)**
Lexington Books; Lexington, MA
1983; 235 pp.

Mayer, Terry S.
Commodity Options **(E)**
New York Institute of Finance;
New York, NY
1983; 350 pp.

Bookstaber, Richard M.
*Option Pricing and Strategies
 in Investing* **(I)**
Addison-Wesley Publishing;
1981; 226 pp.

Jarrow, Robert and Rudd, Andrew
Option Pricing **(A)**
Dow Jones-Irwin; Homewood, IL
1983; 235 pp.

Cox, John C. and Rubenstein, Mark
Option Markets **(A)**
Prentice Hall; Englewood Hts., NJ
1985; 498 pp.

Fabozzi, Frank J.
Winning the Interest Rate Game:
  A Guide to Debt Options **(E)**
Probus Publishing; Chicago, IL
1985; 300 pp.

Lagbuszewski, John and
Sinquefield, Jeanne
Inside the Commodity Option
  Markets **(I)**
John Wiley & Sons; New York, NY
1985; 374 pp.

McMillan, Lawrence G.
Options as a Strategic Investment **(E)**
The New York Institute of Finance;
Second Edition, 1986; 684 pp.

Smith, A. L. H.
Trading Finacial Options **(I)**
Butterworths; London, England
1986; 200 pp.

Bookstaber, Richard M.
Option Pricing and Investment
  Strategies **(I)**
Probus Publishing; Chicago, IL
1987; 233 pp.

Fitzgerald, Desmond M.
Financial Options **(I)**
Euromoney Publications;
London, England
1987; 262 pp.

Ritchken, Peter
Options: Theory, Strategy and
  Applications **(A)**
Scott, Foresman and Co.;
Glenview, IL
1988; 264 pp.

Gastineau, Gary
The Options Manual **(I)**
MacGraw Hill; New York, NY
Third Edition, 1988; 440 pp.

Labuszewski, John W. and
Nyhoff, John E.
Trading Options on Futures **(I)**
John Wiley & Sons; New York, NY
1988; 264 pp.

Luft, Carl and Sheiner, Richard K.
Understanding and Trading Listed
  Stock Options **(E)**
Probus Publishing; Chicago, IL
1988; 231 pp.

In addition, the reader may be interested in the following articles which include the original presentation of the more commonly used theoretical pricing models:

Black, Fischer and Scholes, Myron
"The Pricing of Options and Corporate Liabilities"
Journal of Political Economy
Vol. 81, No.3; May/June 1973; pp.637-654

Black, Fischer
"The Pricing of Commodity Contracts"
Journal of Financial Economics
No. 3, 1976; pp. 167-179

Cox, John C., Ross, Stephen A., and Rubenstein, Mark
"Option Pricing: A Simplified Approach"
Journal of Financial Economics
No. 7; 1979; pp. 229-263

Garman, Mark B. and Kohlgagen, Steven W.
"Foreign Currency Option Values"
Journal of International Money and Finance
December 1983; pp. 231-237

Barone-Adesi, Giovanni and Whaley, Robert E.
"Efficient Analytic Approximation of American Option Values"
Journal of Finance
Vol. 42, No. 2; June 1987; pp. 301-320

Index

Adjustment, 103-104, 109, 113
  how to make, 226-229
  when to make, 189-191
Arbitrage, 226, 371-373
Assignment, 4-5, 10, 295
At-the-money option, 11, 307
  at expiration, 313-315
  in bull and bear spreads, 248-

Backspread, 156-159, 163-164, 178-179, 186, 237;
  expiration, 317-320
Backwardation, 147
Barone-Adesi, Giovanni, 291C
Beckers, Stan, 75n
Bell-shaped curve: *See* Distribution, Normal
Bid/ask spread, 231-232
Binomial model: *See* Cox-Ross-Rubenstein Model
Black, Fischer, 51
Black Model, 51, 336-337
Black-Scholes Model, 51-53, 335-336
Box, 274-277, 371
  effect of early exercise, 294-295
Butterfly, 164-168, 178-179, 186, 238
Buy/write, 251-255

Calendar spread; *See* time spread
Cap, 255-256
Carrying costs, 45, 49, 50, 56, 73, 73n, 146-147, 266-268, 284
  effect on American options, 291-293
  See also Interest rates

Chicago Board of Trade (CBOT), 2-3, 145, 147, 153
Chicago Board Options Exchange (CBOE), 277n
Chicago Mercantile Exchange (CME), 3, 145, 149, 151, 232
Clearing firm, 12-14, 124
Clearing house, 12-14, 124
Collar, 257
Commodity Exchange, Inc. (COMEX), 124, 149
Condor, 255
Contango, 146
Contingency order, 199
Conversion, 264-266, 371
Conversion/reversal market, 266
  See also Synthetic market
Covered write, 251
  See also Buy/write
Cox, John, 288
Cox-Ross-Rubenstein Model, 288-290, 338-341
Curvature; *See* Gamma
Cylinder, 257

Delta, 100-101, 116-120, 136
  as a probability, 120
  effect of price change: *See* Gamma
  effect of time and volatility, 126-129
  implied, 127, 129
  inversion, 236-239
  of a conversion or reversal, 272-274
  of volatility spreads, 177-178
  of a synthetic position, 260

389

position, 141
risk, 211
using to create a graph, 191
Delta neutral positions, 101, 103, 112,
    119, 124, 126-127, 129, 235, 250,
    272
Diagonal spread, 176, 239n
Distribution
    binomial, 288, 290
    implied, 303-304
    lognormal, 70-72, 301-305
    normal, 62
    of underlying prices at expiration,
    64-66

Edge, 44
Exercise, 4-5, 10
Exercise price, 2, 3, 54
Expected return, 43-44, 72-73
Expiration date, 2, 3, 54-55
Extrinsic value, 6, 252
    Negative, 11
    See also Time value

Fence, 257
Floor, 256
Frictionless markets, 107-109
Frontspread, 159n; See Ratio vertical
    spread

Gamma, 121-126, 136
    as an aid in making adjustments,
    124
    effect of changing market condi-
    tions, 124-126
    of volatility speads, 177-178
    position, 141
    risk, 211-212
    using to create a graph, 191-192
Garman-Kohlhagen Model, 337-338
Garman, Mark, 75n
Guts, 163

Hedge ratio, 53-54
    See also Delta
Horizontal spread; See Time spread

In-the-money option, 11
Interest rates, 45, 49, 50, 56, 107-108,
    131-132,146-147, 266, 269, 273,
    279-280, 287, 299-301, 300n
    risk, 269
Intrinsic value, 6
"Investor's Daily," 39n
Iron butterfly, 225

Jelly roll, 277-280, 280n, 371

Kappa; See Vega
Klass, Michael, 75n

Liquidity, 215, 230-231, 241, 243
Long, 2, 17
    spread, 167, 168
Lot position
    using to create a graph, 192

Margin, 14
    See also Variation
Mean, 66-70, 72, 343-344, 345
Models, 46-47; American vs.
    European, 291, 293

Naked positions, 235-236
New York Futures Exchange (NYFE),
    149, 301
New York Mercantile Exchange
    (NYMEX), 2-3
"New York Times," 39n
NOB spread, 147, 149
Non-continuous trading, 315-317

Omega; See Vega
Option
    as a substitute for an underlying
    position, 54
    American, 4, 283, 285, 288, 291,
    295-296
    call, 2
    European, 4, 132, 284-285, 285n, 288,
    295-296
    put, 2
    type, 2-3

value at expiration, 21-26
Options Group, The (TOG), 137-140
Order execution, 197-202
Out-of-the-money option, 11
Overwrite, 251

Parity, 11
Parkinson, Michael, 75n
Premium
  implied volatility, 85
  long and short, 177
  price of an option, 4, 6
  price change, 75-76

Quadratic model; See Whaley Model

Random walk, 60-62
Range forward, 257
Ratio spread, 161
Ratio vertical spread, 159-160, 164,
  178-179, 186, 236-237, 306
Reuters Information Services, 137-140
Reverse conversion (reversal),
  264-266, 371
Rho, 135, 136n, 300
Risk
  conversion/reversal, 268-274
  execution, 269
  interest rate, 269
  limited vs. unlimited, 26, 220
  pin, 269-271
Riskless hedge, 53
  See also Hedge ratio, Delta
Ross, Stephen, 288
Rubenstein, Mark, 288

Scholes, Myron, 51
Sell/write, 253-254
Serial option, 3
Settlement, 266
Stock-type vs. futures-type, 15-16, 57n,
  111, 131-132, 293
Short, 2, 17
Spread, 168
Sigma, 132
  prime; See Vega

Spread
  creating a graph, 191-198
  intra-market, 145-146
  value at expiration, 27-33
Standard deviation, 66-70, 73, 343-344,
  345
  daily and weekly, 74
Straddle, 159-161, 167-168, 178-179,
  186, 219-220
Synthetic, 280-281
Strangle, 161-164, 1780179, 186,
  219-220
Strike price; See Exercise price
Synthetic
  equivalents, 260-261, 371
  in a volatility spread, 281-282
  market, 263, 267-269
  position, 259-264

Taxes, 107-109
Theoretical edge, 44, 141, 179, 205, 222,
  227-229, 319
  using to create a graph, 191
Theoretical futures position, 119
  See also Delta
Theoretical value, 44-46
Theta, 129-132, 136, 169
  of a European option, 285n
  of time spreads, 169
  of volatility spreads, 177-178
  position, 141
  risk, 211
  using to create a graph, 194, 196
  3-way, 274
Time decay; See Theta
Time premium; See Time value
Time spread, 168-176, 178-179,
  186-187, 189, 238-239, 279-280
  effect of implied volatility, 175-176
Time value, 6, 109, 252
  See also Extrinsic value
Transaction costs, 107-108

Underlying, 2, 3
  price of, 55

Variation, 15-16
Vega, 132-135, 136-137, 172, 179
  of time spreads, 172
  of volatility spreads, 177-178
  position, 141
  risk, 212
  using to create a graph, 194

Vertical spread, 239-251, 276-277
  effect of early exercise, 293-294
Volatility, 57
  and observed price changes, 76-77
  as a standard deviation, 73
  effect on early exercise, 287-288
  effect on time spreads, 172-173
  estimating, 90-93
  Eurodollar, 78
  forecast, 81, 82

future, 79, 85
historical, 79-80, 344, 236-347,
  349-360
implied, 81-84, 85, 92, 109-111,
  208-209, 301-303, 346, 348
long and short, 94, 97
non-constant, 309, 312-313
of similar commodities, 92-93
order of, 312-314
seasonal, 86-88
spread, 150, 280-282, 363

"Wall Street Journal," 39n
Whaley, Robert, 291
Whaley Model, 291, 341-343

Zeta; *See* Vega